LOVERLY

Geoffrey Block, Series Editor

Series Board

Stephen Banfield   Jeffrey Magee
Tim Carter   Carol Oja
Kim Kowalke   Larry Starr

LOVERLY

The Life and Times of *My Fair Lady*

DOMINIC McHUGH

OXFORD
UNIVERSITY PRESS

OXFORD
UNIVERSITY PRESS

Oxford University Press, Inc., publishes works that further
Oxford University's objective of excellence
in research, scholarship, and education.

Oxford   New York

Auckland   Cape Town   Dar es Salaam   Hong Kong   Karachi
Kuala Lumpur   Madrid   Melbourne   Mexico City   Nairobi
New Delhi   Shanghai   Taipei   Toronto

With offices in

Argentina   Austria   Brazil   Chile   Czech Republic   France   Greece
Guatemala   Hungary   Italy   Japan   Poland   Portugal   Singapore
South Korea   Switzerland   Thailand   Turkey   Ukraine   Vietnam

Copyright © 2012 by Oxford University Press, Inc.

Published by Oxford University Press, Inc.
198 Madison Avenue, New York, NY 10016

www.oup.com

Oxford is a registered trademark of Oxford University Press

Library of Congress Cataloging-in-Publication Data
McHugh, Dominic.
Loverly: the life and times of My fair lady /Dominic McHugh.
p.   cm.—(Broadway legacies)
Includes bibliographical references and index.
ISBN 978-0-19-982730-5
1. Loewe, Frederick, 1901–1988. My Fair Lady.
2. Lerner, Alan Jay, 1918–1986. My Fair Lady.
3. Musicals—United States—History and criticism. I. Title.
ML410.L7986M34   2012
782.1′4—dc23   2011035377

Publication of this book was supported in part by a grant from the
AMS 75 PAYS Endowment of the American Musicological Society.

1 3 5 7 9 8 4 6 2

Printed in the United States of America
on acid-free paper

For

MUM AND DAD

CONTENTS

● ● ●

FOREWORD

• • •

When I received the proposal that would evolve into the book you are about to read, I immediately recalled Mozart's apocryphal but no less prescient remark after meeting with the seventeen-year-old Beethoven: "Keep your eyes on him—someday he will give the world something to talk about." The analogy may be imperfect, but Mozart's prophecy remains fundamentally apt to describe the thoroughly accomplished young author of *Loverly: The Life and Times of "My Fair Lady,"* Dominic McHugh, of the University of Sheffield. Indeed, McHugh has produced the first comprehensive and most accurate account of how this great and perennially popular show came to be, and *Loverly* will give us much to talk about, just as the revered subject of this book has for generations added immeasurable wealth to the American musical treasury.

In telling the story of how Alan Jay Lerner (1918–86) and Frederick Loewe (1901–88) created what one opening night critic described as "a new landmark in the genre fathered by Rodgers and Hammerstein," McHugh, in contrast to most of his predecessors, turns to Lerner's 1978 memoir, *The Street Where I Live* "only where no other source exists." Although never less than engaging and indispensable, and although we have grown accustomed to accepting Lerner's recollections at face value, McHugh's approach is a welcome one. By looking more closely at Lerner's street—without, however, drawing comparisons with his stage characters as I am doing here—McHugh's reliance on his documentary exploration reveals that Lerner's memory shares much in common with that of Honoré and Mamita in *Gigi,* who think they "remember it well" but clearly do not. Among many polite but firm refutations in the course of *Loverly,* McHugh carefully points out that contrary to Lerner's claim in his memoir, Mary Martin did appear to be a "natural" for the role of Eliza. Lerner wrote at the time that "everyone else after Mary has to be second choice" and that despite Lerner's assertion Rex Harrison was the first choice for Higgins, in fact Lerner and Loewe approached both Noël Coward and Michael Redgrave before turning to Harrison.

Instead of following Lerner at every turn as most previous writers have done, McHugh offers a meticulous exploration of voluminous contemporary sources, including letters, memos, lyric and libretto drafts, and scores both discarded and replaced. The saga begins with the Theatre Guild (entirely omitted in Lerner's expansive narrative) and its attempt to find a talented composer and lyricist, starting with Richard Rodgers and Oscar Hammerstein in 1951, who had produced the great Guild hits *Oklahoma!* and *Carousel* (and the miss *Allegro*) in the 1940s. About a year after Rodgers and Hammerstein concluded, as Hammerstein later allegedly reported in a conversation with Lerner, that "it can't be done," the Guild solicited Frank Loesser, Cole Porter, and Irving Berlin before turning to Lerner for the book and lyrics and Loewe for the music. If I may borrow a song title from the completed show, they "did it."

McHugh next details the two stages of Lerner and Loewe's attempt to adapt Shaw's *Pygmalion,* the abandoned project of 1952 and the successful second effort from 1954 to 1956 that led to the historic opening night March 15, 1956, which was produced by Herman Levin rather than the Theatre Guild. The next chapters look at Shaw's original play of 1914, the 1938 film adaption directed by Gabriel Pascal that became the principal source for the stage version, Lerner's outlines prior to script changes during the crucial rehearsal process, the development of the score based on a rich treasure of musical source material, and the finished show's stage and film legacy to date. In his final chapter McHugh reviews selected commentary on *My Fair Lady* and offers a provocative and well-argued interpretation of "the nature of the ambiguous relationship between Eliza and Higgins."

We don't know if Porter, among the composers approached by the Theatre Guild to adapt *Pygmalion* to the musical stage, regretted not taking on this daunting assignment, but Rex Harrison's recollection that "Porter reserved himself a seat once a week for the entire [six-year] run" suggests the possibility that he had. Thanks to a surviving letter—supplied to me by Dominic, naturally—we now know that when the first season tickets arrived Porter wrote to Lerner expressing his deep gratitude for obtaining his "'subscription' seats." Although *My Fair Lady* was not customarily regarded as revolutionary in its own time or since, its perfect blend of story, words, and music along with its verve and originality have earned the show an honored place in the history of the musical. After he first saw it Fred Astaire wrote an effusive note to Lerner to share his enthusiasm for what he considered "simply the best show that has ever been produced." More recently, although he dismissed Lerner's work for its lack of interest compared with his predecessors Lorenz Hart and Ira Gershwin, Stephen Sondheim found Shaw's characterization "more layered and surprising," and even questioned the notion of doing this musical at all. Sondheim, who was just a few years too young to have been asked to adapt *Pygmalion*, recalled in his "attendant comments" in *Finishing the Hat* (2010) that *My Fair Lady* was "the most entertaining musical I've ever seen (exclusive of my own, of course)."

Many of us might say the same about *Loverly,* a book that tells us how Lerner and Loewe transformed Shaw's fine play into an enduring musical capable of pleasing such diverse critics as Porter and Sondheim, and of course millions of musical theater aficionados for more than fifty years.

GEOFFREY BLOCK
Series Editor, Broadway Legacies

PREFACE AND ACKNOWLEDGMENTS

● ● ●

If there's one musical that deserves to be assessed in a series titled *Broadway Legacies*, it's surely *My Fair Lady*. From the moment of its premiere, critics and audiences alike took the show to their hearts and embraced its wit, its sense of drama, its poignancy, its vivid characters, and its tremendous score. It belongs to a select group of musicals that can truly be said to be artistic land-marks in the genre—a category that also includes shows like Jerome Kern and Oscar Hammerstein II's *Show Boat*, Richard Rodgers and Hammerstein's *Oklahoma!*, Leonard Bernstein and Stephen Sondheim's *West Side Story*, and Sondheim's *Company*—as well as enjoying outstanding commercial success (its original Broadway run lasted 2,717 performances).

Yet to date, *My Fair Lady* has been the subject of comparatively little schol-arly literature, and its composer and lyricist have been similarly marginal-ized. The only book dealing with their entire output is Gene Lees's *Inventing Champagne: The Musical Worlds of Lerner and Loewe*, which broke new ground in establishing a text on one of Broadway's most important partnerships. However, its reliance on gossip and hearsay, its absence of any musical illus-tration or analysis, and the decision not to cite sources for the information contained in the book, render it sometimes unreliable. Keith Garebian's *The Making of My Fair Lady* similarly makes some useful observations and is a fine introduction to the show for general readers, but it is inadequately annotated for scholarly purposes. Gerald Harold Weissman's 1957 dissertation "The Musicalization of Pygmalion into *My Fair Lady*" (master's thesis, Stanford University, 1957) benefited from input from Lerner, who allowed the author to see an early outline of the show, but the critical discussion is largely limited to how Shaw's play was adapted into a musical. The only substantive studies of the show are a single chapter each in Joseph Swain's *The Broadway Musical* (New York, 1990) and Geoffrey Block's *Enchanted Evenings* (Oxford, 1997; rev. ed. 2008), both of which offer original views on the show. In particular, Block's account is the first to make full use of Loewe's autograph manuscripts (housed at the Library of Congress), while Swain provides a personal analysis of the score and libretto. But because both of these are single chapters in larger books on the genre as a whole, there is an understandable limit to the amount of space that Block and Swain can devote to the show.

When I began my research in this field, it was not difficult for me to decide to focus on this undoubted masterpiece (not least because it has always been my favorite musical). The real question was how to go about it. We are fortunate in recent years to have seen a steady increase in the amount of quality scholarship on the Broadway musical available in print. Alongside Block's seminal *Enchanted Evenings*, the books that have most guided me on my way include Stephen Banfield's *Sondheim's Broadway Musicals*, a magisterial study of the work of perhaps the most influential composer and lyricist of the past forty years; James Leve's volume on Kander and Ebb in the excellent Yale Broadway Masters series; and three books that focus on a single musical each—Tim Carter's *Oklahoma!: The Making of an American Musical*, Jim Lovensheimer's *South Pacific: Paradise Rewritten*, and bruce d. mcclung's *Lady in the Dark: Biography of a Musical*. Although the individuality of each of these authors takes their work in different directions, what they share is a seriousness of purpose that shows itself through the depth of research informing their every word. Naturally, the specific focus of Carter, Lovensheimer, and mcclung's wonderful volumes on one show made them especially valuable models for me to use.

One of the trickiest aspects of dealing with a much-loved show like *My Fair Lady* is that almost everyone seems to have a story to tell about it. In contrast to the surprising dearth of scholarly literature on such a widely admired show, there is a huge amount of gossip attached to it. I quickly realized that not all of it can be proven to be true, however, so in chapters 1 and 2 I try to describe the background to the musical's genesis from scratch. The foundation of my revised account lies in several hundred unpublished letters from various archives around the world, most notably the papers of Herman Levin, who produced the show. Chapter 1 describes Lerner and Loewe's early frustrated attempts to adapt Shaw's *Pygmalion* into a musical in 1952, and chapter 2 goes on to show how they eventually managed it in 1954–56. In chapter 3 I take a brief look at the background to Shaw's play and try to clear up some of the confusion about the 1938 film of *Pygmalion*, which contains some changes: for instance, although the play does not show Eliza's lessons with Higgins, the film does. The *Pygmalion* movie is also the source of the reunion of Higgins and Eliza at the final curtain and is not a "happy ending" appended by Lerner to the musical; he just adopted it. I then explore Lerner's draft outlines for the show, which document his developing thoughts as to the show's structure, and go on to look closely at changes made to the script that was used during *My Fair Lady*'s rehearsals. What begins to emerge is a shift of focus, even this late in the day, from a show depicting a conventional Broadway romance to a story with a much more ambiguous center. Lerner went out of his way to make the relationship between Eliza Doolittle and Henry Higgins as ambiguous as possible, and a great many of the changes to the script made during the final weeks before the show opened in previews served this specific purpose. Chapters 4, 5, and 6 point toward the same purpose in the development of the score. I examine in great detail the unusual wealth of music manuscript material available for *My Fair Lady* in the Library of Congress's Frederick Loewe and (in particular) Warner-Chappell Collections, which contain everything from the composer's sketches for unused songs to the dance arranger's scores for the cut ballet. By showing the relationships between different manuscripts, I aim to give a flavor of how much of a collaboration the development of a Broadway musical's score is; it involves arrangers and orchestrators in as much of an authorial role as the composer is, though there is no doubt that Loewe took a keen interest in everything that was being written and orchestrated. Again, various changes of lyric hint at an obscuring of the Higgins-Eliza relationship (though, sadly, Lerner destroyed all his lyric sketches for the show, depriving us of a complete portrait of the lyrics' composition), as do the rejection of numerous conventional love songs well before they reached even the rehearsal process. In chapter 7 I examine the musical's complex legacy on stage, which has been unusual in the number of attempts to re-create the original production. Finally, in chapter 8 I visit some of the secondary literature on the show and in particular examine the nature of the ambiguous relationship between Eliza and Higgins. Just as some of the famous stories about the show are not included in the opening chapters, I do not scrutinize the show from every possible angle here, but rather hope to open up the debate for the future.

If *My Fair Lady*'s primary message is that education can change your life, I certainly owe a debt of gratitude to the numerous people who have taught me everything I know. First, thanks are due to the librarians at the many archives I visited, including Charles Perrier at the New York Public Library; Harry Miller and the staff at the Wisconsin Historical Society; the staff at Yale University Library; the Special Collections Librarian at St John's College, Cambridge; Ned Comstock at USC; and most especially Mark Eden Horowitz, Walter Zvonchenko, and their colleagues at the Music and Theatre Divisions of the Library of Congress. Mark's generosity with his time and help knows no bounds, and I have benefited both from his intimate acquaintance with his collections and his extraordinary knowledge of the musical theatre in general. His friendship has been a guiding force of this book.

Special thanks go to Jerold Couture of the Loewe estate and David Grossberg of the Lerner estate: by giving me permission to copy original musical materials they have allowed me to go into far more depth with this study than would otherwise have been the case, as well as lending support and enthusiasm along the way. Alan Jay Lerner material is reproduced by permission of the copyright owners, the estate of Alan Jay Lerner and family. Thanks to Alfred Music and Warner-Chappell for allowing me to publish extracts from the score. Quotations from the papers of Herman Levin are reproduced by kind permission of his daughter, Gabrielle Kraft. Passages from Hanya Holm's notes are used with permission of the estate of Hanya Holm, thanks to her granddaughter, Karen M. Trautlein. Quotations from Theresa Helburn's papers are used with thanks to the family of her niece, Margaret Kocher. Material from Sir Cecil Beaton's diary is reproduced by kind permission of Hugo Vickers, Beaton's Literary Executor. Many thanks are also due to Rosaria Sinisi for allowing me to reproduce passages from Oliver Smith's letters.

I'm honored to count Liz Robertson (Lerner's widow) as a close friend and enthusiastic supporter. Helpful hints about the Theatre Guild Collection at Yale came from Tim Carter of the University of North Carolina at Chapel Hill. I'm also grateful to the distinguished Broadway orchestrator, composer, and conductor Larry Blank for sharing his years of experience and giving me the benefit of his wisdom and musicianship, not to mention his friendship. The staff of the Music Department at King's College, London, have been supportive throughout my seven-year education there, and thanks are due especially to John Deathridge and Christopher Wintle. Ever since attending his lectures on Mozart and eighteenth-century music performance practice as an undergraduate, I have admired and been inspired by the scholarship of my PhD supervisor, Cliff Eisen. Without question, by coaxing me into following his footsteps down the path of primary research (albeit in the opposite direction across the Atlantic) he enabled me to make my doctoral dissertation, and its adaptation into this book, a much more rigorous study than it would have been, while his encouragement and care at every stage have been invaluable. I'm also grateful to Stephen Banfield and Nigel Simeone, distinguished scholars in this field, for their helpful comments on my dissertation during my doctoral viva. More recently, I am grateful to my new colleagues at the University of Sheffield for their support of my research.

At Oxford University Press, I have to thank Norm Hirschy from the bottom of my heart for being so extraordinarily kind and patient throughout the publication process. In spite of my extreme naivety on the subject of publishing books, Norm has always been quick to answer all my questions (many of them incredibly mundane), thoughtful in his responses, supportive when difficult decisions had to be made, and generally a dream to deal with. No less important to this process has been Geoffrey Block, who is not only the most important scholar in the field of American musicals but also a talented and inspiring editor for this series. It has been a wonderful experience for me, and I'm touched that Geoffrey and Norm have put so much effort into helping me bring this book to fruition. Thanks, too, are due to the three anonymous reviewers, my copy editor, and the entire production team at Oxford.

Of my friends, particular thanks are due to: Tracy and Darren Bryant; Rex Bunnett and the late John Muir; Richard C. Norton and Gary Schocker; Elliot J. Cohen; Michael Feinstein; Ethan Mordden; Ian Marshall Fisher; Larry Moore; Terry and Sue Broomfield; Sir Cameron Mackintosh; Sir Tim Rice; my close friends Dorothy and Michael Bradley, Lynne Huang, Marina Romani, and Arlene Tomlinson; Richard Tay, who has been an especially strong supporter and dear friend; and members of my family, including my brother Alistair and his partner Natallia, and my wonderfully supportive Auntie Lin and Uncle John. Special thanks are due to my beloved, long-suffering partner, Lawrence Broomfield, who is the foundation of all my successes. Nevertheless, I owe everything to my parents. By introducing me to *The Sound of Music* and *My Fair Lady* at the age of four, they opened a window into a whole new world, and without their generosity, love, and care I would never have been exposed to such a wealth of culture throughout my life, understood the value of education, or become the person I am today. This book is dedicated to them.

LOVERLY

1

FALSE STARTS AND ARTISTIC PROMISE

• • •

ESTABLISHING A MYTH: PYGMALION FROM OVID TO SHAW

The Pygmalion myth has its roots in classical Greek legend. Ovid tells us (in Dryden's translation of *Metamorphoses*) that Pygmalion "loathing their lascivious life, / Abhorr'd all womankind, but most a wife: / So single chose to live, and shunn'd to wed, / Well pleas'd to want a consort of his bed."[1] The misogynist Pygmalion is a sculptor, and in spite of scorning women in general his "fear of idleness" induces him to carve a beautiful maiden out of ivory. Pleased with his work, Pygmalion "commends, admires, / Adores; and last, the thing ador'd, desires." This neat progression from feeling pride in the product of his work to finding it an object of desire culminates in Pygmalion's prayer to Venus, begging her to make the statue come to life. The goddess takes pity on Pygmalion and blesses the union of the sculptor and his creation by granting them a son, Paphos. Later versions refer to the sculpture as Galatea, while in his 1767 retelling Goethe calls her Elise, based on variations of the story of Dido (Elissa). The myth was of interest to visual artists (Rodin, Goya), inspired numerous works of literature (from William Morris's "Earthly Paradise" to Mary Shelley's *Frankenstein*) and was the subject of operas by Rameau, Cherubini, and Donizetti, as well as Kurt Weill's 1943 musical *One Touch of Venus*. Yet its most famous incarnation will probably always be George Bernard Shaw's 1913 play, *Pygmalion*, and the latter's adaptation into the musical *My Fair Lady*.

Though the road from Ovid's *Pygmalion* to Shaw's was a long one, we can already see in the original tale the roots of Henry Higgins's personality. Both Pygmalion and Higgins feel nothing short of contempt for the opposite sex, and yet—or perhaps as a result of this—they both lavish their special talents on creating the ideal image of a woman. At the same time, there is a major divergence from the original myth in the final scene of Shaw's play. The birth of Paphos after the union of Pygmalion and Galatea is the conclusion of the legend, but the end of the play leaves the audience with an unanswered question: Do Henry Higgins and Eliza Doolittle form a romantic union after the curtain has come down?

When creating their 1956 musical adaptation of *Pygmalion* as *My Fair Lady*, Alan Jay Lerner and Frederick Loewe's greatest challenge was to deal with the complex nuances of the Higgins-Eliza relationship. Although the current study is far-reaching in the topics it embraces, the evolution of this aspect of the show is a unifying theme. It is hardly surprising that Shaw's *Pygmalion* should be compared to Ovid's version, or that *My Fair Lady* should be compared to both; since Ovid and his successors bring the lead characters together, it is natural to expect this to be reflected in Shaw's version. Yet the fact that the playwright himself was so vehement in his rejection of the romantic union of Eliza and Higgins—famously writing an epilogue to clarify what he intended by the final scene—means that we are left with a compelling ambiguity in the text that can be played one way or another, according to the preferences of the reader, director, or performer.

From initial planning to the opening night in March 1956, it took Lerner and Loewe almost five years to work out how to maintain this ambiguity while employing the paraphernalia of 1950s musical comedy. To have Higgins and Eliza marry would be too conventional, but to rob their relationship of romance would take away the intrigue and tension that were to prove part of the musical's winning formula. The pages that follow describe the *My Fair Lady* story, starting with the approach of various composers to Shaw with the idea of turning *Pygmalion* into a musical and his persistent refusal, through Lerner and Loewe's two separate attempts to write the show before finally getting it right and bringing it to the stage. Although the precise details of how they molded the musical and dramatic material are discussed in later chapters, it is striking even from the narrative in this chapter and those following that Lerner and Loewe were initially thinking along more conventional lines, right down to pursuing Mary Martin, one of Broadway's most in-demand musical comedy stars after her success in Rodgers and Hammerstein's *South Pacific* (1949), for the role of Eliza Doolittle. But in the end, imagination rather than convention was what made *My Fair Lady* special.

WRITING BROADWAY HISTORY: DOCUMENTARY SOURCES FOR THE GENESIS OF *MY FAIR LADY*

My Fair Lady was the most successful musical of its day, yet surprisingly little is known about the creation of the piece. Although the story of its genesis has often been retold, the main source of information for most accounts until now has been Alan Jay Lerner himself. The first third of his memoir, *The Street Where I Live,* is devoted to a highly entertaining report of how he came to write *My Fair Lady* with Frederick Loewe and the journey that team undertook to bring it into being.[2] However, Lerner's story was written after a significant lapse of time, and the author was prone to romanticize events or completely omit them from his book. Furthermore, little has been said in print about the attempts of other composers to write about the show or of the contribution of the Theatre Guild (producers of Rodgers and Hammerstein's *Oklahoma!* and *Carousel*) in trying to get the project off the ground.

Rather than regarding Lerner's autobiography as the primary source of information about the genesis of the show, this book depends largely on contemporary documentary sources, acknowledging Lerner's version of events only where no other source exists. While there is no major collection of correspondence belonging to either Lerner or Loewe currently held in any public collection, the Theatre Guild's role in the musical is illustrated by the company's papers at Yale University, which also houses details of Loewe's projected show with Harold Rome during 1953–54. Background on Cecil Beaton was obtained from his diaries and correspondence at St John's College, Cambridge, and similar information about Michael Redgrave was found at the Victoria and Albert Museum. Hanya Holm's personal notes and correspondence at the New York Public Library brought new insights into the choreography for the show, especially the creation of the ballet; and the bulk of the story was constructed from the papers of Herman Levin, the producer of *My Fair Lady*, held by the Wisconsin Center for Film and Theater Research (also home to Moss Hart's papers).

Some of these sources have been written about previously. In particular, Steven Bach's excellent biography of Moss Hart takes advantage of the Levin and Hart papers, and the riveting epilogue of David Mark D'Andre's doctoral dissertation on the Theatre Guild gives by far the most detailed account of Lerner and Loewe's initial attempt to write the show.[3] Both of these sources remain problematical, largely due to a reliance on Lerner's book to fill in the gaps, and no attempt has been made to marry up all the currently available documentary evidence on the genesis of *My Fair Lady* until now.

Although it would be a mistake to focus too sharply on Shaw when assessing Lerner and Loewe's musical, an account of the genesis of *My Fair Lady* must begin with his *Pygmalion*, the play on which it is based. The first two chapters of this book deal with two key phases, with the summer of 1954 as the cut-off point between them. The first period concerns the approaches of various parties to Shaw to turn *Pygmalion* into a musical and his persistent refusal to allow this; his giving the screen rights for his plays to Gabriel Pascal, the Hungarian film maker; Pascal's decision to make *Pygmalion* into a musical in the wake of the success of his 1938 film version of the play; his joining forces with the Theatre Guild to commission various composers to attempt to write the piece; the signing of a contract by Lerner and Loewe to write the musical, with the hope of having Mary Martin as Eliza Doolittle; Lerner and Loewe's backing out of their contract, having failed to find a way to do the piece; and finally, the Theatre Guild's eventual abandonment of the project in early 1953.

The second period, discussed in chapter 2, involves Lerner and Loewe's decision to try again with the show during the early autumn of 1954, following Pascal's death; their hiring of Herman Levin to produce it instead of the Theatre Guild, and the latter's unsuccessful battle to wrest the rights to *Pygmalion* back from them; Lerner and Loewe's drawn-out search for an actor to play Henry Higgins, as well as other cast and production team members; the creation of the score and script in the background of all these practical dealings; and the mounting of the piece on the Broadway stage on March 15, 1956 after a rehearsal period in New York and tryouts in New Haven and Philadelphia. A brief account is also given of Lerner and Loewe's activities between late 1952 and the middle of 1954, when they each attempted to write one or more shows with another collaborator. In a sense, then, this is the story of two *My Fair Ladies*: one aborted version, and one completed version. By clarifying the genesis of the show in this way, we can understand more fully how the piece came into being and also see how certain decisions—such as the shift of focus from writing a vehicle for Mary Martin to creating a vehicle for Rex Harrison—ultimately changed the content of the script, score, and lyrics.

A SHAVIAN MUSICAL: *PYGMALION* UP TO 1950

While Oscar Straus's 1908 adaptation of George Bernard Shaw's *Arms and the Man* (1894) as *Der tapfere Soldat* (*The Chocolate Soldier*) proved that a musical based on a Shaw play had the potential for popular success, it merely confirmed the playwright's opinion that his works should be left well alone. To Theresa Helburn's suggestion in 1939 that he should give the Theatre Guild permission to allow Kurt Weill to turn *The Devil's Disciple* into a musical, Shaw declared that after *The Chocolate Soldier*, "nothing will ever induce me to allow any other play of mine to be degraded into an operetta or set to any music except its own."[4] Nor had Shaw been impressed in 1921 when Franz Lehár had

Rehearsal for the Broadway production of My Fair Lady,
January 1956 (Photofest)

the notion that *Pygmalion* would be an excellent basis for a musical work. In his response, Shaw mentioned the Straus adaptation and stated firmly that "A *Pygmalion* operetta is quite out of the question."[5] Yet the playwright was not against the idea for whimsical reasons. As he explained, during the time of *The Chocolate Soldier*'s domination of the stage, nobody wanted to produce *Arms and the Man*. He continued: "*Pygmalion* is my most steady source of income: it saved me from ruin during the war, and still brings in a substantial penny every week. To allow a comic opera to supplant it is out of the question." Shaw's eagerness to protect himself financially should be borne in mind when considering his refusals to allow more of his works to be set to music. Anxiety over the potential loss of money was Shaw's main concern from the very moment he heard of the proposed *Chocolate Soldier* project in 1907.[6]

The Shaw estate would ultimately receive a huge sum of money from *My Fair Lady*, however, and his objections often seemed to be more on artistic than practical grounds. For instance, a musical *Pygmalion* was also the subject of RAF serviceman E. A. Prentice's request to Shaw in 1948. A stern reply was dispatched, forbidding "any such outrage" and adding that "If *Pygmalion* is not good enough for your friends with its own verbal music, their talent must be altogether extraordinary." He advised instead that they might put on Mozart's *Così fan tutte*, or Offenbach's *La Grande-Duchesse de Gérolstein*.[7] At around the same time, Gertrude Lawrence approached Shaw about a potential musical adaptation of *Pygmalion*, following her success as Eliza Doolittle in the play. Noël Coward was to write the score, and Fanny Holtzmann, the New York attorney for both Lawrence and Coward, communicated with Shaw on their behalf. Again, the playwright was sharply dismissive, calling it "crazy nonsense" and saying that "Noël could not conceivably interfere in my business."[8]

These refusals came even after he had entrusted the cinematic adaptation of his plays to Gabriel Pascal, who made his film of *Pygmalion* in 1938, so we may take it that Shaw was firm in disliking the idea of his works being set to music, regardless of who approached him. But it is apparent from these letters that various people thought *Pygmalion* was excellent material for a musical. The initial obstacle was the playwright himself, but on his death in 1950 the possibility arose again, this time with a more realistic hope of it being brought to fruition.

THE THEATRE GUILD AND THE SEARCH FOR A COMPOSER

October 1951–May 1952

The first public mention of a musical adaptation of *Pygmalion* for Broadway came in the *New York Times* on May 20, 1951. In a gossip column dealing with show business, the journalist Lewis Funke wrote about Mary Martin's immediate plans to take her hit 1949 show *South Pacific* to London. Funke went on to write that Cheryl Crawford, who had previously produced Weill's *One Touch of Venus* for Martin, "has spoken to her about a musicalized version of *Pygmalion* . . . [I]t is understood that "feelers" have been put out to the Shaw estate on the subject. Miss Crawford, understandably, might even be nurturing the idea that she could interest Rodgers and Hammerstein in the project."[9] The story was taken up on October 5, 1951, by another *Times* columnist, Sam Zolotow, who wrote that "In Richard Rodgers' opinion, the chances are 'fairly good' for him and his team-mate, Oscar Hammerstein II, to acquire the rights to *Pygmalion* from the Shaw estate. Their objective, of course, would be to convert the celebrated play into a musical. . . . Mr. Rodgers conceded that Mary Martin was a possibility [for the lead role]." The article continues by explaining that although an identical project had already been considered jointly by Mary Martin and Cheryl Crawford, the latter would no longer be part of the production.[10]

It seems that Rodgers and Hammerstein decided not to take the *Pygmalion* idea any farther, but the Theatre Guild started to explore the potential of the material, as can be seen in various letters from the Guild's papers at Yale University. The Guild was approached by Gabriel Pascal, with a view to co-producing the show. While in Hollywood on the Theatre Guild's behalf, Armina Marshall on October 24, 1951, wrote to her husband, the Guild's executive director Lawrence Langner, to report on a meeting with Pascal. He said that he had the rights to make a musical adaptation of *Pygmalion*, and claimed that he could persuade Frank Loesser, composer and lyricist of *Where's Charley?* and *Guys and Dolls*, to write the score.[11] But it seems that Loesser was unwilling or unavailable (perhaps because he was preoccupied with his next show, *The Most Happy Fella*); on January 4, 1952, Langner reported that he had now contacted Cole Porter about writing the show, and said that he would meet him on January 8.[12] Again, though, the Theatre Guild had drawn a blank, because, as Langner suggested, Porter "anticipated difficulty in writing 'English' lyrics." So on February 15 Langner wrote to Pascal with a list of composers they would be happy to employ, in order of priority: Irving Berlin, Frank Loesser, Gian Carlo Menotti, Harold Rome, Frederick Loewe, Harold Arlen, and Arthur Schwartz.[13] Conveniently, Langner was about to leave for the Bahamas, where their first choice, Irving Berlin, happened to be vacationing. But he, too, evidently declined. Nevertheless, the *New York Times* had reported on January 27 that the Theatre Guild was likely to produce the show, and the public announcement of their interest shows the seriousness with which they were pursuing the project.[14]

Langner and Pascal now turned to Lerner and Loewe, who had written four Broadway shows together: *What's Up?* (1943), *The Day Before Spring* (1945), *Brigadoon* (1947), and *Paint Your Wagon* (1951). The timing of the first three of these is ironic, since it reflects that of Rodgers and Hammerstein's first three shows together, and the fates of their respective shows were opposite: *What's Up?* was a flop that opened in the same year as their record-breaking *Oklahoma!*; *The Day Before Spring* fared only slightly better than its predecessor and has fallen into obscurity, unlike the contemporaneous *Carousel*; and Rodgers and Hammerstein's third show, *Allegro*, was their first critical and financial disappointment, opening in the same year as *Brigadoon*, Lerner and Loewe's first great success.

Without *Brigadoon*, who knows what may have become of the Lerner and Loewe partnership. Neither *What's Up?* nor *The Day Before Spring* produced anything approaching a hit song, and indeed much of the score for the former is lost.[15] Lerner and Loewe had also collaborated on *Life of the Party* in 1943, and this piece did not even make it to Broadway, so by 1947 they were badly in need of success. Thankfully *Brigadoon* became one of the longest-running musicals of the decade and gave birth to a number of standards, including "The Heather on the Hill" and "Almost Like Being in Love." It took four years before the pair teamed up again for *Paint Your Wagon*, and here a troublesome rehearsal and tryout period led to a disappointing show. Even though a number of the songs became well known, including "They Call the Wind

Maria" and "Wandrin' Star," the Wild West setting was a poor fit for Loewe, and Lerner failed to resolve numerous problems with the book.

The team's track record is ample demonstration of the reason they were included on the list of possible collaborators for the *Pygmalion* musical and also why they were not at the top of it. To turn to the old pros Irving Berlin and Cole Porter first was natural, since they had each had relatively recent smash hits with *Annie Get Your Gun* (1946) and *Kiss Me, Kate* (1948), respectively; Berlin was also represented on Broadway with *Call Me Madam* (1950). Since the task consisted of adapting a classic of English literature, one can see in particular why the composer of *Kiss Me, Kate* (partly based on Shakespeare's *The Taming of the Shrew*) would be asked: obviously, a lyricist of sharp wit and a composer with a lightness of touch were needed. Although less experienced as a composer-lyricist—his early years were spent writing lyrics to other composers' music—Frank Loesser was also an easy fit, given the artistic brilliance and box office success of *Guys and Dolls*. On the other hand, the triumph of *Brigadoon* had established Lerner and Loewe's credentials, and the European pedigree of both composer (who was born in Berlin) and lyricist (who was educated in England) must have seemed an obvious fit for Gabriel Pascal and the Theatre Guild.

Pascal met with Lerner and gained his assurance of the *Brigadoon* team's interest in the project during the time they were in Hollywood filming that particular show. It is certain, according to David Drew, that Lerner had earlier considered setting the play with Kurt Weill during the 1940s, so the material was not unknown to him.[16] Lerner's memoir leaves out the Theatre Guild and suggests that Pascal approached him of his own accord, but in her memoir about the Pascal-Shaw relationship, Pascal's widow, Valerie, writes more credibly that Lawrence Langner proposed Lerner and Loewe as the creative team. After a private screening of the film *Pygmalion*, she adds, they became enthusiastic about it. She then states that Lerner and Loewe "came to our house in California on March 21, 1952. During lunch they seemed very eager to tackle the musical, provided Mary Martin would accept the role of Eliza Doolittle. Without her, they felt the musical would not stand up."[17] However, a telegram of March 22 in the Theatre Guild papers shows that it was only at this point that Langner wrote to Pascal to arrange the screening of his film for them, also making reference to having had a "very successful meeting with Lerner and Loewe" and having "succeeded in getting them very interested and excited," so the film was probably not the start of their fascination with the project.[18]

In May, serious talks took place about casting for the part of Eliza Doolittle; at this point, Eliza rather than Higgins was thought of as the lead role, and it was to be a showcase for a great star. The two biggest female musical comedy actresses of the time were Ethel Merman, who had enjoyed success in Gershwin's *Girl Crazy*, several Porter shows including *Anything Goes*, and Berlin's *Annie Get Your Gun* and *Call Me Madam*; and Mary Martin, who had grown in prominence during the 1940s with shows such as Weill's *One Touch of Venus* before her career-defining appearance in Rodgers and Hammerstein's *South Pacific*. Merman's stage persona was ill suited to Eliza Doolittle, but as strange as it might seem in hindsight, the subtler Mary Martin was in fact a strong possibility. This part of the story has been whitewashed over the years, however. In *The Street Where I Live* Lerner claims that Martin heard he was writing a *Pygmalion* musical with Loewe and demanded to hear the songs against the writers' will. Lerner states that in November 1954, Martin and her husband, Richard Halliday, "had read that we were doing *Pygmalion* and [said] that they would love to hear what we had written." Lerner relates that when the meeting took place, "they listened in silence and departed almost immediately after the last song." Later, the lyricist asked Halliday what Martin's reaction had been, and he reported that she had commented, "Richard, those dear boys have *lost their talent*."

But in reality Lerner himself wanted Martin for the role two years earlier, in 1952, and actively pursued her.[19] In a letter to Pascal (who was to go to London to speak with Martin personally) on May 10, the lyricist stated that

> no matter how excited I get about the play, I always stop when I come to the question: can we get Mary Martin? Although there are undoubtedly others who could play it, I do feel anybody after Mary is second choice. Liza is one of the great parts for a woman ever written. In music it will be even greater. And Mary is obviously the greatest star the musical theatre has produced—and there's no doubt about that. Somehow it seems like a perfect marriage. It doesn't bother me at all that she is American because if the King's English as taught to her by the Prof doesn't seem completely compatible with her, neither was it with Liza in the play. And the cockney she can do easily. From a show business point of view it would be a great tour-de-force for her. Then, too, Mary is the only one I know who has naturally that odd combination of the little girl and the great lady. I can't think of another part when both these qualities could be better employed— or on the other side, when Mary could run more of a gamut of all her talents. This is one play that should be written *for* her and *with* her.

Lerner assured Pascal that he would fly to London with Loewe to discuss the show with Martin when they had the outline completed, and then moved on to propose Michael Kidd as the choreographer for the show—again, someone who would be pursued more than once in this capacity. The lyricist felt that Kidd's sense of humor (as evinced by his work on the stylized choreography for *Guys and Dolls*) would be perfect for helping to depict the cockneys and aristocrats, and commended his great sense of the theater; Lerner had already gained the choreographer's interest in the project. After reiterating his enthusiasm about the play, Lerner ended: "I'm ready to do anything short of homicide to see Mary as Liza."[20]

Langner's letter of May 22 corroborates that Lerner and Loewe's chief desire was for Martin to play Eliza. He also underlined the team's excitement about the project and stated that they had already written a scenario.[21] The letter continues by suggesting alternatives to Mary Martin, should she turn the project down (as Lerner suspected, according to the letter). These included the Hollywood star Judy Garland, whose film work was on the wane and was willing to do the show for six months, but Lerner and Loewe did not like the idea; Garland's Hollywood contemporary, the soprano Deanna Durbin; and the leading musical comedy actress Dolores Gray. Of the latter suggestion, the letter indicates that Lerner was willing to accept her if an "exciting man" could be found for Higgins; George Sanders and Noël Coward were suggested. Eventually, Lerner indeed pursued Coward for the part of Higgins, first in the summer of 1952, then in late 1954, and again for the London production, but he met with refusal every time.

The letter also mentions the possibility of starting the show in England and then opening it on Broadway later on, which excited Lerner and Loewe. They were available to start work immediately and suggested first Robert Lewis (who had directed *Brigadoon*) and then John C. Wilson (director of two hit shows, Cole Porter's *Kiss Me, Kate* and Jule Styne's *Gentlemen Prefer Blondes*, as well as producer of Lerner and Loewe's own *The Day Before Spring*) to direct the production. Finally, the letter clarifies the terms on which Lerner and Loewe were to participate in the project—initially they demanded 8 percent without Mary Martin and 6 percent with her, but Pascal over-optimistically thought they would accept 6 percent regardless of their desire for Martin—and underlines their tremendous enthusiasm yet again.

With the fire sparked inside them, ultimately Lerner and Loewe's association with *Pygmalion* was unstoppable, and the Theatre Guild proceeded to arrange a production of Shaw's play for June 1952 to give them some extra inspiration. On May 30, the *New York Times* announced the Guild's intention to produce a *Pygmalion* musical, and would in the meantime stage the play with three musical theater names: Dolores Gray (who had appeared in Jule Styne's *Two on the Aisle*), Tom Helmore (whose Broadway credits included *The Day Before Spring*), and John C. Wilson.[22] The next day, Lewis Funke's column added to the report, saying that "Unless plans become badly unhinged some-where along the way, it appears likely that Alan Jay Lerner and Frederick Loewe will be the team to do the musicalizing. . . . Should all end with signa-tures properly affixed, production will begin as soon as the pair have success-fully wooed the muse."[23] But in the meantime, the Guild still needed to find a star for their show.

NEGOTIATIONS BEGIN: LERNER, LOEWE, AND MARTIN

June–October 1952

All seemed to be going swimmingly. In June 1952 Langner and Marshall went to London to speak with Mary Martin, who remained their first choice for Eliza, and to meet with Elizabeth Barber of the Shaw estate to negotiate terms over the rights to *Pygmalion*. On June 17 Langner wrote to Theresa Helburn to say that according to Barber, Gertrude Lawrence—star of Weill's *Lady in the Dark* and Rodgers and Hammerstein's *The King and I*, in addition to numerous works written by her childhood friend Noël Coward—was also in-terested in playing the role of Eliza Doolittle, and in fact was upset at not being asked in the first place. In Langner's letter the first mention is made of Cecil Beaton as a possible designer.

The letter also indicates that "long discussions" were taking place about Mary Martin but that negotiations with her were stuck until more of the cast and production team could be formed. "We are trying for Rex [Harri-son]," writes Langner, "but if he is not interested we understand Michael Redgrave sings well and is interested." Evidently, Martin would not consider signing the agreement to appear in the show until the following Monday, by which time it was anticipated that more artists would have committed to the show; indeed, the star's power over the team was extraordinary. The next day, Marshall wrote to Helburn in the wake of a meeting with Barber to say that the Guild's relationship with the Shaw estate was solid, also indicating that there was a general consensus to keep the potentially meddlesome Pascal out of the picture (everyone in London "resented him inching in," Marshall added).[24]

In reply to Langner on June 20, Helburn reported that Gertrude Law-rence's performance in *The King and I* was currently drawing so many com-plaints from audiences about her flat singing that Rodgers and Hammerstein wanted her to leave the show, and the Guild should not therefore consider her for the role of Eliza.[25] Helburn also revealed that Lerner and Loewe were haggling over their royalties for the show and that they were "spreading the report that they will have the complete charge of the show and no one else will have anything to do with it!" At that time, Shaw's *Pygmalion* was staged by the Guild, with Dolores Gray as Eliza; Loewe attended the opening night and was impressed with Gray by the end of the show, laying the ground for casting her as Eliza if Martin turned down the role. Finally, the letter mentions that Lerner and Loewe had already approached Rex Harrison, who was very much interested.

Then, on June 25, Langner sent a telegram to Helburn confirming that Mary Martin was attracted to the role but would do nothing until she had heard some music, just as she had heard some of Rodgers and Hammerstein's songs for *South Pacific* before agreeing to play Nellie Forbush. At that time a contract was drawn up but left unsigned.[26] The telegram also mentioned that Maurice Evans (an English actor noted for his Shakespearean performances and who would go on to star in Bock and Harnick's musical *Tenderloin*) was interested in playing the part of Higgins and that Langner would see Michael Redgrave on the same subject the next day. Less than an hour later, Langner sent a second telegram, saying that "On second thoughts, don't advise awaiting Mary."[27] He went on to urge Helburn to settle the deal with Lerner and Loewe at 6 percent using Dolores Gray instead of Mary Martin, since to use a male star of the caliber of Redgrave or Harrison would also cost them percentages, adding to the production's financial risk. Eventually, this would be the cause of a rift between the producers and writers.

Langner wrote again to Helburn on June 27 to report that Lerner and Loewe were willing to go to London (though they ultimately did not go) to play some of the songs they had written, and went on to say that Maurice Evans was interested in the role of Higgins if it fitted in with his other plans (he was about to star in *Dial M for Murder* on the stage).[28] He also intended to speak with Harrison, but Redgrave was no longer a possibility because he had commitments for the foreseeable future. Cecil Tennant of the British agency MCA was to seek out other actors for the smaller roles, and Cecil Beaton confirmed he was interested in doing the designs, though Langner "preferred the American ones better." In terms of a director, three names are mentioned: Peter Brook, who was thought to be "a great gamble, knowing so little of American musical plays"; John C. Wilson, who was Langner's preference; and Noël Coward, who seems to have been a suggestion of Martin's, but who, according to Langner, "never directs any plays except his own."

The beginning of July brought new concerns for the Guild. Helburn wrote to Langner on July 1 about her worries regarding Lerner, who had caused problems for producer Cheryl Crawford the previous year during the creation of *Paint Your Wagon* by making executive decisions about such issues as casting behind her back.[29] The letter also reports that "The haggling still goes on over the Lerner-Loewe royalties, but they are very keen to do it and will probably come down eventually. I think they are down to 7 percent now so there is only one more percent to go." According to David Mark D'Andre, "Soon her fears began to materialize as rumors reached her that Lerner and Loewe were claiming to be solely in charge of the production. When Helburn challenged them, both men backed down, and a nasty situation was averted."[30]

On July 18 Langner relayed Rex Harrison's remarks about the show, following the Guild's decision to approach him for the part of Henry Higgins: "I think it is only fair to you and myself . . . to wait until some music and lyrics are completed, so that I can hear them and possibly record them myself. After this we could decide whether or not to continue the idea."[31] Harrison himself wrote to Langner on August 7 to say how much he was looking forward to hearing the score.[32] Thus the first choice for Higgins would eventually be the last, though other names later came up in the interim.[33]

THE PROJECT FLOUNDERS

October 1952–January 1953

Lerner and Loewe continued to work on the show and on October 28, 1952, they signed a contract with the Theatre Guild.[34] However, having made such an apparently final decision, they suddenly withdrew. Lerner's explanation of this decision in *The Street Where I Live* is that he met Oscar Hammerstein II at a political rally, discovered that Hammerstein's difficulties with the script when he had tried to write the show with Rodgers coincided with his own, and decided to withdraw on this basis.[35] In the absence of any further evidence, we might more tentatively say that a problem with the book was probably the reason for the decision to abandon the show. This is confirmed by a letter sent by the Guild to Lerner on October 20, 1954, in which Helburn and Langner state that "You withdrew from the project because you said you were unable to lick the book."[36] But it is also worth bearing in mind that the severing of the contract also coincided with the dissolution of the Lerner and Loewe partnership for the time being, as each went to work with another collaborator on another project, so it seems likely, as Steven Bach has suggested, that they quarreled with each other and the script was not the only issue.[37]

Following this, the Theatre Guild and Pascal started pursuing other composers and lyricists, the names on their list including Arthur Schwartz (*The Band Wagon*), Harold Rome (*Wish You Were Here*), Richard Adler and Jerry Ross (*The Pajama Game*), André Previn (one of MGM's staple conductors and composers), and Harold Arlen (*House of Flowers*).[38] According to D'Andre, "Pascal offered to contact Burton Lane and Yip Harburg [of *Finian's Rainbow* fame], but Helburn and Langner thought it would be better to try Leonard Bernstein, Betty Comden, and Adolph Green. Pascal was very enthusiastic about this idea and met with Bernstein two times. Bernstein gave a verbal agreement that he would start work on *Pygmalion* in the fall."[39] On February 8, 1953, the *Times* confirmed that "the Theatre Guild has not forgotten about its proposed project to present a musical version of Shaw's *Pygmalion*. True, the team of Alan Jay Lerner and Frederick Loewe no longer is trying to do the book, score and lyrics. However, overtures now are being played elsewhere."[40]

But at this point Theresa Helburn started to wonder whether the idea of turning *Pygmalion* into a musical was quite as felicitous as it had at first seemed. A musical version of J. M. Barrie's play *What Every Woman Knows* had opened at New York's National Theatre under the title *Maggie* and had been condemned by Brooks Atkinson in the *New York Times*.[41] On February 20, 1953, Helburn wrote to Langner that the review "makes me feel more than ever the difficulty of making an almost classic play as a musical. Isn't *Pygmalion* really fundamentally more difficult than Barrie's play? I think we should consider this carefully before concluding the contract, unless the writers have terrific ideas."[42] It is difficult to know whether Bernstein, Comden, and Green—the dream team of *On the Town* (1944) and *Wonderful Town* (which opened in February 1953 less than a week after Helburn's letter)—actually got around to writing anything for *Pygmalion*, but according to D'Andre, the Theatre Guild relinquished the rights to the play in May, seemingly bringing an end to the projected musical.[43]

CHANGING PARTNERS: LERNER AND LOEWE GO THEIR SEPARATE WAYS

October 1952–September 1954

In the meantime, Lerner and Loewe had both moved on. For the first time since joining forces with Lerner in the early 1940s, Loewe started to write with a different lyricist. In 1953 he set to work with Harold Rome on a musical to be called *A Dancin' Day*, based on Sir Alexander Korda's 1949 film, itself adapted from the play *Saints and Sinners* by Paul Vincent Carroll. On May 27, the *New York Times* ran a story by their correspondent Sam Zolotow saying that Loewe was to write the music for a new show based on *Saints and Sinners*, with Jerome Chodorov and Joseph Fields to write the book (fresh from their success in writing the book for Bernstein's *Wonderful Town*) and Leo Robin (lyricist of Jule Styne's *Gentlemen Prefer Blondes*) to write the lyrics.[44] Loewe, Chodorov, and Fields went on to be involved with the project, but Robin was soon replaced by Harold Rome, composer and lyricist of the shows *Call Me Mister* and *Wish You Were Here*. Rome's papers at Yale University reveal some details of the progress of *Saints and Sinners*. On July 8 an agreement was entered into with Alexander Korda and Paul Carroll for the rights to the show.[45] Then on August 28 Zolotow reported in his column that Moss Hart was to read the script and that if he agreed to direct the show (as he would later take charge of *My Fair Lady*) his brother Bernard Hart and Joseph H. Hyman would produce it together, just as they had done with several plays directed by Hart during the 1940s including *Dear Ruth*, *Christopher Blake*, and *The Secret Room*.[46]

By September 18 circumstances had changed. Zolotow again wrote about the show, this time saying that Moss Hart had read the book and was interested, but because Chodorov and Fields were busy with their new show, *The Girl in Pink Tights*, the *Saints and Sinners* project had been deferred until the next season.[47] In fact, a letter from October shows that Loewe's lawyer was encountering trouble with the rights to *Saints and Sinners*. The composer had been negotiating with Paul Carroll on the understanding that he was the sole rights holder for the material. But it seems that British Lion Productions, the studio that made the 1949 film, was objecting to the deal, so the first of many delays was incurred.[48] On December 9 Zolotow once again turned his attention to *Saints and Sinners*, reporting that Jack Hylton, the British producer of the London productions of classic musicals such as *Call Me Madam* and *Kiss Me, Kate*, would be in charge of the show.[49]

By January 26, 1954, a financial deal had been reached between all parties. It is interesting to observe that Loewe was clearly the driving force behind the musical at this stage—a big difference from the traditional depictions of the Lerner-Loewe collaboration, in which Lerner is usually made out to be the more active of the two. For *Saints and Sinners* the composer had paid the initial $1,000 to Carroll, which Jack Hylton (who is confirmed as the producer) was to repay, along with any further money payable to the British Lion Film Corporation.[50] Within a few months, however, Hylton had withdrawn from the show. On June 11, Zolotow reported that although composition was almost complete, Hylton would no longer produce, with Harold Prince a possible replacement; he again commented on the ongoing search on July 21, now mentioning Burgess Meredith as a possible producer.[51] But there was still none in place by September, leading Benjamin Aslan, Loewe's lawyer, to request that Carroll's representatives accept a smaller payment for the rights to the show than he was ultimately owed, since it was conventionally the producer's job to pay this sum and no one had yet been found.[52]

At this point, Lerner and Loewe reunited on the *Pygmalion* project, and no further work seems to have been carried out on *Saints and Sinners* until 1956. It was not completely abandoned, though. The *New York Times* reported on January 8, 1955, that Fields and Chodorov had "not forgotten *Dancin' Day*" but that Rome and Loewe must complete the score first. Rome's papers indicate that the project was revived in September 1956, six months after the opening of *My Fair Lady*, when the four collaborators had to pay up or relinquish the rights to Carroll's play. In October it was decided that the musical would be made into a film, rather than a stage show, something that was later mentioned in the *New York Times*; and by March 1957 a deal had been reached with Romay Pictures Inc., which would make the film.[53] Nothing more seems to have come of it, however—perhaps because of the gradual demise of the movie musical in the 1950s, or perhaps because Loewe was busy on his new musical with Lerner, *Gigi*—and there is no further mention of it in the Rome papers. An undated typescript for the show has survived, though; some of Loewe's manuscripts for the songs were sold at an auction at Christie's in Los Angeles in 1999; and the Library of Congress possesses a thirty-minute composer's "demo" recording of ten numbers from the show.[54] Therefore, more time was evidently spent on this project than has been previously acknowledged, and it would even be theoretically possible to piece the material together to produce some kind of liberal realization of the work. Both script and composer's demo indicate that the score inclines toward the earlier style of the Loewe of *Brigadoon*, however, and one can see why the composer of *My Fair Lady* and *Gigi* decided to let it go.

Meanwhile, Lerner—ever the insatiable workaholic—had begun work on new projects with Arthur Schwartz. On March 17, 1953, the *New York Times* reported that the pair had "reached an agreement with Al Capp to make a musical of his popular cartoon, *Li'l Abner*, for presentation on Broadway next season. . . . Mr. Schwartz will compose the music and Mr. Lerner will work out the book and lyrics. Together, they will serve as producers of the venture."[55] The article went on to relate how the idea of making a musical out of Capp's cartoons had previously been explored by Joshua Logan, the director of *South Pacific*, and that this would mark the first collaboration between Lerner and Schwartz, who had been a prolific writer of songs for Broadway for more than twenty years.[56] The article also reported that Lerner was writing another play for Schwartz, and that the pair was working on a film adaptation of Lerner and Loewe's 1951 stage show *Paint Your Wagon*—clear confirmation of a rift between the original collaborators, with three projects outlined for the new Lerner-Schwartz combination. Their *Wagon* film had been mentioned in the *New York Times* as early as February 1953, when it was slated to be "the first

Ian Richardson as Higgins in the 1976 Broadway revival of
My Fair Lady *(Photofest)*

feature-length entertainment film to be made in the Cinerama process," though ultimately the musical did not make it to the screen until 1969 when extra songs were added by Lerner and André Previn.[57]

The *Los Angeles Times* had also reported on the movie on February 11, stating that it was "all but set for *Paint Your Wagon* to go before the cameras June 8 as the first Cinerama production here, and a big musical it will be." In addition to the Lerner and Loewe numbers from Broadway, the article continued, "Lerner and Arthur Schwartz are to write eight new songs."[58] Seven of these songs have survived in piano-vocal manuscript and are in the Arthur Schwartz Collection at the Library of Congress. Two of them lack lyrics, but collectively these numbers represent a substantial amount of work. "Bonanza!" is a lively jig in 6/8 time, and like all these songs, it shows Schwartz's lightness of touch in combining the thirty-two-bar song form with the atmosphere of the Wild West. "Californey Never Looked So Good" is a similarly upbeat and optimistic number, and though the lyrics for "Kentucky" have not survived, the use of common time, the tempo indication of *Allegretto,* and the persistently underlined D-major tonality suggest a positive depiction of the state. No words remain for "Paint Your Wagon," either, but it is marked "Slowly" and features the conventional dotted-rhythm accompaniment of western music, apparently used (as far as one can tell) to poignant effect. Although "Noah was a Wisdom Man" maintains the western *tinta* of the rest of the numbers, it also serves as a reminder of the Dietz-Schwartz songs of the 1930s revues, both in its fast harmonic rhythm and witty lyrics ("For after days afloat, it has been wrote, / Nobody wanted to leave the boat"). The finest numbers, however, are "Over the Purple Hills" and "There's Always One You Can't Forget," both of which are gentle, romantic ballads in E-flat major.[59]

At their best, one can see how the fruits of the Lerner-Schwartz alliance might have boded well for future collaborations. Evidently the pair were able to work together fairly quickly, for they came up with these seven songs in only a few months, and a script is also extant in the private collection of Paul Schwartz, the composer's son.[60] No less importantly, it is easy to understand why Lerner might have turned to Schwartz: as a composer, one of his stylistic facets was the ability to create a lot of expressive internal harmonic movement in a song, something that he shared with Loewe. Had the film come to pass, Lerner and Schwartz might have gone on to create a string of works together, and of course the announcement of two stage works in addition to *Paint Your Wagon* shows that this was their intention.

But at this point, a somewhat surprising swap of composers took place. With no progress apparently having been made on *Li'l Abner,* Schwartz signed up to write the score for a show called *By the Beautiful Sea,* starring the Broadway veteran Shirley Booth (who had previously featured in Schwartz's *A Tree Grows in Brooklyn*). Louis Calta's *New York Times* column reported on November 12, 1953, that the composer Burton Lane, who had earlier collaborated with Lerner on the Fred Astaire film *Royal Wedding,* had abruptly withdrawn from *By the Beautiful Sea* "because of changes made in the story line," and that

Schwartz would now take over. His work on the new show (due to open in late February 1954) would "not interfere with the plans for *Li'l Abner*, the musical based on Al Capp's comic strip," which, according to Calta, "will go into rehearsal next August."[61]

But Schwartz's defection to another show seems to have invoked Lerner's ire, according to the composer's son, Jonathan Schwartz. Years later, the latter explained how his father had been in need of money and could not afford to wait for the notoriously slow Lerner to get around to working on their projected stage musicals, hence he went to write *By the Beautiful Sea*.[62] Lerner broke off the relationship with Schwartz and teamed up with Lane, who had left the *Beautiful Sea* show, to write *Li'l Abner*. On June 21, 1954, it was reported that *Abner* was one of three musicals under consideration by director Robert Lewis. According to Zolotow's *New York Times* column, "Herman Levin expects to have the Alan Jay Lerner–Burton Lane show in shape for a November rehearsal date."[63] Another article of August 15, 1954, confirmed that Lerner was "Now busy collaborating with Burton Lane on the forthcoming stage musicalization of the *Li'l Abner* comic strip."[64]

But it was not to be. On seeing Gabriel Pascal's obituary in early July, Lerner thought once more of *Pygmalion*, and on meeting up with Loewe again on the persuasion of Lerner's then-wife, Nancy Olson, he realized they could work together on the play.[65] Composer and lyricist put everything else aside and set to work. The entrance of Herman Levin into the story at this stage was crucial, since although the *Li'l Abner* musical did not come to pass in this form (it eventually reached the stage in 1956 with a book by Norman Panama and Melvin Frank, music by Gene De Paul, and lyrics by Johnny Mercer), it was Levin's determination that brought *My Fair Lady* about in the face of adversity. Lerner informed Levin that he was putting *Li'l Abner* to bed for the time being and that he wanted Levin to produce *Pygmalion* instead, with Loewe as the composer.[66] The producer was understandably surprised but trusted Lerner, and there was now no looking back.

2

FROM PAGE TO STAGE
• • •
THE GENESIS OF *MY FAIR LADY*

PYGMALION WITH LEVIN, LERNER, AND LOEWE

October–December 1954

On October 11, 1954, Herman Levin announced to the press that he was to produce Lerner and Loewe's musical version of *Pygmalion*. Sam Zolotow reported that the Lerner-Lane treatment of *Li'l Abner* had been deferred and that "*Pygmalion* may be put on here."[1] This caused dismay and shock in the Theatre Guild camp, and Theresa Helburn and Lawrence Langner wrote a letter about the matter to Lerner. He responded on October 19:

> My reaction is puzzlement and bewilderment. Pascal, not The Theatre Guild, was the owner of the rights, and it was he who approached us about the project in California, much before any arrangement with The Theatre Guild . . . Gaby was negotiating with Thompson and Allen before he died. Suppose that negotiation had been concluded and they had approached Fritz and me and we had accepted? Would you have written us as you did? Of course not. The property belonged to Pascal as it now belongs to his estate, and it is with his estate we negotiated.[2]

Lerner's letter went on to explain that he and Loewe did not return to the Theatre Guild with the project because of the difficulties they had over the royalty agreement. He claimed that everybody else "held firm on their royalty and only the author was asked to accept less than minimum. My ego was not troubled, but my sense of fairness was definitely jarred." He ended, triumphantly: "Suffice to say I have improved my lot with Herman Levin." The response from the Theatre Guild was strong: "To say that we have been played a dirty trick is not a fair characterization of what has happened."[3] But in spite of the Guild's fury at having been left out of a project on which they had once worked so hard, Levin, Lerner, and Loewe moved on with the show.

The correspondence from Levin's papers begins on October 2, 1954, with a letter from Noël Coward in London to Levin in New York, in which he stated that he was about to play cabaret seasons in London and New York, where he was due to arrive in the first week of December. The significance of this becomes clearer in Levin's reply from October 15: "When you get here the first week in December, I hope that you will be able to spend an hour with Alan Lerner, Fritz Loewe and myself. We want to tell you of a project that may interest you." Clearly Lerner and Loewe had revived the original idea of having Coward as Henry Higgins, but this letter almost ends all mention of Coward's connection with the Broadway production. The meeting may have taken place, but on January 25, 1955, Coward sent Levin a very final refusal in which he indicated that he was committed elsewhere well into 1956.[4]

No leading man for the show, then, but preparations were underway. Levin's next move was to contact the designer Oliver Smith, his old friend and colleague from musicals such as Jule Styne's *Gentlemen Prefer Blondes* (1949) and Harold Rome's *Bless You All* (1950), both of which Levin co-produced with Smith (who also designed them). On October 17, 1954, Smith wrote to Levin from Hollywood (where he was designing the film version of Rodgers and Hammerstein's *Oklahoma!*) in the wake of a brief visit to New York, giving some tantalizing details about the *Pygmalion* musical: "Please write me about *Pygmalion*. Are the rights cleared? I want to start soon working on ideas. I have some wonderful research here which will be absolutely terrific. . . . Send me a scenic outline so I can begin to think about *Pygmalion* soon."[5]

Smith's eagerness to start work on what would become *My Fair Lady* is palpable. It is also interesting that he was the first member of the production team to be hired; indeed there appears to have been no debate as to which designer to use for the show. Levin replied to Smith on November 1 with a surprisingly early production date: "From what Alan and Fritzie tell me, *Pygmalion* is coming along beautifully, and if it continues that way and we can get our casting done in time, we should be in rehearsal by February 15th."[6] So although very few letters from this period survive, Levin was evidently intent on getting the show on the stage within a few months: although he concedes that "I can't promise the February 15th date, and we all know that February 15th could become September 15th"; he also asks, "If we do go in February . . . will you still be able to do it?"

The producer continues with a further important piece of information: "I'm having lunch with Cecil Beaton today, because I feel very strongly that he is the best one to do the costumes." From this, one might infer that Levin was responsible for choosing Beaton for the show, though of course he had been in the running with the Theatre Guild's potential version in

1952; however, Lerner claims that the choice was "unanimously agreed" upon and that the conversation with Beaton took place during Lerner, Loewe, and Levin's trip to London in early 1955.[7] Also crucial to the genesis of the show is a final reference in the letter from Levin to Smith: "It's much too early to send you a scenic plot," he says, "because, though they've got the book outlined, they have been working mostly on songs." Although Lerner never claimed to have written the script by this point, it seems surprising that so little had been prepared by way of a scenic outline: How were the songs motivated, if not by the plot? We know at the very least that a detailed synopsis had been produced for Mary Martin in 1952. Of course, Levin may have deliberately wished to resist unveiling specific information about the show while so much had yet to be decided, but it does indicate, if nothing else, that his February 1955 rehearsal date was rather optimistic.

The next we hear of the show is a telegram of November 19, 1954, in which Barron Polan (an artists' agent) wrote to the actor Michael Redgrave, supposedly at the suggestion of the conductor Lehman Engel, to ask whether he was interested in playing Henry Higgins.[8] Redgrave responded on November 25 to confirm that he was indeed intrigued by the proposal: "I hope that Mr. Levin will send me the script and, of course, the score." Allusion is made to Lerner and Loewe's initial attempt at turning *Pygmalion* into a musical two years earlier, when he had been approached by the Theatre Guild. "I have never heard any more about it," he said, adding that he was still "very much" interested.

This letter made its way to Levin, who replied to Redgrave on December 1. By this time, the rehearsal start-date was put back to August 15, 1955, and he announced to Redgrave: "We are talking to Cyril Ritchard about directing the book, to Michael Kidd about doing the choreography and to Cecil Beaton about doing costumes."[9] Levin also told the actor that he would be visiting London in two months' time, and asked him whether he would be available to begin the show in August. No further documentation is forthcoming about later stages of the Levin-Redgrave negotiations, but Redgrave evidently decided to commit to another project. An extract from his diary (held in the Victoria and Albert Museum's collections) of January 16, 1955, shows that Levin called him even after he had turned down the role, in an attempt to persuade him to do it: "Sleeping when Corin [Redgrave's son] tells me a call from NY is thro' . . . It is Levin from NY about *Pygmalion*. He . . . suggests I could get out of Clurman-Giraudoux commitment.[10] But in spite of Levin's persistence, Redgrave apparently still refused, and the producer turned to Rex Harrison.

THE THEATRE GUILD RETALIATES

December 1954–June 1955

In the meantime, the Theatre Guild was determined not be excluded by Lerner and Loewe. They gained the support of Richard Halliday, Mary Martin's husband, who felt that "the Guild had a moral claim to participation in the project."[11] A memo of December 15, 1954, records a telephone conversation between the Guild and Halliday, in which the details of the rights to the play become clear. Paul Ramsay of the Chase National Bank was handling Gabriel Pascal's estate, which was convenient for Lerner because Ramsay was an old family friend and was also looking after his recently deceased father's property. Halliday hoped to reconcile all parties, provided that Lerner "came with clean hands." According to David D'Andre, both sides approached Mary Martin, and she "began to show serious interest in the project, especially because she was currently taking speech lessons to learn the Cockney accent."[12] On December 27, Langner wrote to Ramsay to ask about the possibility of purchasing the rights to *Pygmalion* and underlined the Guild's early participation in the show.[13] With some reason, he was clearly annoyed.

The matter came to a head early in 1955. On January 18, Halliday reported to the Guild on the audition of Lerner and Loewe's songs held the previous night in the presence of Levin, Lerner, Loewe, the designer Mainbocher, Mary Martin, and Halliday. According to the memo, both he and Martin were "not satisfied with the lyrics or musical material the score offers her." They thought many things in it were "good," but "Mary in particular did not get any particular lift out of the songs planned for the part of Liza."[14] The memo continues by stating that Martin and Halliday would not commit themselves at this time, even if it meant that Lerner and Loewe took the show to others. Martin still felt that "this is the best role and the best story" for her and confessed that "this is a decision they have reached with great regret." Additionally, the memo mentions a meeting due to take place between Halliday and Harold Freedman, who had been appointed by the Chase Bank to decide to whom to give the rights to *Pygmalion*. Underneath the memo, a handwritten note says that Halliday phoned after this meeting and that "Harold strongly upholds the Guild interest" in the show.

In early February, the narrative took an unexpected turn as Rodgers and Hammerstein, who had considered writing the *Pygmalion* musical all those years earlier, now re-entered the picture and held four conversations with the Guild. On February 8 at 2:30 p.m., Helburn met with Rodgers at her apartment, and proposed that he and Hammerstein now write the show. This would ensure that Martin would agree to play Eliza, which in turn should help guarantee that the Guild be given the rights to the play (though one wonders how enthusiastically Rodgers and Hammerstein would have capitulated to the idea of allowing the Guild to produce their shows again, after having parted ways following *Allegro* in 1947). Rodgers "seemed actively interested" and "promised to discuss the matter further with Mr. Hammerstein." The following day, he rang Helburn and confirmed that Hammerstein was intrigued. A meeting was arranged for February 10, but Hammerstein wished "to be sure that [the] story problems are clear so that he would not encounter any major writing snags." Helburn's assistant then reported to Harold Freedman, who "expressed interest" but wanted to create a safety net to protect them if Rodgers and Hammerstein withdrew after an agreement was reached; Freedman would "have to place a substantial financial forfeit in the contract." Hunter also phoned Halliday, who was "enthusiastic" and "delighted." The bottom of the page declares: "ALL PARTIES SAYING THEIR PRAYERS!"[15]

Perhaps Rodgers and Hammerstein were still not convinced they could overcome the problems they had always had with the book, for there is no further record of their work on the show. In any case, Lerner and Loewe had proceeded to such an extent that they had now completed a significant portion of the show, putting them ahead of the game. In *The Street Where I Live*, Lerner explains that he also tipped the balance by asking Freedman to represent him and Loewe, so that it was no surprise when Freedman advised the Chase Bank to give them the rights for *Pygmalion*. With the permission, the inspiration, and the added satisfaction of succeeding where Rodgers and Hammerstein had given up hope, they were now unstoppable on the road to completing the musical within a year.

THE SEARCH FOR A CHOREOGRAPHER

December 1954–June 1955

Meanwhile, Herman Levin proceeded to put the production together. Among his papers is a telegram of December 21, 1954, from Michael Kidd (choreographer of stage shows such as *Guys and Dolls* and films including *The Band Wagon*) to Lerner, in which he expressed interest in the show and asked if any of the script was available for him to read.[16] In Lerner's autobiography, Kidd is the subject of a memorably embarrassing anecdote. Lerner calls Kidd "a rather unemotional fellow" and says that his reaction to "You Did It" was simply, "That's wrong" (representative of his generally dismissive attitude toward the material). Intriguingly, Lerner also says that "The problem of

The ball scene from My Fair Lady, *showing* (left to right) *Christopher Hewitt (Zoltan Karpathy), Julie Andrews (Eliza), and Rex Harrison (Higgins) (Photofest)*

selecting a choreographer for *Pygmalion* was . . . complicated by the dramatic fact that neither Moss [Hart], Fritz nor I felt the show required a great deal of dancing," so it was difficult to entice someone to play what seemed like a secondary role in the production.[17]

In Lerner's formulation, Hart is categorically included as part of the decision not to have much dancing in the show, and Lerner also claims that when the score was played and sung for the none-too-impressed Kidd, Hart became angry with the choreographer and refused to contemplate teaming up with him.[18] However, since Hart only agreed to direct the show around June 12, 1955, and signed his contract some time after June 18, he can surely have had no major input into decisions such as choosing the choreographer until this later period.[19] Yet Lerner first spoke to Kidd about the show in mid-January—his telegram of January 25 to Levin mentions having had a "long talk with Kidd on Sunday"—and two letters written by Levin on April 1 suggest that the producer, composer, and lyricist intended to meet with Kidd during a trip to the West Coast on April 8, long before Hart was hired.[20] A gap in the Levin correspondence from April 6 to April 30 suggests that the trip indeed took place. It is possible that the meeting between Hart, Lerner, Loewe, and Kidd occurred as Lerner claimed, but all mention of Kidd simply disappears after the April trip to Hollywood, indicating that a meeting of a similarly negative character to the one Lerner describes may have taken place during this time instead, only without Hart.

Linked to this are three letters between Levin and Oliver Smith. On May 30, Smith wrote to Levin that "Gower [Champion] sounds very good for dances," seemingly in reply to Levin's letter of May 17 in which he hoped "to know something more about the director and choreographer situation in about a week." But Levin's irritable response on June 2 not only proves that Kidd was no longer in the frame for the show but contradicts another aspect of Lerner's chronology. Lerner claims that Gower Champion was the first choice for choreographer, but it is clear both from Smith's mention of "Gower" on May 30 and from Levin's reply that the team had turned to him a good six months after first pursuing Kidd. "I still haven't made a deal with Gower," wrote Levin on June 2. "All choreographers, it seems to me, have in the last couple of years been infected with an overdose of self-importance—and he is no exception. Who did the dances for *Show Boat*? I am meeting with him today and have some hopes that the matter will be settled then."[21] Levin's letter does, however, corroborate Lerner's account of the reason for Champion's not becoming the choreographer: "When Herman sat down with [Champion']s representatives, his terms were more than we could afford."[22]

SEEKING ELIZA

January–March 1955
These negotiations with various choreographers—which did not cease until September 1955, when Hanya Holm signed her contract to do the show—were but a small part of the work faced by Lerner, Loewe, and Levin. Casting the lead roles took months of work. At the same time as pursuing Michael Redgrave and Noël Coward, their thoughts were turning to the role of Eliza Doolittle. As part of a telegram to Levin on January 25, Lerner made a reference to Judy Holliday, the future star of Jule Styne's *Bells Are Ringing*, who was apparently an early possibility for the role.[23] Nonetheless, Lerner and Levin soon opened talks with Julie Andrews during her stint in the first cast of the Broadway production of Sandy Wilson's *The Boy Friend* from September 1954.

On April 1, Levin wrote to Oliver Smith to say that "Unless something goes awry, Julie Andrews, who plays the lead in *The Boy Friend*, will play Eliza."[24] During this three-month period of January–March 1955, then, Lerner and Loewe asked Andrews if she was interested in the role, auditioned her, and formally asked her to do the part, and Levin began negotiations with her agent. She signed an agreement to play the part of Eliza on March 31, earning $1,000 per week for the first of her two years under contract, being given second-star billing, performing on the original cast album for $1,000 per day, being permitted a personal dresser, and being allowed a lay-off of eight weeks after the first year.[25]

Yet both Andrews and Lerner appear to disagree slightly with this timescale. In her autobiography, *Home*, Andrews says that as her contract for *The Boy Friend* "neared completion, I began to grow very excited about returning to London [in October]," but was then approached about playing the part of Eliza.[26] However, it is difficult to see how January could be seen as "near the completion" of Andrews's contract, which was not until the end of September 1955. Lerner, too, is curiously vague about when these events took place: he describes how he went to see *The Boy Friend* with Levin and Loewe, met with Andrews, and asked her not to make any commitments until the rights for *Pygmalion* had been acquired.[27] But Andrews differs with this description slightly by saying that she was "amazed" when the offer "came through," implying a time lapse between the audition process (during which period she also auditioned for Rodgers and Hammerstein's *Pipe Dream*) and the offer.[28]

Throughout this phase, the only evidence of another actress possibly playing the role of Eliza is in a letter from the agent Deborah Coleman, who wrote to Levin on February 3 to suggest Vanessa Lee (one of Ivor Novello's leading ladies) for the part, but no further mention is made of Lee elsewhere in Levin's papers.[29] Four days later, Levin wrote letters to two agents to announce that he would be going to London on February 15 to "do some casting on the leads for the musical version of *Pygmalion*."[30] The ambiguity of the phrase "casting on the leads" may suggest that the team was undecided as to whether to use Andrews or not, and there is evidence that Petula Clark was auditioned for the show in March 1955 during the visit to London.[31] But in truth, there seems never to have been a serious alternative discussed for the role once Andrews's name had come up, and as history has shown, she was the perfect choice.

A VISIT TO LONDON

January–March 1955

Aside from the casting of Eliza, Levin's letters of February 7 appear to uncover a massive discrepancy in Lerner's autobiography regarding the visit to London in the early months of 1955. Lerner describes how, in order to fund the trip to England, he sold his share of stock in a gold mine left to him and his brothers by their late father—"And so it was that shortly after the first of the year, we took off to visit the original scenery."[32] He talks about arriving "that cold January night"[33] and meeting up with Rex Harrison (whom he claims was his first choice for the role of Higgins),[34] says that Cecil Beaton agreed to do the costumes during this time,[35] mentions that Harrison agreed to play Higgins after five weeks of procrastination, and avers that Lerner, Loewe, and Levin left London in mid-February.[36] Yet according to Levin's letters of February 7, he intended to leave New York on Tuesday February 15 and arrive in London the next day.[37] Therefore, Lerner's departure date was in fact the arrival date for the producer. Levin's letter continues: "The Messrs. Lerner and Loewe will follow me in a few days." Again, this contradicts the romantic image Lerner conjures up of a "little brigade" of people all traveling together, because clearly they went in at least two separate parties.[38]

As to their activities during the visit, it is difficult to be much more specific, other than to rely on Lerner's account as outlined. A letter from Levin to Cecil Beaton confirms that the two met in London and clarifies that his agreement to do the show depended on being given permission by Irene Mayer Selznick to do it at the same time as working on a production for her.[39] The main purpose of being in England, of course, was to secure the services of Rex Harrison, and negotiations with the actor resulted in a preliminary agreement drawn up by Levin at Claridge's Hotel on March 18.[40] Harrison's terms were that his guaranteed salary would be $3,000 per week, plus 10 percent of the gross box office receipts between $30,000 and $50,000; that he was guaranteed a minimum of six weeks' employment or $18,000 in lieu; that he would be given first-star billing, though the actress playing Eliza Doolittle could be co-starred if Levin chose; that the contract would last a year; and that rehearsals would begin on or after October 1, 1955, subject to two conditions: the closing of the play *Bell, Book and Candle* in which Harrison was starring in London at the time, and a four-week lapse between the end of the play and the start of rehearsals for the musical. The final point in the agreement is a fascinating list of directors with which both parties were happy. The choice was subject to Levin and Harrison's mutual approval, but both were amenable to the following names: John Van Druten, Alfred Lunt, Moss Hart, Robert Lewis, Peter Glenville, Tyrone Guthrie, Hume Cronyn, Cedric Hardwicke, and Cyril Ritchard. It is striking that Hart was third in the pecking order here, since various writers have suggested that his name "headed the list."[41]

The other business to be conducted while in London was to find an actor for the role of Alfred P. Doolittle, Eliza's dustman father. Exactly when Stanley Holloway's name first came up is uncertain; the earliest documentary evidence is a letter from Lillian Aza, his agent, on February 24, 1955, in which she informed Levin of her contact details, having heard that he was interested in using Holloway.[42] No known documentation exists for the actual meeting between them, but Lerner and Holloway's autobiographies largely concur on the matter. Lerner says, "In New York, when we first discussed the part of Doolittle, both Herman and I had the same first thought: Stanley Holloway. I remember him well from my schooldays in England and we both had seen some of his recent motion pictures. Herman called him and we all had lunch together at Claridge's. He loved the idea of playing Doolittle."[43] With his typical inclination to embroider his text with humorous stories, Lerner also relates Holloway's reaction to the team's question as to whether he could still sing after many years away from the stage: "Without a word he put down his knife and fork, threw back his head and unleashed a strong baritone note that resounded through the dining room, drowned out the string quartet and sent a few dozen people off to the osteopath to have their necks untwisted."

On March 14, Lillian Aza wrote to Levin with a list of points to be included in Holloway's contract, following a meeting in London a week earlier.[44] Among other details, Holloway was to be paid $1,000 per week; rehearsals were still scheduled to begin "on or about" August 15; and his billing was to be equal to that of the actors playing Higgins and Eliza "unless the artiste eventually engaged for the part of Higgins is a star of such caliber that he commands larger billing." Aza also required that Levin let her know whether rehearsals were to be postponed until October 1, because Holloway had received an offer of a film contract for that time. Although Aza had asked him to reply before he left England, Levin did not answer until March 25, by which time he was back in New York. He was now able to announce that rehearsals had been deferred to October 1 and clarified that Holloway would receive first featured billing if Levin could not arrange co-star billing.

He also quibbled at Aza's terms regarding the length of contract, which she had specified as lasting "for the run of the play," but Levin requested instead that Holloway be under contract for three years, explaining that this was the tradition under American Equity.[45] Levin ended by promising that "the terms agreed upon will in a short time be incorporated in an Actor's Equity Contract and sent you for Mr. Holloway's signature," but there would follow a delay of several months, during which time the increasingly agitated Aza would keep urging Levin to set a rehearsal date and submit the contract. On March 31 she wrote to him again, requesting that he could leave the show after two years if he should wish, and further arguing his cause regarding billing. "If Rex Harrison demands first billing, then we will, of course, agree," she allowed, "but I do feel Stanley should be billed in the same type as Julie Andrews." After all,

Holloway was far more experienced than the young Andrews. Aza now also added the proviso that Holloway be given first refusal of the role of Doolittle if the show went to London.[46] Five days later, Levin replied in agreement with the latter request but was firm in insisting that Holloway accept first featured billing if co-star billing could not be arranged, an argument that would continue to rancor throughout the run of *My Fair Lady*.[47]

Also on March 31, Levin was sent a letter about Harrison's contract from his agent, Laurence ("Laurie") Evans, who mentioned a proposed trip by Lerner and Loewe to London on June 18. They were to bring Harrison more of his songs once they had written them; Evans had already booked rooms for their trip.[48] The next day, Levin wrote to Evans, though he had clearly not yet received his letter. Levin admitted that "it was awfully hectic the first week that [he] was back" but now had time to bring Evans up to date. He mentioned his forthcoming trip to the East Coast to see Michael Kidd and John Van Druten; he asked Evans to inquire as to a fair financial deal for Harrison's role in the original cast album recording, strongly urged him to speak to Harrison about co-star billing for Holloway, and asked for an update on the business situation regarding *Bell, Book and Candle* (since until Harrison was able to leave the play, *My Fair Lady* could not go into rehearsal).[49] The same day, Levin also wrote to Oliver Smith. He confirmed that a deal had been made with Harrison to play Higgins. "I feel it is ideal casting," he added, "and I have a hunch that you will agree with me."[50] Levin also mentioned that Holloway had signed for Doolittle ("I think he will be wonderful") and that Andrews would almost certainly play Eliza. He asked Smith to call him on Friday afternoon at the Beverly Hills Hotel to "make a date." In a postscript, Levin also confided that Beaton had agreed to do the costumes—"but keep this under your hat. Just in case I find it too tough to make a deal with Arnold Weissberger, we may want to turn to Irene [Sharaff]."

GOING HOLLYWOOD AND PACIFYING HOLLOWAY

April–July 1955

After this, all we hear of Levin's actions while in Hollywood is a series of telegrams between him and John Van Druten, the prospective director, who was known for writing the plays *I Remember Mama* and *I Am a Camera*, as well as for directing the original Broadway production of *The King and I*. His association with *The King and I*, which features a simmering relationship between the king of Siam and the governess Anna Leonowens that is not unlike that of Higgins and Eliza, may well have been the reason for this choice of director.

On April 5, Levin wired Van Druten to confirm his arrival on the Friday and to request a meeting on the following Monday, and eventually the director agreed.[51] As stated earlier, no evidence about any possible conversations with Michael Kidd has survived, but a telephone message sent to Levin on May 9 confirms that Van Druten was busy until October and could do the show only if the production were to be considerably delayed.[52] Thus at the end of his trip to Hollywood, Levin returned with neither a director nor a choreographer.

In the meantime, Aza wrote to Levin again about the rehearsal date, because if Holloway were to be free until the end of October he could accept yet another film contract.[53] Levin ignored the letter, so she wrote to him again fifteen days later and urged him to finalize both the rehearsal date and the contract.[54] This time, Levin wrote back at length explaining the problem regarding Harrison's contract with *Bell, Book and Candle*. In desperation, he pleaded for leeway from Aza on the date but confirmed that rehearsals would not begin until at least November 1 and said that if she would permit him to put a clause in Holloway's contract to allow for Harrison's problem, Levin would send the document immediately.[55] The discussion continued for some time. On May 12, Aza asked that Holloway be allowed to be free until November 30 in order to make his film and mentioned that the opening of Harrison's new film (*The Constant Husband*) had probably stimulated interest in *Bell, Book and Candle*.[56] Five days later, Levin acknowledged Aza's letter but said he needed more information on the situation with Harrison's play before he could grant the permission Holloway desired.[57]

One has to admire Aza's persistence. On May 31, she reported that she had checked with Harrison's agent directly, who said it was unlikely that the play would fold before the end of October,[58] then on June 13 Levin sent Aza a telegram asking her not to commit Holloway beyond November 1.[59] Two weeks later, she wrote back to say that Holloway had signed to do the film because she had not heard back from Levin, and the outside shots had to be done that very week.[60] Even then, though, Aza continued to badger Levin for Holloway's contract, sending him a desperate telegram on July 13, to which he replied: "ALL HINGES [ON] HARRISON. EVANS ADVISES HOPEFUL SATISFACTORY OUTCOME THIS WEEK."[61]

BELL, BOOK AND CANDLE

April–May 1955

As Levin said, everything hinged on Rex Harrison's availability. Although the main issue was allowing him to be free to leave *Bell, Book and Candle*, negotiations continued as to the finer details of the contract. On April 4, Laurie

Evans asked that Harrison be paid $3,000 per recording day on account of 2 percent of the gross sales of the cast album, going on to mention that the play continued to do very good business.[62] Levin replied at length on April 20, after his return from Hollywood, and for the first time suggested making a deal with Hugh Beaumont, the producer of *Bell, Book and Candle*, to effect a firm date for Harrison's departure. The terms of Harrison's contract allowed him to quit when the gross dropped below £1,750 ($4,902), but Levin proposed that Evans agree with Beaumont to allow Harrison to leave on November 1; in return, Harrison would stay on until that date even if the gross had previously dropped below that amount.

Levin also acceded to the proposed terms of Harrison's record contract, while commenting grumpily that "this is the rate usually paid stars who are record personalities." He added, with an air of condescension: "Perhaps I will be given credit for what in my view is generosity."[63] Five days later, Evans replied that the proposed deal with Beaumont was poorly conceived, because even if Harrison continued in the play when the gross dropped to £1,750, the show would have to close because the operating cost was the same amount. The letter also dealt with the issue of Holloway's proposed co-star billing. Harrison was "completely unwilling" to allow this, wrote Evans: "Rex feels that Holloway's name does not mean anything to Broadway audiences and, additionally, that the part of Doolittle should automatically get feature billing." Throughout their association, there was no love lost between the two actors, and Holloway made his opinion of Harrison well known in the press, even when they were still working together.[64]

For a few weeks, the news from London was brighter. In a letter of May 2, Evans told Levin that the box office takings for the play were down to £2,700 ($7,563). Levin replied on May 6 and promised Harrison's contract the following week.[65] Evans wrote yet again on May 9 and mentioned that the gross had dropped to £2,600 ($7,282);[66] Levin found this letter "encouraging" but mentioned that "this whole thing makes me feel a little like a fellow who is waiting around for someone to die. It's the first time I've ever had any reason to want a show to close rather than run forever."[67] At this point, he also admitted, "It may be that we should resign ourselves to going into rehearsal about December 5th." Again on May 18, Evans mentioned that "business at the Phoenix is slowly going down" and that "Lilli has been ill and was unable to play for five nights," the latter a reference to Harrison's wife, who was co-starring with him in *Bell* but with whom relations had broken down.[68]

But five days later, Levin's worst fears were realized. Evans wrote to the producer again to inform him that "Business has gone right up again at the Phoenix and last week they played to over £3,000 [$8,403]!" He reported a conversation between Harrison, Beaumont, and himself in which Beaumont predicted that the play would run until the end of October and advised Levin to "forego any idea of rehearsing before the end of November or even early December."[69] The producer was depressed at the news and offered to pay Beaumont $2,500 in return for Harrison's release on October 1.[70]

BEATON SIGNS UP; ANDREWS AND EQUITY

April–June 1955

In the meantime, negotiations with Cecil Beaton had gone through—one of the few jobs Levin managed to complete with total success during this frustrating time. Beaton had written to Levin on April 6 to inform him that he was represented by Arnold Weissberger.[71] Some time during the ensuing weeks, Levin made a deal with Weissberger, who wrote to him on May 13 to clarify Levin's offer to Beaton. The costume designer was to receive his round-trip fare from England and a fee of $5,000; $150 a week for the run of the original company in New York and on the road; for each touring company, he was to receive a fee of $2,500 and $100 a week, provided that he supervised the execution of the costumes himself (if he did not, he had to pay the fee of someone else and receive only $75 a week); and for the London company, he was to receive a fee of $2,500 and $75 a week.[72] These terms were agreed, and a week later Weissberger sent Levin three copies by hand, promising to take them with him to England for Beaton to sign.[73] By June 13, Weissberger had returned to New York with the contract, and Beaton became the second member (after Oliver Smith) of the production team to officially join the show; Levin received the contracts on June 16.[74]

Although Julie Andrews had signed an agreement to play the role of Eliza as early as March 31, Levin faced a problem regarding her employment in *The Boy Friend*. According to the terms of the American Actors' Equity Association, foreign actors had to wait six months between engagements. Since at the time of drawing up Andrews's initial agreement Levin still hoped to begin rehearsals between October 1 and November 1, and Andrews was contracted to be in *The Boy Friend* until the end of September, Levin required a waiver from Equity. Therefore, on April 21 he wrote a persuasive letter to them, submitting six points in favor of their granting the waiver: that the "importance of the role of Eliza is self-evident" hence they had "selected Miss Andrews only because no other actress has, in our opinion, the ideal combination of acting talent, voice, skill, appearance, background and prior acceptance by the critics and public, possessed by Miss Andrews"; that Andrews was to be co-starred as additional evidence of the importance of the role; that the employment of American Equity members would not be increased even if someone else were hired for the role because they would still be using an English actress; that when Andrews left *The Boy Friend*, an American Equity member would replace her, therefore creating an employment opportunity; and that the production's importance was proven by its budget of $360,000 and its cast and crew of "fifty to sixty actors, about thirty musicians and about thirty stagehands."[75] The council met on April 26 and the following day agreed to Levin's request, provided that at the conclusion of the *Pygmalion* musical, Andrews would add the unexpired time between the two engagements to the six months' waiting period at that time (i.e., a total of one year).[76]

This accepted, Levin now had basic agreements from his three stars, but the problem with Harrison's play continued to plague the entire production. On May 14, Oliver Smith wrote to Levin to say that "it was exciting to hear the show and some of the songs, which sounded very good" to him, and asked the perennial question: "What are your dates at present?"[77] Poor Levin had to give his standard response—"The date situation is confused"—but mentioned November 1 or December 1 as the likely rehearsal starting point.[78] Smith in return promised to hold himself "in a state of cosmic flux." Then on June 2 Levin moved his dates slightly to "somewhere between November 1st and December 10th," adding, "I don't know who's going to direct. That will be the next problem we must solve."[79]

CBS BACKS THE SHOW; HART DIRECTS

May–July 1955

Aside from finding the director, another issue to be addressed was the question of financing the show. Lerner's autobiography explains how the peculiarities of the Shaw estate—the rights to his plays were only to be given to any one person for a maximum of five years—meant that it would be difficult to find conventional backers (who were used to participating in profits for many years) for the show, and that it could not be made into a motion picture. If the production were to fail, the stakes would be too high.[80] Therefore the team turned to CBS, because a television company could still broadcast either the musical or the play version of *Pygmalion* even if the show flopped, and therefore it would still be worth investing in the play for the fixed period of five years. On May 23, Levin drew up a suggested deal with CBS, whereby they would put up $300,000 plus an overcall of 20 percent ($60,000); CBS would get the rights to televise the show, while the stage version would get television and radio publicity, with the possibility of television coverage of the opening night.[81] The television company followed up on its position on June 15: it was adamant that it would not pay any of the profits due to the Pascal Estate (which owned the screen rights to Shaw's plays), that it wanted the right to take control of the musical if Levin abandoned it, and that it wanted an allocation of house seats.[82] Negotiations continued until July 18, when Levin entered into a final agreement with them.[83]

The month of June was significant primarily for the signing of Moss Hart to the musical. On June 13, Levin wrote to Laurie Evans and mentioned that a deal had been struck. "You probably don't know it," he continued, "but he has been my personal first choice all along." Levin felt he was "the best possible director we could get" and reported that "he has been enormously and excitingly helpful," concluding, "I know that Rex, when they begin to work together, will feel as I do and as the authors do."[84] (Levin also mentioned that Lerner and Loewe had "written some new stuff which I think is just great.") Finally, after seven months of searching, the show had a director.

Cecil Beaton was pleased at the news: "I am *delighted* Moss Hart will direct," he told Levin on June 24. "I have never worked with him before but always had real admiration for his sense of the theatre."[85] This letter also reveals several interesting aspects about Beaton's ideas for the show. He insisted that Levin tell Hart and Smith "how strongly I trust that the production will be set at the time it was written," going on to say how the fashions before the First World War "can be so nostalgic and charming, and will be a great challenge." Beaton went into specifics about the costumes and continued: "I am sure Oliver will argue that the furnishing can be made so much more amusing in the manner of the Early Vogue Covers," adding that the style of 1890–1900 "has really been done to death" and that "that lemon has been squeezed of its last drop!" As well as mentioning his forthcoming arrival in New York to design Irene Selznick's show—"a full time job: I'm liable to be called at any given moment of day or night so cannot promise that you will have much of my time for the first few weeks"— the designer requested that Beaton ask Smith "if he thinks that muted colors might be a bit of a change and yet have their own gaiety. We're all a bit exhausted by orange, scarlet and magenta musicals—and like old Litmus paper refusing to react any more. Do let me have the rough scenic layout as soon as possible."

SECONDARY ROLES; THE FRENZY CONTINUES

June–July 1955

While dealing with these sorts of requests about the production, Levin also began to think more about casting the smaller roles. During his visit to

London, he had auditioned a young actor by the name of Frank Lawless for the role of Freddy Eynsford-Hill, and Levin requested photographs of Lawless from his agent, Basil Geoffrey, on June 12. It seems negotiations fell apart after Levin's trip to England in the summer of 1955, perhaps because Geoffrey demanded a fairly hefty $250 per week for Lawless from the very start.[86] Levin also received a letter from Lou Wilson, Julie Andrews's representative, remind him of the actress's "whistling prowess," which he suggested could be of use to Lerner and Loewe in the cockney scenes.[87] Eventually, of course, the fruits of this suggestion came to bear in "Wouldn't It Be Loverly?"

But still the trouble remained that Rex Harrison could not leave *Bell, Book and Candle* and therefore the musical could not proceed. On June 28, Levin, Loewe, Lerner, and Louis Dreyfus met to discuss the situation and decided to approach Beaumont with the idea of releasing Harrison from his contract in return for a cash payment. It was put to Beaumont that Levin could not "arrange theatre bookings in America, may lose his director, choreographer, as well as other important production personnel. It is further complicated because Harrison is so anxious for a holiday during August that there is some danger that he will agree to continue in the show from September on if [you] will give him the holiday he seeks."[88] Just over a week later, Levin spoke to Laurie Evans on the phone and clarified his position in a letter written immediately afterwards: "Here it is: I am perfectly willing to fly to London if there is a reasonable chance of coming to a deal with Beaumont . . . I am willing to take part in any Byzantine charade whatever, if a satisfactory solution can be found . . . I assure you that if the amount can be agreed upon, I will recompense Rex's company for the payment to Beaumont. I think Beaumont is entitled to receive what can reasonably be anticipated as the loss occasioned by closing. If, after your talk with him and with Rex, it makes sense for me to come over, I'll do so at once."[89] Evidently, Levin was optimistic about the outcome of this deal, for the very same day he wrote to Beaton: "It looks to me as if everything will work out on the rehearsal date—the middle of November—so the time element and conflicts should all be smoothed out."[90] Levin also reported that "Alan and Fritz will certainly be in London in about a month" and that "Alan is preparing a rough scenic layout and I am sure we will send it out within the week."

Yet the frenzy was far from over, as a series of telegrams between Levin and Evans on July 12 and 13 prove. First Levin asked Evans desperately: "HAVE YOU ANY NEWS? LAST WORD I HAVE IS THAT BEAUMONT WILL DO NOTHING. CAN YOU GIVE US ANY HOPE?" Evans replied that the situation was unchanged but that he was hopeful of a satisfactory outcome that week. The next day Levin replied that he would come to London when the moment was propitious, and that Lerner would come in a couple of weeks' time if Evans thought it helpful. Later on July 13, Evans wired back to say that Beaumont would not discuss a closing date but that he was negotiating for Harrison to have the right to give notice after the gross of the play had dropped below £1,700 for two consecutive weeks. On July 15, Levin wrote to Evans to agree to this, "though, of course, it does not solve our problem. Nothing is a final solution except the fixing of a date when Rex can leave *Bell, Book and Candle*."[91] Levin also enclosed a letter that he had written to Beaumont to say that he intended to come to London between August 12 and 15 in the hope of meeting him; the timing was important because while starring in *Bell*, Harrison was also directing a play called *Nina*, which was due to open early in August (though it was eventually brought forward to July 27).[92] Levin wrote another letter to Evans the same day, reiterating his intention expressed to Beaumont that it would be better to arrive after *Nina* had opened and requesting that Evans book hotel rooms for him, Lerner, and Loewe.[93] On July 18, the producer answered Evans's letter, stating that since *Nina* was opening on July 27, the team might as well come to London on August 5 as planned since "Time is important to all of us." Levin asked him again to call Lillian Aza and calm her down. "She is concerned about a starting date for Holloway, and I must say, with some justification. She should have a signed contract by now, but how can I give her one?"[94] Aza herself received a letter from Levin sent on July 18, in which he stated his plan to come to London on August 5 and bring Holloway's contract with him: "I know this is difficult for you—it is difficult for me also," he said. "I don't know what else I possibly can do."[95]

Although the next day Levin informed Evans that he had made reservations to leave New York for London on August 6, on July 28 Levin wired him to postpone the trip.[96] In the meantime, Levin had received word from Beaumont that he would be happy to have a meeting, but that his responsibility was to protect everyone associated with *Bell, Book and Candle*.[97] Evans informed Levin that Harrison was leaving London on August 7 for a two-week vacation and suggested delaying the *Pygmalion* trip until August 21, but Levin was initially reluctant.[98] However, on July 28 Levin sent Evans a telegram cancelling the trip and the hotel rooms.[99]

Curiously, another leading British actor, John Gielgud, sent a letter to his friend Hugh Wheeler that same day, in which he stated: "Oliver Smith rang from N.Y., would I like to do Higgins in the musical of *Pygmalion* as Rex is now problematic. I remain flattered but refuse to be rushed."[100] It is difficult to know how serious an offer this was, since the plans of Lerner, Loewe, and Levin still revolved around Harrison's presence in London, and Smith was only the designer (albeit a sometime co-producer of other Levin projects); it is possible, perhaps, that Levin was tentatively exploring names other than Harrison if the latter continued to be unavailable.

LEVIN VS. BEAUMONT

August 1955

Harrison continued to dominate the producer's activities in August. On the first day of the month, Levin cabled Evans to tell him that he was trying to work out a deal with MGM for a film project they were hiring Harrison to do. It was possible that MGM could give Levin a lever for removing Harrison from *Bell, Book and Candle* and setting a rehearsal date for *Pygmalion*. "However," continued Levin, "we [are] concerned [about] his doing [a] film and immediately begin[ning] rehearsals [for a] big musical. Is he aware [of the] magnitude of [the] physical undertaking?"[101] Finally, some headway was achieved on August 12, as Evans informed Levin that Beaumont was asking for £10,000 in return for Harrison's release on November 19—the hint of a concrete date at last.[102]

Five days later, Levin recorded a conversation he had had on the telephone with Charles Moskowitz of MGM, discussing the penalty provision in the anticipated deal for Harrison's release.[103] The next day, Evans called Levin to discuss the latter's insistence on several conditions before he would allow MGM to make a deal with Beaumont to release Harrison to make the film. Levin was adamant that Harrison be delivered on January 2, 1956, or that MGM would have to pay a penalty for every day thereafter if he were late; he also wanted assurance that the actor would be able to leave *Bell, Book and Candle* in time for him to spend a week in New York with Lerner and Loewe for the preparation of the *Pygmalion* musical. Levin also felt that unless he could get a specific rehearsal date as part of MGM's deal with Beaumont, he may as well negotiate directly with Beaumont himself.[104]

Ultimately, this is precisely what he decided to do. The way he broke the deadlock at this point was vital to the progress of the show. Evans sent Levin a telegram on August 26 to confirm his reservation at the Savoy and an appointment with Beaumont on the following Monday, indicating that Levin was to arrive in London on Sunday.[105] The meeting took place. A memorandum of August 30 indicates two possible deals: either (a) Beaumont would release Harrison on October 29 in exchange for first right of refusal of the British Rights of *Pygmalion* and one-half of 1 percent of the gross of the New York production (though these terms would not apply if Harrison were able to leave *Bell, Book and Candle* under the terms of his original contract); or (b) Beaumont would release the actor on December 3 under the same terms, except that the payment of the percentage of the gross would cease after Beaumont had been paid $25,000.[106] The latter option was agreed upon on September 1. At last, Levin could plan to begin rehearsals in early January with the assurance that Harrison would be available.[107]

CONTRACTS

September 1955

With this news, the producer could set to work finalizing Equity contracts with the production team and actors. Rex Harrison signed on September 2.[108] Julie Andrews signed on September 8.[109] and Stanley Holloway signed on September 13.[110] Levin also managed to find his Freddy Eynsford-Hill in John Michael King, whose contract is dated September 23.[111] On September 27, Robert Coote agreed to play Colonel Pickering, a curiosity of the initial terms being that the management could require Coote to understudy Henry Higgins, although this never came to pass.[112] In June Levin had made a deal with the Trebuhs Realty Company to move into either the Imperial, St. James, Majestic, or Shubert Theatre for the Broadway run, and he maintained a hope even on September 2 that the Imperial might still be an option; on September 9 he signed a contract with Anthony Brady Farrrell of the Mark Hellinger Theatre.[113] The following week, a contract was drawn up with the Shubert Theatre in New Haven for the first of the out-of-town tryouts between 4 and 11 February.[114] Levin then proceeded to book the Shubert Theatre in Boston for the second, longer tryout, but on 2 November this contract was cancelled and he made a deal to hire the Erlanger Theatre in Philadelphia between February 13 and March 10 instead.[115] In an interview with the *Boston Daily Record* in November 1957, the producer would explain a "sentimental" reason for the change: "I happen to be a Philadelphia boy, that's the only reason we played there instead of Boston."[116]

Levin worked mesmerizingly fast during September. On September 12, he drew up Franz Allers's contract as conductor of the show, following an initial agreement of June 27.[117] A veteran of Broadway, Allers had been musical director of the original productions of previous Lerner and Loewe shows *The Day Before Spring*, *Brigadoon*, and *Paint Your Wagon*, and would go on to do the same job for *Camelot*, the 1980 and 1981 revivals of *Camelot*, and the 1981 *My Fair Lady* revival, which would once again star Rex Harrison and Cathleen Nesbitt (as Mrs. Higgins). Also on the musical front, a letter of September 20 from Dr. Albert

Sirmay of Chappell and Co. Publishers confirmed that Robert Russell Bennett would take charge of the orchestrations for the show; Chappell had already signed up to produce and publish the sheet music on August 31.[118] Cecil Beaton and Oliver Smith's final contracts were also drawn up during this period, as was Abe Feder's for the lighting and Hanya Holm's for the choreography.[119]

True to form, Rex Harrison continued to make Levin anxious during this time. He started to drag his heels regarding the record contract with Columbia, who had entered into an agreement on September 7 to finance the entire production.[120] On September 13, Levin wrote to Laurie Evans to hurry the signing of the record album rider for Harrison's contract, and he received an answer two days later. "I am afraid Rex is quite adamant that he will not commit himself before he arrives in New York," said Evans. Levin assured him that "the terms of compensation for him are the same as those paid Ethel Merman, Mary Martin, etc."; it seems this issue was the reason for Harrison's delay.[121] Levin also asked Evans "whether Rex is working on his voice. Did you contact Roy Lowe at the Drury Lane? Is he working with Rex now?" In reply Evans said that Harrison had not yet worked with the vocal coach because there was no actual material to study yet; and in any case, "he doesn't ever want to become a light baritone and he doesn't feel there is any value in simply doing scales, vocal exercises etc."[122]

Mention was made at this time of a forthcoming trip to London by Lerner and Loewe, who had not visited England in August as planned. On September 27, Levin informed Evans that the pair would be leaving for England on October 15, later advising him to "keep Roy Lowe on call, available to meet with Lerner and Loewe as soon as they get to London."[123] Eventually, Levin persuaded Harrison to sign the record company contract, which was sent to him on October 12. Levin also informed Evans that Beaton intended to go to London on November 1, partly to order Harrison's costumes; this is confirmed by Beaton's diaries from the period.[124]

PROGRESS

October–November 1955
Developments continued in October. The veteran actress Cathleen Nesbitt (whose Broadway appearances in the early 1950s included the plays *Gigi*, *Sabrina Fair*, and *Anastasia*) agreed to play the role of Mrs. Higgins, signing her contract on October 4. Christopher Hewett was hired as a lead understudy on October 10 but resigned from the show around opening night.[125] While Lerner and Loewe were in England, Hanya Holm planned

to go to London, Paris, and Berlin to do some research for the choreography and, as mentioned earlier, Beaton went to England to arrange for Harrison's costumes to be made "authentically" in London.[126] To Oliver Smith, Levin suggested exploiting the connection with CBS by borrowing "some ancient-looking phonographs and recording equipment for Higgins's study" from them, one of a number of imaginative ideas made by the evidently excited producer during the show's later gestation period.[127]

Levin was also good at taking care of the press. To Laurie Evans he wrote: "As soon as you know when Rex is arriving here, I will appreciate knowing that as well. I think we can arrange a pretty good publicity break."[128] Evans informed him that Harrison intended to have a vacation in North Africa, spend Christmas in Paris, and leave Europe by air on December 27, arriving in New York the next day; he also mentioned that Harrison's vocal training with Roy Lowe was taking place daily.[129] Similarly, Lillian Aza was asked when Stanley Holloway was to arrive. In her reply, she mentioned a meeting that had taken place with Lerner and Loewe, in which she found them "as charming as ever."[130] She informed Levin that Holloway would fly into New York on December 28, but with only three weeks to go before rehearsals, the actor suddenly decided to go by sea instead because "he finds he has a lot of baggage and also feels the rest will do him good." He now intended to get to New York on December 27.[131]

The arrival of Julie Andrews for rehearsals, however, was less straightforward. In her autobiography Andrews explains how she had only three months between the end of *The Boy Friend* and the beginning of *My Fair Lady*'s rehearsal period, and that this time was further reduced by a period back in America to film the Arthur Schwartz television musical *High Tor* in which she starred with Bing Crosby. Desperately needing to spend more time with her family (whom she had barely seen in over a year and would in all probability rarely see in the ensuing two-year run of *My Fair Lady*), she decided to spend both Christmas and the New Year in England, even though the two male leads intended to arrive on Broadway in late December.[132] This caused some consternation for Levin, Lerner, and Moss Hart. On November 18, the producer wrote to Charles Tucker, Andrews's agent, to urge her to consider coming on December 28 instead of January 2, the day before rehearsals were due to begin. "It would seem to me that this makes sense," he wrote sternly, "not only from the standpoint of the show but from the standpoint of her relationship to the rehearsals, her part and the show itself. The few extra days may be enormously valuable."[133]

But Levin's importunacy was in vain. Tucker defended Andrews at length in a letter of November 23, assuring Levin that he would do anything he could to help, but that the request was impossible. He reminded Levin of Andrews's youth, and informed him that she had been very homesick during the Broadway run of *The Boy Friend*; she wanted to spend the New Year with her family because she did not know when she might see them again.[134] Things came to a head on December 5 when another letter was dispatched from New York directly to Andrews in London. "I am sure you know in advance that our desire to have you here on that date is no capricious whim on our part," wrote Lerner, before launching into a lengthy explanation of why Andrews should arrive in New York at the same time as Harrison and Holloway. "You are a star now, Julie," he said somewhat portentously, and "it would be most impolitic to have them, who are two great and established artists, follow the usual pattern and you not do so." He told her that "much can be accomplished in those few days," such as "freshening" her Cockney and dealing with publicity, and later expressed concern about her being rested and about potential delays to flights around the New Year if bad weather occurred.[135] The letter closed: "Will I see you December 27th? Please. Please." But emotional blackmail and rough handling did not work on Andrews, who took the holiday, which she needed and to which she was entitled, and arrived as she originally planned on the second day of January.

Casting continued apace as, among others, Levin hired Philippa Bevans as Mrs. Pearce on November 15; Rod McLennan as a member of the ensemble (he went on to play a Bystander in the opening scene, as well as Jamie and the Ambassador) and understudy on December 5; Olive Reeves-Smith as Mrs. Hopkins and Lady Boxington on December 9; and Viola Roache (as Mrs. Eynsford-Hill and Mrs. Higgins's understudy) on December 12 (the date when Robert Coote's final contract was also signed).[136] Richard Maney was hired as the company's Press Agent on November 26, commencing on January 9, 1956; he would be an active participant throughout the show's original Broadway run, as a lengthy folder of material in Levin's papers proves.[137] An agreement was drawn up with Trude Rittman on November 30 to be the Dance Arranger, and on December 2, Ernest Adler was signed on to create "all hair stylings and coiffures" for the production.[138] The signing of Rittman was especially important: she had arranged the dance music for Rodgers and Hammerstein's *Oklahoma!*, *Carousel*, and *South Pacific*, and the "Small House of Uncle Thomas" ballet from *The King and I*. After working together on *Brigadoon*, Loewe brought her in again for *Paint Your Wagon* as well as the later stage adaptation of *Gigi* (1973). In *Fair Lady*, she was so completely trusted by the composer that he allowed her to create the lengthy choreographic sequences without his intervention, nor was her work confined merely to the dance music.[139]

The recording of the original cast album, with (left to right) Robert Coote, Rex Harrison, and Julie Andrews (Photofest/Columbia Records)

Meanwhile, although Cecil Beaton had successfully ordered the costumes he required for Rex Harrison, there was a question of how to get them from England to the United States. Beaton felt it was awkward for him to ask Harrison to take them there himself as a favor and suggested that Levin should ask the actor.[140] Levin replied that since Harrison was traveling by plane, this was impossible, and asked whether it would be possible to send them by "some other means, perhaps air express or air freight?"[141] The producer also made a suggestion regarding Julie Andrews's hair: "It occurs to me that it might be a good idea if it were made an auburn shade." Within the following week the problem with Harrison's clothes was solved, as the actor himself volunteered to carry them in his luggage; the producer wrote to Harrison to thank him and to promise to pay the excess baggage, which came to around $450.[142] To Beaton, Levin also followed up his comment about Andrews's hair: "My idea was only a suggestion," he informed Beaton. "I gather from your letter that you have brightened the tone of her hair considerably. I thought that her own hair seemed rather drab."[143] During December, Levin also approached several companies regarding the construction of the scenery for the show. The contract went to the Nolan Brothers of West Twenty-fourth Street, who provided the sets for $65,000.[144]

December 1955–March 1956

The year's correspondence ends with letters from Levin to the key actors in which "the *Pygmalion* musical" is finally referred to as *My Fair Lady*; that to Robert Coote on December 28 appears to be the earliest example.[145] The question of what to call the show was one of the most important decisions to be made. Lerner addresses the issue in his autobiography, saying that the early suggestions *Liza* and *My Lady Liza* "went to their final resting places in the trash basket" because "it would have seemed peculiar for the marquee to read: 'Rex Harrison in *Liza*.'"[146] He claims that *My Fair Lady* was considered and discarded because "it sounded like an operetta" and that Loewe liked *Fanfaroon* as a title "primarily I believe because it reminded him of *Brigadoon*." *Come to the Ball* was also considered. Later, Lerner claims that "toward the second week of rehearsal," Levin came to the theater and demanded that Lerner, Loewe, and Hart decide on a title, at which point they agreed to choose *My Fair Lady* because it was the one they disliked the least.[147]

But this chronology is difficult to corroborate with documentary evidence. During the autumn of 1955, the show is typically referred to as *My Lady Liza*, and most of the contracts refer to this as the title. Then on November 29 Lerner wrote a long letter to Harrison, in which he mentioned the issue of the title in the postscript: "*Fanfaroon* has not been abandoned, although there is stiff opposition," he wrote. "But *My Lady Liza* will definitely not be it. I know this will break your heart, because you seem so terribly fond of it."[148] Although Lerner claims in *The Street Where I Live* that the final decision was made during the second week of rehearsals, in fact it must have happened between December 16 and 28.[149] *My Fair Lady* it was to be, and on December 30 Levin sent the record producer Goddard Lieberson an outline of the billing sheet for the show for use on the cover of the Original Cast Album with the new title stamped proudly across the middle.[150]

Not surprisingly, the primary documentary sources for the remainder of the time leading up to the opening night on Broadway are less detailed than that for the preceding months. With the cast and crew in the same place for most of the time between the start of rehearsals (January 3), the opening night in New Haven (February 4), the Philadelphia tryout (February 15) and the Broadway opening (March 15), there was little need for written correspondence between the key players. This means that we have to fall back on the memoirs of figures such as Lerner, Andrews, Harrison, Holloway, Kitty Carlisle Hart (the director's wife), and Doris Shapiro (Lerner's assistant) to fill in many of the gaps, as well as newspaper reports and playbills. Nevertheless, a number of letters from this period remain, because Levin kept things ticking over while the show was being staged and rehearsed.

On January 4, he wrote to Laurie Evans in London to tell him that "Rex arrived in good shape; rehearsals started yesterday; and everyone is working hard."[151] The cast was working upstairs at the New Amsterdam Roof, 214 West Forty-second Street in New York for the first four weeks until embarking for New Haven at the end of the month.[152] The entire ensemble gathered onstage for the first time on January 3. Lerner tells us that "Around the edges of the stage Moss had arranged an exhibition of sketches of the scenery and the costumes, and the press was allowed in to do their first-day interviews. . . . The cast read the script aloud, with Moss reading the stage directions. Whenever they came to a song, Fritz and I performed it. After the first act the enthusiasm was high."[153] The exception was Rex Harrison, who felt that the character of Higgins had been put too much into the background in the second act. The solution was to add the song "A Hymn to Him," better known as "Why Can't a Woman Be More Like a Man?" Supposedly, the inspiration for this song came from Harrison himself, while walking down Fifth Avenue during the rehearsal period. Lerner reports that they had been "reviewing our past marital and emotional difficulties and his present one. . . . Suddenly, he had stopped and said in a loud voice that attracted a good bit of attention: 'Alan! Wouldn't it be marvelous if we were homosexuals?!' I said that I did not think that was the solution and we walked on. But it stuck in my mind and by the time I reached the Pierre I had the idea for 'Why Can't a Woman Be More Like a Man?'"[154] The lyricist adds that it was finished by the end of the eighth day of rehearsals.

Hart's rehearsal schedule was distinctive, incorporating an afternoon and evening schedule to leave the mornings free for other aspects of the production process. Andrews reports that "We began working every day at 2:00 p.m., took a break for dinner at 5:30 p.m., and then reassembled from 7:00 until 11:00 in the evening. Stanley Holloway and I kept up the British tradition of a cup of tea at 4:00 in the afternoon, and soon everyone was enjoying that welcome little break."[155] Lerner explains that the choice of this rehearsal schedule was deliberate: "Most directors like to begin in the morning at ten o'clock and rehearse until one or one thirty, returning at three and continuing until seven. Moss did not. He felt that by the end of the day the cast was usually so tired that little was accomplished in the last two hours," hence the decision to start at 2 p.m.[156] Another oft-repeated story about the show is that during rehearsals, Harrison kept brandishing a Penguin edition of Shaw's *Pygmalion* and referred to it "at least four times a day, if a speech did not seem right to him," according to Lerner. He would invariably cry out,

"Where's my Penguin?" and compare the text of the show to that of the play. After a week, Lerner's response was to go to a taxidermist and purchase a stuffed penguin, which he had rolled out the next time Harrison asked the question. "From that moment on, he never mentioned the Penguin again and kept the stuffed edition in his dressing room as a mascot throughout the run of the production."[157]

It was not merely the nervous Harrison who made life challenging for Hart and Lerner during this time; the inexperience of Julie Andrews as an actress in a substantial piece started to cause problems, too. After two weeks of rehearsals "Moss decided drastic assistance was needed. He closed down rehearsals for two days and spent them alone with Julie."[158] Andrews herself adds that "it became obvious . . . that I was hopelessly out of my depth as Eliza Doolittle. . . . And that's where Moss's humanity came in. . . . [He] decided . . . to dismiss the company for forty-eight hours and to work solely with me. . . . For those two days . . . [we] hammered through each scene—everything from Eliza's entrance, her screaming and yelling, to her transformation into a lady at the end of the play. Moss bullied, cajoled scolded, and encouraged.[159] Lerner adds: "On Monday morning when rehearsals began again with the full company, Julie was well on her way to becoming Eliza Doolittle."[160] Though Andrews was now feeling more confident, Stanley Holloway in turn became unhappy that insufficient time was being spent on rehearsing his character, but on confronting the director with this issue he was told by Hart, "Now look, Stanley. I am rehearsing a girl who has never played a major role in her life, and an actor who has never sung on the stage in his life. You have done both. If you feel neglected it is a compliment."[161] The actor was mollified.

One important job to be done during this time was for the show to be orchestrated. On January 5 Levin signed a contract with the arranger Guido Tutrinoli and three days later another with Robert Russell Bennett, who orchestrated the show with Phil Lang (and the "ghost" orchestrator, Jack Mason).[162] It was Bennett who insisted that Lang be credited with the orchestrations along with himself, writing a letter to Levin on February 11 specifically asking it as "a favor."[163] Other things to be taken care of included ordering floral arrangements for the show from the Decorative Plant Corporation, and items such as necklaces and bracelets from Coro Jewelry, paying for the costumes Beaton had ordered in London, and finishing off the costume order with the Helene Pons Studio.[164]

After spending January rehearsing the show in New York, the company moved to New Haven, where the New Haven Jewish Community Center had been hired for rehearsals between January 30 and February 1.[165] Over at the Shubert Theatre, Biff Liff, the stage manager, "wrestled with the scenery," and although chaos ensued with the complicated sets, they were in sufficient order by Wednesday night to have a technical run-through.[166] It was complete by Friday, and the orchestra arrived in the pit for the first time—"and blew Rex sky high," according to Lerner.[167] The actor's inexperience as a singer meant that he was extremely intimidated by the overwhelming sound of the orchestra, and Hart promised he could rehearse alone with the orchestra the following afternoon.

"But his terror of the orchestra did not abate," Lerner continues. "Late that afternoon with the house sold out and a fierce blizzard blowing, Rex announced that under no circumstances would he go on that night." The performance was cancelled, and announcements were made on the local radio stations. However, "by six o'clock that evening hundreds of people had braved the snow and were already queuing up at the box office. The house manager was livid. He swore to us all that he would tell the world the truth. . . . About an hour and a half before what would have been curtain time Rex's agent arrived from New York. . . . No matter what happened that evening on stage, he said, Rex damn well had to go on. Fear of the consequences must have overshadowed his fear of the orchestra because one hour before curtain time, Rex recanted."[168] So in the end, the show did begin that night of February 4 at 8:40 p.m. Although there were some technical difficulties with the turntables and curtains, Lerner says that "the total effect was stunning and when the curtain came down the audience stood up and cheered."[169] *Variety* reviewed the show in its New Haven incarnation and reflected the reception that Lerner indicated, stating: "*My Fair Lady* is going to be a whale of a show . . . [It] contains enough smash potential to assure it a high place on the list of Broadway prospects."[170] Every aspect of the production came in for praise.

After playing in New Haven for a week, the show moved to Philadelphia for a four-week run at the Erlanger Theatre. In preparation for Philadelphia, three numbers were cut, making the running time around fifteen minutes shorter: Higgins's "Come to the Ball," the "Decorating Eliza" ballet, and Eliza's "Say a Prayer for Me Tonight." The reaction to the show continued to be phenomenal. Joseph M. Hyman, who looked after Moss Hart's affairs, wrote to Philip Adler to say that he thought it would be the biggest hit for twenty years.[171] Arnold Weissberger, Beaton's New York lawyer, told Levin that after the adjustments being made to the show, "it now has a 50–50 chance (50 to run for five years and 50 to run for ten years)."[172] The reviews of the opening night performance on Broadway, March 15, 1956, concurred with these early opinions: the *Daily Mirror* called it "one of the all-time great song-and-dancers"; the *World-Telegram and Sun* said that it "prance[d] into that rare class of great musicals"; and the *Herald Tribune* ordered the reader not "to finish reading this review now. You'd better sit right down and send for those tickets to *My Fair Lady*." But perhaps the most unexpected praise came from Lawrence Langner, who had brought the project to Lerner and Loewe on behalf of the Theatre Guild in 1952 and then been shut out of it when they recommenced in 1954. "You remember Mary of Scotland's line—'After I am dead you will find Calais written upon my heart'—that is the way I will always feel about *Pygmalion*. But the perfect job you have done certainly mitigates my suffering. I can only congratulate you on the superb welding of all the component parts with the original so that they seem to be conceived and executed by one master mind."[173] Even those with an axe to grind could not resist the charm of *My Fair Lady*, and the show went on to be Lerner and Loewe's greatest triumph—one which they would never come close to repeating.

3

SHAVIAN BUT NOT SHAW

• • •

DEVELOPING THE SCRIPT OF *MY FAIR LADY*

With *My Fair Lady*, Lerner and Loewe were taking on Shaw's most popular and perhaps greatest comedy. Working out how to make the adaptation was undoubtedly the most difficult aspect of writing the show. In *Pygmalion*, Shaw struck a balance between promoting his socialist outlook and creating a humorous and human vehicle. He did this with an ease that even he did not always manage to equal, and his unquestionable brilliance provided an intimidating precedent for everyone who approached the property with a view to making it into a Broadway musical. No wonder so great a dramatist as Oscar Hammerstein 2nd was interested in *Pygmalion*, and no wonder he eventually gave it up. No wonder, either, that it was the English-educated and ingenious wordsmith Lerner who eventually succeeded in the task, which required someone who could assimilate Shaw's vast, imposing, and provocative work into a musical that would be related to but independent of *Pygmalion*. This chapter explores the background to the play in brief, before referring to documentary sources that track Lerner and Loewe's initial ideas about the format of the show. It then reveals how changes made to the text initially used in *Fair Lady*'s rehearsals resulted in a vital shift of focus in the Higgins-Eliza relationship, and finally goes on to explore the structure of the completed show.

SHAW AND *PYGMALION*

George Bernard Shaw was born in Dublin on July 26, 1856—just a few months short of a century before the premiere of *My Fair Lady*—and moved to London in 1876.[1] Though he did not quite share Eliza Doolittle's plight in his upbringing, the fact that he left school at fifteen and relied heavily on acts of self-education—such as visiting galleries, concert halls and theaters, and reading Shakespeare—to better himself in the world was undoubtedly a motivating factor behind many of his plays, including *Pygmalion*. Obviously, it would be unjustifiable to perceive too strong a link between the two, but Shaw was hardworking, just like Eliza; unlike her, Shaw was able to benefit from financial support from a parent (his mother, who left her husband when Shaw was a teenager). He was also, of course, a unique figure in the history of literature and had a remarkable intellect. But in spite of this difference, there is no doubt that the portrayal of Eliza's desperate financial circumstances, and the ongoing insecurity that this creates within her, came from deep within Shaw's heart. To climb the social ladder was a mutual ambition.

In 1884 Shaw joined the Fabian Society, which championed social reform through debate. Here he was in his element, and in the same year decided to become a playwright. His first stage work, *Widowers' Houses*, was eventually completed and performed in 1892. Its subject matter hints that Shaw started as he meant to go on: a young couple, Harry and Blanche, are thwarted in their love by Harry's disgust at the exploitative behavior of Blanche's father, a slum landlord. The following year, Shaw wrote *Mrs. Warren's Profession*, a controversial play in which he suggests that prostitution is "an economic rather than moral problem, a position that caused the play to be banned from public stages in Britain for over twenty-five years."[2] In both these works, the oppressed and the poor are treated with sympathy, and Shaw's defense of women's rights in *Mrs. Warren* is particularly indicative of his stance on sexual equality. Poverty was also a theme in *Major Barbara* (1905), in which he described it as "the greatest of evils and the worst of crimes." Another important factor is the style of these plays, which mix humor and lightness with a seriousness of purpose.

Both this technical approach and these themes recur in *Pygmalion*, which Shaw started to write in March 1912. It took three months to complete, but it is documented that the basic premise of the play was in his mind from 1897.[3] All along, Shaw envisaged using his muse, Mrs. Patrick Campbell, in the role of Eliza Doolittle, but she took quite some convincing since, as Shaw himself said, she had "never appeared in a low life part." The play received its premiere, in German, in Vienna in 1913, and was also performed in Berlin later that year, so it was not until April 1914 that it received its English-language premiere at Her Majesty's Theatre in London. (Several of Shaw's previous works had also been given their first performances abroad, since the playwright abhorred the tastes of London's critics and "knew [his plays] would be received more sympathetically by theatre managers and critics" in other countries.)[4] Unfortunately, the rehearsal period was overshadowed by a three-way tension between Shaw, Mrs. Patrick Campbell, and Herbert Beerbohm Tree, the actor-manager who ran Her Majesty's Theatre and had been hired to play Higgins after much debate.[5] It did not augur well for the work, which had long been one of Shaw's pet projects.

Pygmalion's first-night reviews were sidetracked by Eliza's line "Not bloody likely" from act 3.[6] The word "bloody" had rarely been used onstage before and was controversial. This inevitably became the focus of the reviews, and Shaw was unhappy that it "had become a major distraction from the more serious elements of the play."[7] The first performance was also spoiled for Shaw by Tree's divergence from the intended ending of the play. Shaw had underlined to the actors that Eliza and Higgins do not finish up together, and the original text of the scene makes this clear, too. Eliza bids a final farewell to the Professor, but quite casually he asks her to buy him a ham, some cheese, a pair of gloves, and a new tie. She retorts, "Buy them yourself." Mrs. Higgins (who is present in the final scene, which takes place at her house in the play, rather than Higgins's house as in *My Fair Lady*) offers to buy the tie and gloves in her place, but Higgins ends with: "Oh don't bother. She'll buy 'em all right enough."[8] However, Shaw wrote to his wife that Tree depicted Higgins "shoving his mother rudely out of his way and wooing Eliza with appeals to buy a ham for his lonely home like a bereaved Romeo."[9] Later in the run, this had developed further, with the actor throwing flowers to Eliza as she left the stage at the end.[10]

PYGMALION: CLARIFYING THE TEXT

Shaw's reaction to this liberal treatment of his script was to amend it. To the end of the 1916 edition of the play he added a "Sequel," in which he explained in prose what he intended by the final scene. *Pygmalion* is subtitled "A Romance," and Shaw makes it clear in the sequel that this description refers not to a union between Higgins and Eliza but to the "transfiguration" of its heroine, a process the writer describes as "exceedingly improbable."[11] In other words, Eliza's unlikely rise through the social ranks is the romantic element of the plot, rather than romance itself. Shaw also relates how Eliza and Freddy get married, briefly live with Higgins and Pickering, and later set up their own florist shop. Relations between the four remain positive, and Shaw says that Eliza is "immensely interested" in Higgins, and even has "secret mischievous moments" in which she wishes she could "just drag him off his pedestal and see him making love like any common man."

But, he continues firmly, "when it comes to . . . the life that she really leads as distinguished from the life of dreams and fancies, she likes Freddy and she likes the Colonel; and she does not like Higgins."[12] Eliza's decision to choose Freddy over Higgins is "well-considered," says the playwright, because she knows that the Professor will always prefer his mother, Milton, and the Universal Alphabet to herself. Since she is young and gifted, she has options. "Will she look forward to a lifetime of fetching Higgins's slippers or to a lifetime of Freddy fetching hers?" asks Shaw, and goes on to answer that she marries Freddy.[13] He adds that her "instinct tells her not to marry Higgins" but "does not tell her to give him up," and underlines that he will remain "one of the strongest personal interests in her life."[14]

Shaw frequently tried to convince performers and audiences of his point of view, but it was often in vain. For a 1920 production at the Aldwych Theatre, he changed the text of the final scene by having Higgins return to the front of the stage after Eliza's exit and exclaim "Galatea!" supposedly signifying that "the statue has come to life at last," but as L. W. Conolly has noted, this implies that "just as Pygmalion marries Galatea so Higgins marries Eliza."[15] So for a projected film version in 1934, Shaw's draft screenplay has Eliza and Freddy kissing (before getting in the car to go to Doolittle's wedding), while Higgins shakes his fist at them.[16] Then in 1938 (when the movie was eventually made) he wrote a different ending again, with Higgins having both a flashback to Eliza in Covent Garden and a "vision of the future" in which Eliza and Freddy are seen in their shop. A policewoman asks Higgins if anything is wrong, and he answers "No: nothing wrong. A happy ending. A happy beginning."[17] In 1939 a new edition of the play was published, in which the final lines were now changed in print. To Mrs. Higgins's observation that "I should be uneasy about you and her if she were less fond of Colonel Pickering," in this version Higgins answers: "Pickering! Nonsense: she's going to marry Freddy."[18] However, the actual ending of the 1938 film has a scene familiar from *My Fair Lady*, in which Eliza returns to Higgins's study while he asks "Where the devil are my slippers, Eliza?" apparently effecting a reconciliation and making no reference to the union of Eliza and Freddy.[19]

In summary, the number of English-language versions of *Pygmalion* is large, even before we take into consideration several foreign film versions that preceded the 1938 British movie. This textual minefield clarifies one of the reasons why turning the play into a musical was so difficult: Which version should be adapted? The original play, in its five-act 1914 version, is quite simple in what it depicts. Act 1 shows Eliza in Covent Garden; she meets Higgins, who bets Colonel Pickering that in three months he could pass her off as "a duchess at an ambassador's garden party."[20] Higgins takes pity on Eliza and gives her a handful of change. In act 2, Eliza arrives at Higgins's house and requests elocution lessons; Pickering asks Higgins to make good his bet, and they decide to teach her. Eliza's dustman father arrives, demanding his rights, and "sells" her for £5. Act 3 shows a tea party at Mrs. Higgins's house, where Eliza disgraces herself with embarrassing stories about her family. Nonetheless, Higgins decides to persevere, and at the start of act 4 we learn that Eliza's formal debut into society (which takes place during the interval) has been a success. However, Higgins credits solely himself for this achievement and ignores Eliza while basking in Pickering's congratulations. Higgins and Eliza quarrel, and she leaves. Act 5 brings the story to a conclusion, at Mrs. Higgins's house. Higgins and Pickering come to report Eliza's disappearance, only to discover she has taken refuge with Mrs. Higgins. Doolittle arrives and announces he is to be married, having been left a legacy as a result of being recommended as a lecturer by Higgins on a whim. After a final confrontation between Eliza and Higgins, Eliza sets out for the wedding with Pickering, Doolittle, Freddy, and Mrs. Higgins, leaving Higgins behind.

What's striking about this synopsis is that there are no elocution lessons, and we are not allowed to witness Eliza's triumph. In the original conception, Shaw's emphases are on the role of woman in society and the way in which education could facilitate social mobility. For the 1938 film adaptation, produced by Gabriel Pascal and co-directed by Anthony Asquith and Leslie Howard, Shaw made some additions and changes.[21] These include a scene at the end of act 1 in which Eliza hires a taxi with some of the money Higgins has given to her, to make the short journey home; a scene in act 2 in which Mrs. Pearce gives her a bath; an example of Eliza's lessons; and a new scene between Eliza and Freddy in act 4, when the former leaves Higgins's house in anger and hurt. The film also introduces Eliza's return to Covent Garden after her argument with Higgins. But without Shaw's knowledge, Pascal and the directors "secretly shot a different ending to Shaw's screenplay," and withheld it from him until the preview for the press "two days before the premiere, too late for him to do anything about it."[22] With the exception of this unauthorized ending, Shaw subsumed many of the new scenes from the film into the play script for a definitive edition in 1941, which has been the source used for most subsequent editions of the work.

Lerner and Loewe saw the Pascal film in early 1952, and its screenplay was ultimately the primary basis for the script of *Fair Lady*. But before deciding to adhere to much of Shaw's structure, Lerner and Loewe considered a more liberal adaptation. There is evidence of this in the correspondence partially discussed in chapters 1 and 2, as well as four outlines (see tables 3.1–3.5) of the show roughly dating from 1952 (Outlines 1 and 2), 1954 (Outline 3) and

1955 (Outline 4). These documents reveal how Lerner and Loewe initially sought to impose musical theater conventions on *Pygmalion* and were willing to tear the text apart to make it work as a Broadway show. Set pieces, locations, and the potential for the lyric moment (i.e., song and dance) were the priorities at this point, rather than the surface of the spoken text.

There is a marked difference in attitude between literary scholars and musicologists when discussing the nature of the adaptation. Typical of Shaw scholars is Paul Bauschatz, who suggests that *My Fair Lady* is both a corruption and an inept treatment of *Pygmalion*. He says it "works badly" and "is structurally flawed."[23] Conversely, musicologists such as Joseph Swain tend to assume that the majority of the dialogue was simply lifted from Shaw's text. Swain says that apart from the musical's lessons montage, Shaw's script "is followed quite faithfully" by Lerner.[24] In fact, the adaptation of *My Fair Lady* shows an unusual conscientiousness compared to the average Broadway musical regarding the retention of the literary style of its source, as well as much of its dialogue, but Lerner, Loewe, and Moss Hart deserve more credit from musical theater scholars for their many innovations.

In confirmation of this, a rehearsal script from producer Herman Levin's papers shows that the musical went into rehearsal with a text that, if anything, contained more of Shaw than the final published script was to include. This is in direct contrast to standard views of the musical that assume it is merely a reduction of Shaw's script, to which some songs have been added. There are in fact well over two hundred differences between these two distinct *Fair Lady* texts, ranging from a change of word order to the omission or addition of a whole speech. The thrust of chapter 3 is on how these late modifications resulted in subtle changes of focal point even during the rehearsal period; but before this comes a discussion of the implications of the early correspondence about *Fair Lady* on its book, and the four outlines of the show predating the creation of the script.

SHAVIAN SOURCES FOR *MY FAIR LADY*

Alan Jay Lerner described at great length in *The Street Where I Live* how the challenge of making a musical out of *Pygmalion* was intimidating. "The more we talked," he wrote, "the more insoluble the problems seemed to become because, unfortunately, the characters in Shaw's play also kept talking, talking and talking. *Pygmalion* is a drawing room comedy and no matter how hard we tried, we did not seem to be able to tear down the walls of the drawing room and allow the play to unfold in a setting and atmosphere that suggested

*Stanley Holloway (Alfred Doolittle) and Audrey Hepburn (Eliza) in the 1964
movie of* My Fair Lady *(Photofest/Warner Bros.)*

music."[25] But as is obvious from Valerie Pascal's memoir of her ex-husband
The Disciple and his Devil, one of the overall solutions to the problem had
already been supplied to Lerner and Loewe by Pascal himself, who encouraged them to see a screening of his 1938 film version.[26] On March 22, Lawrence Langner (of the Theatre Guild) sent a telegram to Pascal and mentioned
that "Lerner and Loewe . . . are seeing [the] picture soon as possible and hope
to settle [a] deal with them for immediate work on [the] musical."[27] This ver-
ifies the fact that they saw the film, and we know from a letter written by
Lerner to Pascal on May 10, 1952, that he had already begun to give much
thought to the adaptation of the story:

> As far as the actual conversion into musical form is concerned, there are
> two basic problems that I see at this moment—both of which [are] easily
> overcome. The first is to get it out of the drawing room and into the open;
> and the second is to tighten the story. By that I mean to give characters
> such as Mr. Doolittle a more important role in the plot and not just be a
> highly amusing interlude as he is now. Too, Freddie should be developed
> into more attractive a fellow so that he can become more of a real threat.
> In the first instance of getting it out of the drawing room Fritz and I have

several ideas which we didn't have time to discuss with you. The scene in Mrs. Higgins' home for example—the "gin to her was mother's milk" scene—could be played at the opening of Ascot. It could be extremely colourful and lend itself to great humour both musically and otherwise. The calmness of the British aristocracy at the races I always thought very funny. Now, of course, following the motion picture, there are the ball scenes and the wonderfully touching sequence when she returns to Covent Garden and nobody recognises her. A scene like that could be developed so that the second scene at Mrs. Higgins' when the Professor finds her after his long search could be obviated. The end of the first act, of course, can be one of the great moments of any musical I can remember. It should be Liza's preparation for the ball, her excitement, her desire to please the Prof., her dressing, her rehearsing, her manners, etc. Musically it should be one of her big, big numbers—ending with her going off with the Prof. for the great and final test. It could be really wonderful, don't you think?[28]

This letter corroborates Lerner's comment in his memoir about "getting the story out of the drawing room," as quoted above. We can sense the desire to "open up" Shaw's domestic story into a form that would work as a musical with a larger ensemble and the need for the "lyric moment" to clinch most scenes via song and/or dance. It also raises the issue of "tightening the story" by expanding the roles of Doolittle and Freddy. The comments on these two characters are interesting, because, excepting for his having two lengthy songs, Doolittle's role is in some ways truncated in Fair Lady, rather than expanded—one might say a surprising treatment of a character whose wisdom and depth has been compared to Shakespeare's Falstaff.[29] Freddy, meanwhile, remains nothing but bland in the musical, even though he plays perhaps more of an active role.

From this, the decision to move the scene of Mrs. Higgins's tea party to the races at Ascot (act 3, scene 1) seems also to have been Lerner's invention. Richard Traubner notes the presence of a scene at the races in the German film version of Pygmalion, which was premiered in Berlin in 1935, but it should be borne in mind that it concerns a rather different incident to that which takes place in the Fair Lady Ascot scene.[30] Bernard Dukore has described how Higgins and Pickering take Eliza to "visit a race track." Bored with the race, Eliza wanders around the course and sees her friend Jonny selling ice cream. "He admires her elegant apparel and leaves his cart to bring her some. While he is gone, a tall, burly man steals a cup of ice cream." When Eliza sees what has happened, she alerts Jonny, who is then hurled "to the ground. . . . Furious, Liza yells at [the man], climbs over the railing in an unladylike manner, and flails him with her parasol." Predictably, Higgins arrives and admonishes Eliza for her behavior. "Taking advantage of the bully relaxing his guard because of the interruption," Eliza strikes him "resoundingly on the head with the parasol."[31]

It is true that the German film introduces a scene in a racecourse that Shaw's *Pygmalion* did not contain, but this incident bears very little relationship to the Ascot scene from *My Fair Lady*. The Eliza of the musical is excited, not bored; she does not see a friend, ask for ice cream, or witness a crime; Higgins does not reprimand her in the musical, but rather stifles a laugh; the specific location of Ascot in the show—and the fact that it is the opening day—is far from insignificant, given the wider social implications; and the key climax in the musical—Eliza causing a public spectacle by losing her control during the horse race—is completely missing. Therefore, it seems likely that Lerner invented the Ascot scene without knowing about the German film.

Lerner's letter makes obvious his intention to embrace several sources for the *Fair Lady* script, including the play, the new scenes that Shaw wrote for the 1938 British film, and additional situations suggested by his own imagination. Perhaps the most interesting aspect is the placing of the interval in Lerner's scenario. Since the play has five acts and its film version has no intermission, the question of how to slice the musical into two acts was important. Obviously, the final moment before an interval should be a climactic one, and at this stage the plan seems to have been to end with Eliza's preparations for and departure to the ball. Going along with this plan, the published *Fair Lady* script includes the ball in the first act and has the interval at the end of it; the cliffhanger is the question of whether Zoltan Karpathy, the Hungarian phonetician who is an ex-pupil of Higgins's, has successfully discovered Eliza's secret. However, the 1964 film version reverts to Lerner's original plan—ending the first half with the departure to the ball—and Trevor Nunn's 2001 production for London's National Theatre also took this course. Whereas ending the act with Higgins's gesture of respect to Eliza when they leave for the ball—he extends his arm to help her through the door—places emphasis on an emotional high in the Higgins-Eliza relationship, ending the act with the ball shifts the focus to the success of the experiment, leaving the characters to work out their problems with each other in the second act. This is just one example of many considerations Lerner had to bear in mind while fashioning the script.

Outline 1: Act 1 only (ca.1952)
None of the outlines discussed here can be dated with absolute accuracy, but it is easy to guess the order in which they were written. The earliest outline comes from Herman Levin's papers and consists of a thorough five-page description of how the first act was to run.[32] Unfortunately, there is nothing at

all on the second act, either because it was never completed or because the second half of the document has been lost. It is enough, however, to see in what ways Lerner already had elements of the show's structure in place, while others are completely unexpected. The outline is reproduced in table 3.1, with the songs and dances separated into their own columns for clarity, and some of Lerner's description of the action has been slightly condensed where a complete reproduction seemed unnecessary.

In Outline 1, we can recognize several songs from the final score, including "The Rain in Spain," "The Ascot Gavotte," and "Just You Wait" (as well as "Say a Prayer," which was cut during the New Haven tryouts). This suggests that Lerner and Loewe had already set to work on the score by the time the outline was written. On the other, the presence of scenes or elements that did not make it into the show (such as opening at Limehouse instead of Covent Garden) implies an early date. Lerner's letter of May 10, 1952 (quoted earlier) indicates that he already had strong ideas of how the structure of the musical might work, and in all likelihood this is the outline referred to in his letter: there is a particular focus on Eliza's character, which would make sense if Outline 1 was the one produced to try and persuade Mary Martin to play the part. If this is so, it means that the songs mentioned above were composed (or at least partly conceived) in 1952, rather than in 1954–55 as is usually assumed, and Outline 1 is certainly the earliest surviving version of the show.

Taken as a whole, it is striking how vastly this plan differs from the final show. Particularly curious is the change of location of the first scene from the flower market in Covent Garden to a space with a more varied crowd of people (including sailors and Chinese) at Limehouse. One senses the desire to introduce Eliza in an atmosphere of Otherness, but it is not quite clear how Lerner intended to provide a legitimate reason for Higgins and Pickering to be there.[33] The omnipresence of Doolittle in this scene—albeit inside the pub much of the time—is significant, showing him to have a greater prominence in Eliza's existence than is the case in the eventual show. It means that the two dominant male forces in her life are around from the very beginning, and the proposed song "I'm a Good Girl, I Am" ends the tableau neatly.

The early encounter between Higgins and Doolittle is also intriguing: Lerner explains in a note that "The purpose of having Doolittle meet Higgins here, even though their joint interest in Liza has not yet been established, is to break up the long dialogue scene that occurs in the play between them in Act II." The sense of progression is much poorer in this version because the motivation for the dialogue is not clear; cutting up a long scene is not enough reason to have Higgins, Pickering, and Doolittle meet early on. The unfinished song "The Undeserving Poor" probably expanded on a theme similar to that of "With a Little Bit of Luck," but we can see how Lerner's original intention was to diverge from *Pygmalion* more drastically than he eventually did: the location and scenario are almost completely different here.

The third scene is initially more familiar from both play and musical: Higgins and Pickering sit in the study listening to phonetic noises in the darkness, and the Colonel is tired of the exercise. But then Lerner introduces something new—a visit from Mrs. Higgins with Miss Clara Eynsford Hill, neither of whom ever sets foot in Higgins's residence in the finished musical. Mrs. Higgins's attempt to encourage Higgins to marry Clara is also an innovation, probably based on Shaw's stage direction in act 3 of *Pygmalion* that Clara "considers Higgins quite eligible matrimonially." (Indeed, in the play she goes on to flirt with him during act 3, which depicts Mrs. Higgins's tea party; much of the scene is transferred to Ascot in *My Fair Lady*.)[34] This gives rise to Higgins's song "Please Don't Marry Me." The number signals the start of a much more conventional discussion of romance in the show, which continues with Pickering's song about the impossibility of living without "the warmth and affection of the opposite sex" in scene 5, Freddy's song about loving Eliza (which obviously became "On the Street Where You Live") in scene 8, Higgins's and Pickering's song of praise and flattery, "Lady Liza," in scene 9, and Eliza's "Say a Prayer" in the final scene of the act. Originally, the latter song had a more overtly romantic lyric that referred to Eliza praying "that he'll discover / I'm his lover / For now and evermore," hence the song belongs in the same category (see chap. 4).

Also of importance is the description of the end of the first act: "Liza appears at the top of the stairs, dressed like a queen. . . . In seemingly regal serenity, she requests Higgins' arm, and the three start off for the ball." In this formulation, Lerner has Eliza *requesting* Higgins's arm, but the published script suggests quite the reverse: "[Higgins] starts briskly for the door. At the threshold, he pauses, turns and gazes at Eliza. He turns to her and offers his arm."[35] The mere presence of this scene is also significant, because Lerner later claimed it was an invention during the New Haven tryouts to cover the cutting of the ballet, "Come to the Ball," and "Say a Prayer."[36] Instead, it seems from this outline to have been a reinstatement of an idea that had been thought of early on.

Outline 2: Complete Early Structure (1952)

Outline 2 probably dates from roughly the same period as its predecessor; the substance of the first act is almost exactly the same in both, hence scenes 2–9 are omitted in the reproduction of Outline 2 in tables 3.2 and 3.3. Evidently, this second outline is an elaboration of Outline 1, as well as adding Lerner's plans for act 2.[37] Aside from the way in which it diverges from the final show,

Table 3.1. **Outline 1, Act 1 only**

Scene	Setting	Action	Song/dance
1	Limehouse	The smoky atmosphere of Thomas Burke's Limehouse—Chinese, sailors, swells who have come slumming. Almost the same as the Covent Garden scene in the play. Doolittle and his cronies are thrown from the pub, and he has a scene with Liza before exiting. She sings. Liza becomes aware of Higgins taking notes of her speech and is afraid her song has caused offence. Scene follows that of the play except that Pickering is younger, wiser and more worldly.	Song by Liza knocking "nobbies." Following Higgins' exit, song by Liza: "I'm a Good Girl, I Am."
2	Outside of Pub	Doolittle and his cronies are thrown out again. They sing. Higgins and Pickering enter on their way home; dialogue between the three. Song continues.	Doolittle and cronies' song: "The Undeserving Poor."
3	Higgins' Study	Phonetic noises heard on the PA in the darkness. Pickering asks to have the lights turned on but Higgins tells him that darkness aids hearing. Mrs. Higgins and Miss Eynsford Hill arrive, the former hoping that the professor will agree to a liaison with the latter. Miss Eynsford Hill is the same haughty, disagreeable character from the play. After they depart, Higgins sings. Liza enters, and the scene follows that of the play, ending with her departure for the bathroom.	Higgins' song: "Please Don't Marry Me."
4	The Upstairs Bathroom	Liza has just got out of the bath and is in Higgins' bathrobe, which trails to the floor. She is wet and shaking like a drowned rat. She sings.	Liza's song: "Just You Wait."

5	Higgins' Study	Higgins is organising the staff as Doolittle enters. Higgins and Pickering recognise him but he does not recognise them. The scene is devoted to getting money in exchange for Liza. Liza enters and the lessons begin. They will be in the form of a montage, as in the film, taking the form of short scenes that fade out. There will be two scenes with the servants in an inset on the side, which will be used to break up the action and help inform the audience of the passage of time. The lessons will be interspersed with music. Near the end, there will be a scene between Liza and Pickering about Higgins. Pickering sings. The climax of the sequence is when Liza can finally pronounce "The rain in Spain stays mainly in the plain" properly. In the joy of the moment, the line turns into a song. Higgins decides Liza should be tried out.	Pickering sings a ballade in which he doubts that any man can live as Higgins does, without the warmth and affection of the opposite sex (tentatively called "The End of a Beautiful Friendship"). Higgins, Liza and Pickering sing and dance "The Rain in Spain," a Spanish one-step.
6	(In One)	On the telephone at the side of the stage, Higgins calls his mother, who stands on the other side of the stage, to tell her he intends to bring Liza to Mrs. Higgins' box in the royal enclosure at Ascot.	
7	Ascot	The ensemble sings in a colourful display of Edwardianism. In the middle of each chorus, there is the running of a race, observed in stony silence. Liza enters and the famous "Tea Scene" from the play occurs here. Liza thoroughly disgraces herself at the end and starts shouting for her horse: "Come on, get the bloody cork out."	Chorus: "The Ascot Gavotte."
8	(In One)	Miss Eynsford Hill, Mrs. Higgins and Freddy are leaving the stands. All but Freddy and Mrs Higgins are in a thorough state of shock. Freddy is absolutely smitten with Liza.	Freddy may have a song about his love for Liza.

(continued)

Table 3.1 continued

Scene	Setting	Action	Song/dance
9	Windsor Park	Liza is sitting on a bench, crying. Higgins and Pickering find her, and even though she wants to withdraw, they persuade her she can go through with it through a song. After three choruses she brighten up and agrees.	Higgins and Pickering's song: "Lady Liza."
10	Full Stage	Montage of lessons done balletically in pantomime, showing Liza learning how to walk, dance and curtsey. Twice during the sequence in an inset on one side, Freddy is seen coming to the door with flowers and sent away. At the end, Liza is doing everything beautifully and the chorus sings.	Ballet. Choral reprise: "Lady Liza."
11	(In One) A Flower Shop	On the night of the ball, Higgins and Pickering, in white tie and tails, are buying boutonnieres. They run into Aristede Karpathy, an ex-pupil of Higgins', and discover to their horror he will be at the ball precisely so he can spot frauds. They are staggered by the news.	
12	Higgins' Entrance Hall	Liza, about to go upstairs to dress, has a song she does to and with the servants. Higgins and Pickering enter and tell Liza she is not going to the ball because of the risk of being spotted. She exits, dumbstruck. Doolittle enters and announces he is to be married in three days. He has come to invite them to the awful proceedings. This will be from the scene that occurs in Act 5 of the play where Doolittle accuses Higgins, by means of Mr. Wannafeller's will, of throwing him into the Middle Class. At that moment, Liza appears at the top of the stairs, dressed like a queen. Doolittle doesn't recognise her. In seemingly regal serenity, she requests Higgins' arm, and the three start off for the ball.	Liza's song: "Say a Prayer for me Tonight."

62

Table 3.2. **Outline 2, Act 1**

Scene	Setting	Action	Song/dance
1	Limehouse	The setting is Limehouse—the smoky atmosphere of Thomas Burke's Limehouse—Chinese, sailors, blowzers, swells who have come slumming, etc. In substance, same scene, with minor additions, that takes place in play outside Covent Garden.	Pantomime.
		In opening pantomime characters of locale appear. Alfred Doolittle and two cronies thrown from pub. He tries begging, to no avail. Liza enters. Small scene with Liza establishing relationship between the two.	Liza's song.
		Song by Liza. Following song, Liza is made aware of man taking notes of her speech. She is afraid she has offended someone in her song. Crowd gathers, includes Pickering. From here to end of scene, same as play.	Higgins' song.
		Higgins has song. Subject: How the English can't speak their own language. He and Pickering exit. Liza muses in song on same basic difference between her and them. Song by Liza. (Pickering will be younger man than in play—younger, wiser and more worldly.)	Liza's song: "The Like of 'im and the Like of Me."
2–11		*Same as Outline 1.*	
12	(In One)	Liza, about to dress, has a song with servants. Higgins and Pickering enter and tell her she is not going. Risk is too great. Pickering leads in this scene in decision. Higgins, unhappy, sees the sense of it, and accepts. Pickering says, after all, she's perfectly equipped now to find a job in a flower shop. Pickering maintains it isn't fair to Liza to allow her to go through with it. Liza, heartbroken, exits. Doolittle enters. (This will be portion of scene that occurs in play in Act V, where he accuses Higgins, by means of Wannafeller's will, of throwing him into the Middle Class. He is to be married in three days and has come to invite them to the awful proceedings.) Liza appears at top of stairs, dressed like a queen. She has decided to risk all. Doolittle doesn't recognise her. Pickering's attitude is, "Does she know what she's doing?" Higgins' is as if he expected her to make this choice—but the smugness doesn't conceal his delight. The three depart for the ball.	Eliza's song: "Say a Prayer for Me Tonight."

Outline 2 is notable largely for Lerner's clarity regarding the derivation of the script's different components. For instance, in act 1, scene 1, Lerner writes "From here to end of scene, same as play," and in the final scene of the act he indicates: "This will be portion of scene that occurs in play in Act V." Elsewhere, reference is made to the "motion picture." So although the events depicted in act 1 of Outline 2 are largely the same as in act 1 of Outline 1, Outline 2 acts as a kind of loose map around the *Pygmalion* play and film that Lerner proposes as the basis for his adaptation.

New musical numbers are indicated here, too. In place of "I'm a Good Girl, I Am," Outline 2 has "The Like of 'im and the Like of Me," which presumably indicates Eliza's view of the social distinction between her and Higgins. It is reprised in act 2 at the end of the scene of the argument between the two characters in the same position as the tearful reprise of "Just You Wait" in the published script; it is interesting that the expressive function of a reprise at this point in the show was in place early on. Also, Pickering's act 1 "ballade" is reprised twice in the second act, signaling his more prominent function in this early version. Scene 4 seems also to be roughly in its definitive state, but scenes 5–8 are quite different because of a crucial change to the story: Doolittle's wedding becomes a focal point. Upon discovering Eliza has fled, Higgins traces her to her father's wedding; the gathering of the significantly "Middle Class" guests outside the church is a way of illustrating Doolittle's social mobility; Doolittle blames Higgins for his new circumstances to his face (as in *Pygmalion*) rather than via Eliza (as in *Fair Lady*); there is no scene at Mrs. Higgins's house (the argument takes place outside the church instead); and Eliza leaves "triumphantly" with Freddy after her argument with Higgins, rather than departing alone and reappearing at Higgins's house in the final scene. The ending, however, seems to have been conceived as the proper conclusion for the musical all along, hinting that Lerner always saw the close of the *Pygmalion* movie as his preferred ending to the piece.

Like Outline 1, Outline 2 portrays romance between Higgins and Eliza in a different way than in the published show. Suddenly, Eliza's feelings seem to matter: Pickering says that "she's perfectly equipped now to find a job in a flower shop," indicating a concern with her future that is not portrayed in the final show, and he "maintains it isn't fair to Liza to allow her to go through with [the bet]." Higgins agrees with this, apparently mirroring Pickering's compassion and common sense, and then is secretly "delighted" when she decides to go on, indicating how emotionally bound up with her he is (though the experiment is unquestionably a huge motivator here too, of course). A significant difference between Outlines 1 and 2 is that whereas the first indicates that Eliza "requests Higgins' arm," this second outline merely has the three "departing for the ball." Ultimately, Lerner would reinstate the gesture with the arm and give it huge significance.

The outline of act 2 continues the overall trend toward overt discussions of love. We see, for instance, the crucial inclusion of a duet for Higgins and Eliza—something missing from the final show, and yet something that would have united them in music in a classic gesture of romance. Pickering's character is strikingly at odds with his *Fair Lady* persona: he is "amused" at Higgins's behavior, intimating that the motivation for the Professor's irritability is romantic jealousy. He reprises his first-act song and "facetiously suggests to Higgins that he try it again with another flower girl—create another woman precisely to his own taste," whereupon Higgins "stomps off" and Pickering "laughs." This outline also reveals initial plans for the ball scene: whereas the definitive show ends the first act in the middle of the dance and tantalizes us with Eliza's fate until "You Did It" at the start of act 2, Outline 2 shows the events in real time. "You Did It," of course, is a great showcase for Higgins and Pickering in which they relate the evening's events to Mrs. Pearce and the servants, but Outline 2 has all this happen onstage instead, and even includes reference to Liszt's Hungarian Rhapsody in the same ironic way that Loewe would eventually evoke it in "You Did It." The third scene of act 2 is also unfamiliar, in the sense that it depicts the trio in a "period limousine" with Pickering driving, but Higgins self-satisfied behavior is familiar from both *Pygmalion* and the published *Fair Lady*.

Outline 3: Scenic Outline (ca.1954)

Outline 3 (reproduced in table 3.4) also comes from Herman Levin's papers. It gives less specific information about the action, has no mention of songs, no title or date, and takes up only three pages. However, the outline does show a mixture of some scenes held over from the previous outline and some advanced to the familiar scenario, implying it must be an intermediate version. Act 1, scene 9 contains a note: "I am hoping that by the time we come to England, we will have a choreographer, and this sequence might be a little more precise than it is at the moment." This strongly implies that the document dates from either the end of 1954 or early 1955, because it is likely to be an explanation to Rex Harrison—whom Lerner and Loewe visited in London—of how the scene might play. Therefore, Lerner's subsequent claim that he and Loewe recommended the composition of *Fair Lady* in autumn 1954 because they had decided they "could do *Pygmalion* simply by doing *Pygmalion*" (i.e., following the progress of the film "and adding the action that took place between the acts of the play"), in fact he simplified the matter.[38] Clearly, more work was done on the story than Lerner would have us believe.

Table 3.3. **Outline 2, Act 2**

Scene	Setting	Action	Song/dance
1	(In One) Entrance to Ballroom	This scene and the following, that of the ball, are underscored by music, the guests being introduced to the hostess, and then entering the ballroom. Liza enters with Higgins and Pickering. Karpathy's curiosity is aroused. (Almost exact scene as in motion picture.)	Musical underscoring.
2	The Ball	Of course—the Waltz! The entire action of the ball is told in pantomime to music, or song. Group of women express curiosity about Liza to Karpathy. Several times Karpathy tries to dance with Liza. Each time Pickering and/or Higgins step in between and dance her away. Finally he is successful. He asks her into adjoining room, and they leave the floor. Higgins and Pickering wait it out, aghast. Liza and Karpathy return. Karpathy acts as if he knows something. The women ask him. He tells them she is a fraud. Before he can continue, King and Queen of Transylvania enter with the Prince. All bow and curtsey. King admires Liza. Liza is notified the Prince would like to dance with her. She does. Liza and Prince lead the dance. When ensemble joins in, women gather around Karpathy to find out who she is. In a rapid recitative they try and guess who she is, what nationality she is. Karpathy says no to each question and then gives the answer: She is Hungarian. Not only Hungarian, but a princess. (A few strains of the Hungarian Rhapsody are heard in the orchestra.) Karpathy and the group stand back in awe, as the spotlight shines on Liza and the Prince. On the other side of the stage, Higgins and Pickering wipe their brows and start dancing around together, as the curtains close.	Dance: waltz.
3	(In One) Front View of Period Limousine	Pickering driving. Higgins sitting next to him. Scene is practically a monologue by Higgins expressing his contentment with himself and his triumph. Very smug indeed. (Combination of dialogue from play and motion picture.)	
4	Higgins' Study	Basically same scene as Act IV of play, with deletions. When Liza is alone she reprises "The Like of 'im and the Like of Me."	Eliza: reprise.

66

5	(In One) Outside Higgins' House	Freddy is waiting (as in motion picture). Liza enters. Same basic scene between them as in picture. Scene will end with song by Liza. (Note: there is a possibility that at the end of Scene 5, Freddy, finding the door open, will come into the house and that the above scene between them will take place in Higgins' study. The ultimate decision will depend on the subject of Liza's song.)	Eliza: song.
6	Insert Stage Right: Higgins in Bed	He awakes to discover Liza has gone. He is outraged by her lack of gratitude. Pickering in pajamas and housecoat, enters, as Higgins calls his mother. On STAGE LEFT, Mrs. Higgins appears on telephone. Higgins tells mother his troubles. Remembers while on phone that Doolittle is getting married today. Higgins, convinced Liza will be there, goes off to dress. Pickering is highly amused at Higgins. Reprises ballade. (This scene combination of bedroom scene in picture and beginning of Act V, in play.)	Pickering: reprise.
7	Outside St George's	Doolittle enters in cutaway, surrounded by raggedy cronies. A very proper Middle Class, all dressed the same are waiting to welcome him on the other side of the stage. Doolittle has song. Subject: "Middle Class morality and the end of the good old days." Higgins and Pickering enter looking for Liza. Doolittle informs them she is not there yet. He has few more vituperative outbursts against Higgins and enters church. Liza enters. This will be basically same scene as in play, Act V. Pickering exits into church, leaving them alone in the middle of the scene. Only addition to scene is during discussion Liza likens herself to her father, who has been intimidated into doing something he does not want to do. She refuses to be thus intimidated. The important moment of the scene, when Liza turns on Higgins and suddenly realises she can deal with him on an equal footing—the moment in which Liza acquires a soul and is finally a completed woman. This will be done as a duet. The substance of it will be Liza saying that she is a brand new woman and needs him no longer, and Higgins telling her she is magnificent. At the end of the song, Higgins has dialogue from play, wherein he tells her he likes her like this, that five minutes ago she was a millstone around his neck and now she is a tower of strength . . . that he said he'd make a woman of her and by George he did. Freddy enters. Liza triumphantly says goodbye, and she and Freddy exit together. Doolittle and bridal party enter from the church. Pickering enters with them and exits with Higgins.	Doolittle's song. Liza and Higgins: duet.

(continued)

Table 3.3 *continued*

Scene	Setting	Action	Song/dance
8	Higgins and Pickering walking home	Higgins is in a blue funk. A flower girl tries to sell them flowers. Pickering facetiously suggests to Higgins that he try it again with another flower girl—create another woman precisely to his own taste. Higgins furiously stomps off. Pickering laughs at him and reprises ballade.	Pickering: reprise.
9	Higgins's Study	This will be the exact same last scene as that of the picture . . . Higgins puts on recording of Liza's voice . . . then breaks record and sits slumped in chair facing the audience. Liza enters and continues where record left off. Same last line as picture, where Higgins would like to run to her and take her in his arms, but not knowing how, sinks back in his chair and says: "Liza, where are my slippers?"	

Although the first scene in Outline 3 has been moved back to Covent Garden from Limehouse and several of the other scenes are in a familiar form, scene 6 still has a telephone call between Higgins and his mother that does not appear in the published show or in *Pygmalion*. Scene 8 has a Policeman who was eventually not included, and scene 9 still contains a scene in which Higgins persuades Eliza to continue with the experiment, followed by the ballet which stayed in the show until New Haven. Act 2, scene 4 is "undetermined"; apparently, Lerner had not yet finalized the scene where Higgins and Pickering discover Eliza's disappearance and resolve to track her down. This part of the story is not shown in the *Pygmalion* play or film and is a key example of Lerner "filling in the action" between the play's acts. The next scene is also interesting in that it appears to preserve the action of *Pygmalion* by including Doolittle, who departs from the show after the return to Covent Garden in the published version, and Pickering, whose final appearance in *Fair Lady* is in scene 4. The Colonel also appears in the ensuing scene, along with some "Street Folk"; the purpose of this tableau is unclear, however, though the final scene is in its familiar form. In summary, Outline 3 moves us much closer to the definitive structure of the musical, but several scenes were still in a different form. Of particular relevance is the scene of Higgins's near-"seduction" of Eliza in act 1, when he persuades her to continue with the experiment: this shows that Lerner was continuing to overplay the Higgins-Eliza relationship, even though as a whole his plan moves back toward *Pygmalion* as a model.

Outline 4
Finally, Outline 4 (table 3.5) comes from the papers (housed in the New York Public Library) of the show's choreographer, Hanya Holm. It undoubtedly postdates her agreement to create the dances for the show because it includes a reference to "Miss Holm." This places it somewhere between late September 1955 and the rehearsal period in January 1956, probably nearer the former than the latter. By this stage the structure of the show was much more strongly in place. Reflecting this, Outline 4 is very thorough in mentioning the locations, times, musical numbers, and characters involved in each scene, in contrast to the previous outlines.

At first glance, it may seem that Outline 4 represents the published show, but there are several important additions and omissions. At the start, there is reference to a song for the Buskers. Assuming that this is not the orchestral "Opening" that depicts Covent Garden after the Overture, this could have been an additional scene-setting song in the style of "Wouldn't It Be Lovely?" Neither of Doolittle's songs has a title, hinting

Table 3.4. **Outline 3**

Act 1

Scene No.	Setting	Characters/Action/Notes
1	Covent Garden—March	Higgins, Liza, Pickering, Freddy, Mrs. Eynsford Hill, Cockneys and "Swells".
2	(In one) The façade of a tenement section— immediately following	Liza, Doolittle and two of his Chums.
3	Higgins' Study	Higgins, Pickering, Mrs. Pearce and Liza.
4	(In one) The façade of a tenement section—a month later	Doolittle and Middle-aged Cockney Woman, who lives in tenement.
5	Higgins' Study	This will be a montage of Liza's lessons, featuring Higgins, Liza and Pickering. Mrs. Pearce and Six Servants (four women and two men) appear in a cut-out, supposedly the kitchen, between episodes. Doolittle enters in the middle of the scene. Because the lessons are interrupted by the Doolittle scene, Liza will have time to make one change.
6	(In one—split stage)	From one side of the stage, Higgins is phoning his mother, who appears on the other side. In this scene will be Higgins, Pickering, Mrs. Higgins and Mrs. Higgins' maid.
7	The royal enclosure at Ascot— late June	Higgins, Liza, Pickering, Mrs Eynsford Hill, Mrs. Higgins, Freddy and Ensemble.
8	(In one) Outside Higgins' house—later that afternoon	Freddy (who has come to woo Liza), Mrs. Pearce and Policeman. (Note: There will be some "street folk" in this scene. We don't know how many or their identity as yet.)

70

#	Setting	Cast / Description
9	Higgins' Study—immediately following.	Liza, Higgins and Pickering. This will be a scene in which Higgins persuades Liza to go on, in spite of the catastrophe at Ascot. When she agrees, we intend a short balletic pantomime of more lessons, all to take place in the study. There will be dancing teachers, those who teach her how to walk properly, hairdressers, couturieres, etc. We discussed this scene in great detail with Oliver, and he has some interesting ideas scenically.
10	(In one) Outside the ballroom of the Transylvanian Embassy	Higgins, Pickering, The Host and Hostess, Karpathy (Hungarian, Higgins' ex-pupil), A Few Couples.
11	The ballroom	Higgins, Liza, Pickering and possibly the King, Queen and Prince of Transylvania, Karpathy and Ensemble.

Act 2

#	Setting	Cast / Description
1	The entrance hall of Higgins' house—early the following morning	The Six Servants and Mrs. Pearce, who have been waiting up for news of the ball, and Higgins, Liza and Pickering, who return from the ball.
2	(In one) Outside Higgins' house. About an hour later.	Freddy and Liza.
3	Covent Garden—around 5 o'clock in the morning	Cockneys, Doolittle (in his usual clothes) and Liza.
4	(In one)	Undetermined.
5	Mrs. Higgins' drawing room. The next day.	Mrs. Higgins, Liza, Higgins, Pickering, Doolittle in cutaway.
6	(In one) London street	Higgins, Pickering and a few "Street Folk."
7	Higgins' study. Immediately following.	Higgins and Liza.

they had not yet been written, and scene 4 does not have the reprise of his first number either. Scene 5 has a "montage of lessons" song (which became "Poor Professor Higgins") both before and after "Just You Wait," whereas it only appears after Eliza's song in the published version. Another obvious difference is that "I Could Have Danced All Night" had not yet been written and an earlier song, "Shy," was in its place. On the other hand, scene 6 is similar to the published script, except that Higgins appears to have been the person talking to his mother outside the racecourse, rather than Pickering; obviously, the latter character benefited from an extra moment of humor in the final show, especially in light of the extent to which Pickering's role had been reduced from the initial outlines.

Lord and Lady Boxley (scene 7) later became Lord and Lady Boxington, and in this version the Policeman in scene 8 has been replaced by possible Street Strollers. The sequence of musical numbers in scene 9 was still in its original form, unsurprisingly, but the next few scenes seem to be roughly in their published state. A crucial exception is Liza's apparent exclusion from the group reprise of "Wouldn't It Be Loverly?" Scene 4 is now in place, with the exception of "A Hymn to Him" (which was added much later), and only the location of scene 5 is unfamiliar: this outline has it in Mrs. Higgins's garden, rather than her conservatory (in the final show). It is also worth noting that the reprise of "You Did It," with which Higgins interrupts Eliza's "Without You," is already fixed and not a late addition as Lerner claimed in his memoir. The setting for Higgins's final song is also unfamiliar: the location by the Thames is still an anomaly since, as noted above, a scene in Higgins's house cannot "immediately follow" one on the Embankment because the two are geographically displaced. The final scene is crowned by a reprise of "Shy" rather than "I Could Have Danced All Night" because the latter had not yet been written. It is interesting to note that this aspect of the structure of the show—the reprisal of Eliza's first-act putative "love song"—was already firmed up. One might easily have thought that the last-minute return to the "I Could Have Danced" music was a way of bringing the curtain down on what the composer and lyricist guessed could be the show's hit song, but gesture was clearly the highest priority all along. In conclusion, Outline 4 reveals that although the musical follows *Pygmalion* quite closely, many factors had to be created or changed along the way, as the numerous differences between this late outline and the published script demonstrate. By extension, this shows how deliberate, considered, and thoughtfully contrived the piece is.

The main text to be considered in this section is the document labeled "Rehearsal Script" in Herman Levin's papers.[39] There are a couple of hundred differences between the musical's identified rehearsal script and the published script, and these afford an insight into the last-minute polishing done by Lerner and the director, Moss Hart, during the rehearsal period. Curiously, the authorship of Lerner's book has sometimes been called into question, with the suggestion that Moss Hart was in effect the co-author. For instance, his wife, Kitty Carlisle Hart, mentions that Lerner and Hart "went to Atlantic City for a week to work on the script" and adds that when she asked Hart about it, he replied that "he was hired as the director, and the fact that he was a writer-director didn't make any difference." On the other hand, Steven Bach reports that Lerner's production associate Stone Widney—who was present during the writing and rehearsal stages—remembered Hart contributing "very little to the book." No evidence remains in Moss Hart's papers in Wisconsin of the director's additions either, and the issue cannot easily be resolved. Therefore, for the purposes of this book Lerner is referred to as the author of the script, even though there is no doubt that Hart's contributions were vital to its success.[40]

Diction seems to be one of the main concerns of Lerner's revision of the script. Often he changed just a couple of words or the word order to make it as convincing as possible, especially in the cockney scenes. For example, Eliza's "Two bunches of violets trod into the mud" (rehearsal script [hereafter *RS*], 1-1-1) becomes simply " . . . trod in the mud" (published script [*PS*], 2).[41] This is a small change, but it makes the line sound shorter and more abrupt, as well as introducing a grammatical mistake (Shaw's *Pygmalion* has "into").[42] Rather than detailing all such changes, however, this section deals mainly with the ways in which the differences between the rehearsal and published scripts had implications for the central relationships in the piece.

Defining Doolittle

The biggest changes made during rehearsals were to the part of Alfred Doolittle, Eliza's father, one of the show's most vibrant characters. His relationships to the other characters shifted in focus, and some of the darker aspects of his personality were obscured. For example:

DOOLITTLE: Well, I'm willing to marry her. It's me that suffers by it. I've no hold on her. I got to be agreeable to her. I got to give her presents. I got to buy her clothes something sinful. I'm a slave to that woman, Eliza. Just because I'm not her lawful husband. And she knows it, too. Catch her marrying me! Come on, Eliza. Slip your father half a crown to go home on. An unmarried man has to deaden his senses much more than a married one.

PS (17)

DOOLITTLE: Well, I'm willing to marry her. It's me that suffers by it. I'm a slave to that woman, Eliza. Just because I ain't her lawful husband. *[Lovably]* Come on, Eliza. Slip your father half a crown to go home on.

The first extract gives a sense of the extent of Doolittle's misery at not being married to the woman with whom he lives. He says that he has no hold over her, and that he is obliged to buy her presents in order to keep her, because he has no legal rights. His final line ("An unmarried man . . .") is tinged with a melancholy that we might not normally associate with the jovial "Lerner" Doolittle, but it is absolutely consistent with Shaw's arguably more elegiac Doolittle. The replacement speech still contains reference to "slavery," but it is not explained, losing the opportunity for a darker moment.

The subject of Doolittle's relationships, especially with Eliza's current "stepmother," was originally discussed more explicitly. Particularly important is the indication in *RS* that Eliza is aware that her parents were not married: when Mrs. Pearce asks Eliza about her parents, she replies, "I ain't got no mother. Her that turned me out was my sixth stepmother, and my father isn't a marrying sort of man if you know what I mean" (*RS*, 1-3-23). Lerner simplified this to "I ain't got no parents" (*PS*, 30), almost as if she is simply an orphan, yet the original is more revealing, because we learn about Eliza's insecure upbringing. It also discloses that she is aware her parents were not married, something her father later claims (to Pickering and Higgins, albeit in *RS* only) that she does not know. Again, the cut line derives from Shaw, who mentions Eliza's "sixth stepmother" but does not have the comment about Doolittle not being "a marrying sort of man."[43]

The encounter (a couple of scenes later) between Higgins and Doolittle is white-hot. Deciding how to carve this scene must have been quite a challenge for Lerner: money changes hands for Eliza and Doolittle "sells" his daughter, which paints him in an unpleasant light, yet he has to remain a *likeable* rogue.

One theme that Lerner originally explored more extensively was the "unde-serving poor," a label that Doolittle gives himself early on in the scene. An example is the line "They charge me just the same for everything as they charge the deserving" (RS, 1-5-33), which was later removed; here, Doolittle explains why he needs money. Later, he rejects Higgins's offer to train him to be a preacher: "Not me, Governor, thank you kindly . . . it's a dog's life any way you look at it. Undeserving poverty's my line" (RS,1-5-34, derived from *Pyg-malion*, 55). Soon afterwards, when Pickering says that he assumes Doolittle was married to Eliza's mother and is firmly put straight on the subject, Doo-little adds: "No, [i]t's only the middle class way. My way has always been the undeserving way. But don't say nothing to Eliza. She don't know" (RS, 1-5-35). This reintroduces the reality of Eliza's background hinted at in the previous scene, and underlines the fact that she is illegitimate while more generally showing that she was brought up with a different sense of morality than the place in which she now finds herself (the additions are not from Shaw).

Consistent with the changes made to act 1, scene 5, the relationship between Eliza and Doolittle is much darker in the rehearsal version of the Ascot scene too, even though he is physically absent. Eliza originally had a long speech (deriving from *Pygmalion*), dealing with the news that her father is an alco-holic (RS, 1-7-58). Mrs. Eynsford Hill expresses sympathy, but Eliza replies that "it never did him no harm" and assures her that he did not "keep it up regular." Doolittle only did it "on the burst . . . from time to time," and Eliza points out that he was "always more agreeable" afterwards. Her mother would send him out to drink himself happy if he was out of work. Eliza's motto is simply that "if a man has a bit of conscience, it always takes him when he's sober. . . . A drop of booze just takes that off and makes him happy." This state-ment represents Shaw at his most acute.[44] The comment not only exposes Eliza's social status, it also gives a shocking insight into the emotional condi-tions in which she was raised. *PS* removes this element of the scene, retaining reference to Doolittle's drinking habits only in passing for a joke ("Drank! My word! Something chronic," 106). In consequence, *PS* maintains light comedy throughout the Ascot scene rather than adding new insights.

Doolittle's final appearance, in the Covent Garden scene in act 2, was also changed, specifically during his last exchange with Eliza. This confrontation is an invention of the musical, though it does have an equivalent in *Pygma-lion* through Doolittle's presence in the final scene. (In the play, Freddy, Mrs. Higgins, Pickering, and Eliza all depart for his wedding; crucially, Eliza does not attend the ceremony in the musical, and Lerner implies a final rift between them.) During rehearsals, Lerner excised several lines showing the "philosophical" Doolittle. He says that he was "free" and "happy" and didn't

Table 3.5. **Outline 4**

Act 1

Scene	Setting	Principal Characters	Musical Numbers	Other
1	Covent Garden—outside opera house. March.	Higgins, Pickering, Liza	First song: Buskers. Second Song: "Why Can't the English?" — Higgins. Third Song: "Wouldn't it be Loverly?" — Liza, Four Cockneys around Fire, Dancers (number to be determined by Miss Holm).	If required to fill out crowd at opening of scene, there will be enough time for the dancers to change from evening dress to Cockney costumes.
2	Tenement district—pub on one side, Liza's house on the other. Immediately following.	Liza, Doolittle, Alfie, Harry.	Song: Doolittle Alfie, Harry.	
3	Higgins' study. The following morning.	Mrs Pearce, Higgins, Pickering, Liza.	Song: "I'm an Ordinary Man" — Higgins.	
4	Tenement district. Late April.	Doolittle, Alfie, Harry, Mrs. Hopkins.		
5	Higgins' study. The next day.	Higgins, Liza, Pickering, Mrs Pearce, Four Maids, Two Manservants—Doolittle.	Song: Montage of Lessons. Second Song: "Just You Wait"—Liza. Song: Montage of Lessons. Second Song: "The Rain in Spain." Third Song: "Shy"—Liza.	There will be a blackout after "Just You Wait." Lights come up on same scene a few days later. "The Rain in Spain" will be sung late at night. All three are in various stages of exhausted dishevelment.

76

6	Outside Ascot. Shortly after.	Mrs. Higgins, One or Two Footmen, Higgins—perhaps One or Two Passersby.
7	Ascot. Immediately following.	Higgins, Mrs. Higgins, Liza, Pickering, Mrs Eynsford Hill, Lord and Lady Boxley, Freddy, Full Ensemble.	Song: "Ascot Gavotte"—Chorus. Dancing by Ensemble.
8	Outside Higgins' house. Later that afternoon.	Freddy, Mrs. Pearce—and perhaps a few Street Strollers (to be determined).	Song: "On the Street Where She Lives"—Freddy.
9	Higgins' study. Later that day.	Liza, Higgins, Pickering, Mrs. Pearce.	Song: "Come to the Ball"—Higgins. Ballet (or pantomime): The preparation of Liza—Liza, Higgins, Dressmakers, Dancing Teachers, Beauty Specialists, etc. Second Song: "Say a Prayer for me Tonight"—Liza.
10	Promenade of the Ball. Fall.	Pickering, Higgins, Karpathy, Three or Four Ladies of the Ensemble.	

(continued)

Table 3.5 continued

Scene	Setting	Principal Characters	Musical Numbers	Other
11	The ballroom. Immediately following.	Higgins, Pickering, Liza, Karpathy, King and Queen of Transylvania, Full Ensemble.	Dance: Waltz Finale—Higgins, Karpathy, Liza, Full Ensemble.	

Act 2

Scene	Setting	Principal Characters	Musical Numbers	Other
1	Entrance hall of Higgins' house. The following 3 a.m.	Liza, Higgins, Pickering, Mrs. Pearce, Four Maidservants, Two Manservants.	Song: "You Did It"—Higgins, Pickering, Servants. Second Song: "Just You Wait" (short reprise)—Liza.	
2	Outside Higgins' house. Immediately following.	Freddy, Liza.	Song: "On the Street Where She Lives" (reprise)—Freddy. Second Song: "Show Me"—Liza and Freddy.	Liza should be in a street coat and will have time during Freddy's reprise, if not to slip off her dress and put on another, at least to slip it off and put on the coat. She could put on the dress that goes under after this scene, if necessary.
3	Covent Garden. 5 a.m. that morning.	Liza, Doolittle, Alfie, Harry, Full Ensemble.	Dance: The flower market coming to life. Song: "Wouldn't it be Loverly" (reprise)—same group around smudge pot fire as in 1-1. Second song: Rousing number by Doolittle and Ensemble. Dance by Ensemble.	Doolittle will be in his striped trousers. Everybody else in Cockney garb, except, of course, Liza.

4	Upstairs corridor Higgins' house. The following morning.	Higgins, Pickering, Mrs. Pearce, Four Maidservants, Two Manservants.		Higgins is discovered in the process of getting dressed and completes his attire in the course of the scene. Pickering is already fully dressed.
5	Garden of Mrs Higgins' house. Later that day (Fall).	Mrs. Higgins, Liza, Freddy, Higgins.	Song: "Without You"—Liza. Second Song: "You Did It" (short reprise)—Higgins.	
6	Along the Embankment of the Thames. Sunset same day.	Higgins, Passersby (number to be determined).	Song: Higgins.	
7	Higgins' Study. Immediately following.	Higgins, Liza.	"Shy" (reprise)—Liza's voice on recording, and then Liza herself.	

want to be interfered with. He had no relatives, but now he has "fifty, and not a decent week's wages among the lot of them." He used to live for himself, but now he's "middle class" and has to "live for others." He concludes: "The next one to touch me will be your blasted professor. I'll have to learn to speak middle-class language from him instead of speaking proper English" (RS, 2-3-17). This is an interesting speech that depicts Doolittle's fate as part of a wider social commentary within the show; his previous life was one of freedom, whereas financial security has entailed social burden—a direct contradiction to Higgins's philosophy, where the Cockney dialect binds the working classes and clear diction facilitates social liberation. The other addition to the speech follows the news that Doolittle is to be married to "Eliza's stepmother": "She wouldn't have married me before if she'd had six children by me. But now I am respectable. Now she wants to be respectable. Middle-class morality claims its victims" (RS, 2-3-17). Again, Doolittle reinforces the idea of his social shift as being something imprisoning rather than giving him an opportunity, describing himself as a "victim" and making it clear that social respectability (not love or affection) is the reason for the marriage.

Initiating the Eliza-Higgins Relationship

The all-important battle between Higgins and Eliza was intensified throughout the script during rehearsals. In act 1, scene 3, Lerner added several lines after Mrs. Pearce's question about whether Eliza is to be paid for taking part in the experiment. Higgins claims that Eliza will "only drink if you give her money," much to her indignation; she appeals to Pickering, who comes to her defense and asks whether it occurs to Higgins that Eliza "has some feelings." The Professor replies that he does not think she has "any feelings that we need bother about," but Mrs. Pearce interjects and asks him to "look ahead a little" (PS, 30–31). Yet again, these lines show Lerner going back to Shaw's text to add nuance to the musical.[45]

Higgins's character is further developed in his song, "I'm an Ordinary Man." The dialogue leading into the number was changed quite substantially during the rehearsal period. In particular, his original line, "Do I look like the kind of person who roams about anxiously searching for some woman to upset his life?" (RS, 1-3-25), is noticeable in the way that Higgins seems to reject the idea of having a female lover at all. The replacement is less clear-cut, relating a history of relationships with women that have gone badly as the reason for his bachelorhood: "I find that the moment I let a woman make friends with me she becomes jealous, exacting, suspicious and a damned nuisance. I find that the moment I let myself become friends with a woman, I become selfish and tyrannical. So here I am, a confirmed old bachelor, and likely to remain so" (*PS*, 35). Unusually, this is an example of *PS* making Higgins's possible status as a lover more tantalizing, rather than more obscure.

The revised speech is quite an improvement, because Higgins bares his soul in an unprecedented fashion, and thereby reveals his emotional repression: his relations with the opposite sex have been a disaster, and in his way he has been damaged by them. As before, Lerner reinstates several lines from Shaw. But he still omits the following statement of Higgins's: "You see, she'll be a pupil; and teaching would be impossible unless pupils were sacred. I've taught scores of American millionairesses how to speak English: the best looking women in the world. I'm seasoned. They might as well be blocks of wood. *I* might as well be a block of wood."[46] It is no accident that these lines were omitted from *My Fair Lady*: Lerner's Higgins cannot exaggerate his immunity to the opposite sex if the musical's ambiguous treatment of the Higgins-Eliza relationship is to be effective.

Two scenes later, the subject of Higgins's relationship with Eliza is again discussed openly, this time by Doolittle just before he departs the house: "I don't know what your intentions is, Governor, but if you'll take my advice you'll marry Eliza while she's young. If you don't, you'll be sorry for it after. But better her than you, because you're a man and she's only a woman and don't know how to be happy anyhow" (*RS*, 1-5-36, partly based on *Pygmalion*, 56). This was later altered to a shorter speech in which Doolittle advises Higgins simply to give Eliza "a few licks of the strap" if he has any trouble with her. Originally, however, Doolittle explicitly states his assumption that Higgins desires Eliza. Such a line seems oddly out of place in the musical, but it makes sense in the context of other comments from *RS*, in which a union between Higgins and Eliza seems almost inevitable. So different was its tone, in fact, that Higgins does not even react to Doolittle's comment about marrying Eliza. That Lerner changed this only during rehearsals suggests that the shift to romantic ambiguity was not yet complete.

The next person to inquire about Higgins's business with Eliza is his mother. In the original act 1, scene 6, Higgins and his mother discuss the experiment outside the race course; but the final version has Pickering in Higgins's place. The most surprising part of the *RS* version of the exchange is when Mrs. Higgins asks, "Henry, do you know what you would do if you really loved me?" and Higgins replies, "Marry, I suppose" (*RS*, 1-6-51). It seems that even during the rehearsal period, the subject of Higgins's possible matrimony was still openly discussed between the two characters, positing the Professor more overtly as a romantic lead. Later in the scene, Mrs. Higgins raises the issue again, asking where Eliza lives and on what terms she lives there (*RS*, 1-6-51). Higgins replies that she is "very useful," "knows where things are," and "remembers my appointments." But, he concedes, "she's there to be worked at." Higgins confesses it's his "most absorbing experiment" to date and that he thinks about Eliza "even in my sleep." An element of this exchange was brought back for the film version of the show, in which a scene is added outside Ascot after the race and Higgins admits that he and Pickering are "at it from morning until night . . . teaching Eliza, talking to Eliza, listening to Eliza, dressing Eliza . . ." But in addition, Higgins tells us (in RS alone) that "Even in my sleep I'm thinking about the girl and her confounded vowels and consonants. I'm worn out thinking about her, and watching her lips and her teeth and her tongue, not to mention her soul, which is the quaintest of the lot." Most of this comes from Shaw, but—significantly—Lerner replaces Shaw's "As if I ever stop thinking about the girl" with "Even in my sleep . . ."[47] That Higgins's nights are absorbed in thinking about Eliza, coupled with the sensuous language he uses to talk about her lips, teeth, and tongue, signifies an infatuation that does not stop at intellectual intrigue.

The replacement scene still touches lightly on the status of the Higgins-Eliza relationship, but Pickering is instantly dismissive of the idea of romance between the two when Mrs. Higgins asks if it is a love affair: "Heavens no! She's a flower girl. He picked her up off the kerbstone" (72). This encounter increases the ambiguity of the relationship between Eliza and Higgins because Pickering, who lives with both of them, does not seem to have detected a romance. Nevertheless, his comment does not rule anything out, muddying the waters brilliantly.

Freddy

Another character whose personality was modified is Freddy. His main function in the Ascot scene is to provide Eliza with the bet on Dover, the horse that will bring about the memorable climax to the sequence. In PS he does this fairly discreetly, merely informing Eliza that he has a bet and offering it to her. However, in RS he is given a prominent entrance (RS, 1-7-55). When he arrives holding a ticket, his mother pounces on him and says: "You know you can't afford it, dear." He replies that he "had to" because the odds were "too good to resist." In this original formulation, Freddy is depicted as a compulsive gambler. As the musical evolved, Freddy increasingly became the polar opposite of Higgins, so that the Eliza-Higgins-Freddy love triangle had a stronger dynamic. Arguably, the idea that Freddy is the sort of person who gambles for thrills and cannot resist the odds on Dover makes him a risk taker and a more masculine, virile character. Therefore, it is easy to see why Lerner removed this element of Freddy's personality and made him into a faithful but dull lover for Eliza.

His role in act 2 was similarly adjusted: his speech leading into the verse of "Show Me" was originally longer, including the lines "You're beautiful and delicate and warm and desirable. Every night I look up at these very stars and dream of being near you. Eliza, you don't know how potty I am about you" (*RS*, 2-2-12). It fits into the overall remodeling of Freddy's character that this was removed; the rhetoric of "beautiful and delicate and warm and desirable" shows a sensibility far more intensely romantic than Freddy is ultimately capable of, while his nightly dreams of being "near" Eliza insinuate a potent sexuality that is incoherent with the rest of his behavior. Here, we can see once and for all how Lerner watered down Freddy's personality to render him an impossible choice of suitor for Eliza, thereby introducing the parting of ways with the published epilogue to *Pygmalion*, in which the two are united in marriage.

Intensifying the Higgins-Eliza Relationship

The final three scenes of act 1 underwent the largest number of changes during rehearsals and previews, especially scene 9 of *RS*, which takes place "simultaneously with the preceding scene" (that is, at the same time as "On the Street Where You Live") and shows us the aftermath of the Ascot scene. As the curtain rises, we see Mrs. Pearce comforting Eliza who, significantly, says, "I failed him." As before, this makes the emotional connection between Eliza and Higgins stronger and gives her the air of someone who has failed the man she loves. The rest of the scene involves three musical numbers: "Come to the Ball," in which Higgins seductively persuades Eliza to return to her lessons; the ballet, in which she receives dancing instruction, better posture, a cosmetician, and "the best hairdresser in London" (1-9-66); and "Say a Prayer for Me Tonight," in which Eliza tells the servants of her anxieties.

Lerner's solution to the need to replace this long sequence of music with something much shorter—and in the process, go back to the original scenario for the scene as described in Outline 1—changed several emphases. Scene 9 of *PS* takes place "six weeks later" than the Ascot scene, whereas *RS* places the races in July and the ball in October. Therefore, Higgins's work has involved much more pressure in the final version, giving him only a few weeks rather than a quarter of a year. Furthermore, although we perhaps lose out by not witnessing the pain gone through to complete Eliza's education, the status of the Eliza-Higgins relationship is kept far more consistent by removing all flagrant suggestions of their emotional attachment. A subtle but important gesture is added, however. Eliza arrives at the top of the stairs in her gown; Pickering says that she looks beautiful, and then goes on to prompt Higgins to agree with him. According to the stage directions, "Eliza turns to

Higgins hopefully," and Higgins, "having decided the gown is quite all right," declares that it is "Not bad at all" (91). Eliza's "hopefulness" is the salient point here, replacing the spoken line in *RS* about having failed *him* with the implication that she has dressed beautifully for *him*. Then come two of the most resounding gestures in the musical. First, having refused Pickering's offer of port a couple of minutes previously, implying that he is not nervous about the ball, Higgins "looks furtively around to make certain Pickering doesn't see him" and "pours himself a quick glass of port." In itself this shows a more human side to Higgins, but what follows is even more surprising. As he starts for the door, "he pauses, turns and gazes at Eliza. He returns to her and offers his arm. She takes it and they go out of the door, Pickering following after." Through this action, Higgins acknowledges Eliza's dignity for the first time, going through the door *with* her rather than before her. This shows Lerner at his most brilliant and imaginative (the scene is a complete deviation from *Pygmalion*): one of the longest scenes in the play, including three musical numbers, is replaced by one of the shortest, yet in this instance gesture serves the overall drama more effectively than twenty minutes of song and dance.

Resolving the Higgins-Eliza Relationship

The first scene of the second act is one of the most crucial in the show, and it was changed in numerous ways during rehearsals, nearly always to adjust this climax in the Eliza-Higgins relationship. First, Higgins's initial speech of reaction to Eliza's admission that she is worried about "what is to become of her" was originally slightly shorter. One might take the addition of the line "Oh, I shouldn't bother about that if I were you" (*PS*, 110) as a comfort to Eliza—suggesting that she has nothing to worry about—but at the same time, it also has an air of dismissal, as if her future is not worth contemplating. The rephrasing of the subsequent line from "You'll settle yourself somewhere or other" (*RS*, 2-1-8) into "I should imagine you won't have much difficulty in settling yourself somewhere or other" also hints at a split meaning: the first part becomes softer, but "somewhere or other" maintains Higgins's apparently indifference towards Eliza's precise fate (though this indifference could be perceived to be feigned).

Addressing a similar issue, Eliza has a line in *RS* that was then cut: she says to Higgins, "I wish you'd left me where you found me" (2-1-8). This intensifies the character's grief and fear, and in particular illustrates her realization that she is now too self-aware either to resume her former life or to fit comfortably into middle-class society. The climax to the scene (from "Damn Mrs. Pearce" on, *PS*, 114) was also slightly changed for *PS*. Crucially, Higgins does not

Julie Andrews (Eliza) and Rex Harrison (Higgins) (Springer/Photofest)

"damn" Eliza in the original version of this speech. This makes a huge differ-ence; never before has Higgins so flagrantly shown his lack of regard for Eliza than in this direct insult, and it is no wonder that the scene ends with her breaking down into "uncontrollable sobs." The other change is the addition of the word "my" in reference to Higgins's comment about "lavish[ing] hard-earned knowledge" (*PS*, 114) on her, thereby intensifying his resentment.

This trend is continued in the revision of the scene in which Higgins and Pickering discover that Eliza has fled (something not shown in *Pygmalion*). Again, the most important changes involve explicit discussion of Higgins's feelings for Eliza. Pickering suggests that "Eliza could have met some bounder at the ball and eloped with him." Higgins calls this "an idiotic notion" but is clearly perturbed by the idea because he soon asks Pickering: "Was there some chap or other she paid particular attention to? Or he to her?" They discuss a "toothy Spaniard" who Higgins noted was "quite attentive," but Pickering assures him that he "didn't speak a word of English," to which Higgins responds—"to himself"—"Good. Good" (RS, 2-4-24). Yet again, we can see how the issue of romance between Higgins and Eliza was to have been more unambiguous.

When the two meet again at Mrs. Higgins's house, the battle continues, and once more Lerner made some effective changes during rehearsals. Originally, Mrs. Higgins's advice to Eliza was simply to "Remember, last night you danced with a prince" (2-5-28), but the published version turns this into "Remember, last night you not only danced with a prince, but you behaved like a princess" (140). The alteration adds dignity and power to Eliza, raising her status because of her own behavior rather than by association with a man. By contrast, when Higgins's original insult of "You mean I'm to put on my Sunday manners for this creature I picked out of the mud?" (2-5-29) was changed to "You mean I'm to put on my Sunday manners for this thing I created out of the squashed cabbage leaves of Covent Garden?" the affront to Eliza was made far graver. Lerner also added the tense exchange in which Eliza and Higgins contrast the Professor's manners with those of Pickering; Higgins advocates "having the same manner for all human souls" (PS, 143). This presents rather a stark revelation of Higgins's true character: a man with no respect for anyone. Such a portrayal helps tip the balance of the scene even more in Eliza's favor, since he backs himself into a corner with his foolish words.

Eliza is generally much stronger in PS. For instance, originally she said to Higgins, "It would make no difference to you if I were there or not, and it's cruel of you to pretend that it would" (2-5-31), yet the published text has her say instead, "But I can get along without you. Don't think I can't" (143). The original has Eliza describe her worth in terms of what she means to Higgins while the replacement has her declare her independence from him. The adjustment makes it necessary for Higgins to respond to this new statement: "You never wondered, I suppose, whether I could get along without you," he asks her. But she replies that he will "have to," and he immediately returns to his normal defiant stance: "And so I can. Without you or any soul on earth" (PS, 143). This makes the battle even more interesting, with Higgins acknowledging Eliza's power and contemplating his dependence on her. She takes this to be emotional blackmail, yet in truth Higgins has let down his guard and spoken his true feelings for her—a rare example of romantic intensification in *PS*. Then again, *RS* has Eliza address something that is not dealt with in *PS*: "You can twist the heart in a girl as easy as some could twist her arms to hurt her. Mrs. Pearce warned me. Time and again she has wanted to leave you; and you always got around her at the last minute. And you don't care a bit for her. And you don't care a bit for me. I won't care for anybody that doesn't care for me" (*RS*, 2-5-31). Here, Lerner seems to have considered sketching a new aspect of Mrs. Pearce's relationship with Higgins: we do not otherwise know that she has nearly left him several times, nor do we realize that Eliza and Mrs. Pearce are confidantes who have discussed the Professor's behavior. This fact is not unimportant, since it explains why Mrs. Pearce is not surprised at Eliza's bolting, as well as telling us why she did not prevent her from doing so.

Romance becomes a topic again in the next part of the scene. There was originally a series of lines about Freddy's advances toward Eliza: Higgins "damns his impudence," Eliza says that "he has a right to" love her, Higgins declares that she has "no right to encourage him," but she responds that "Every girl has a right to be loved." Higgins refers to him as a "fool," yet Eliza says that "if he's weak and poor and wants me, maybe he'd make me happier than my betters that bully me and don't want me" (*RS*, 2-5-32). Notwithstanding the reference to marrying Freddy, this exchange unequivocally foregrounds the possible Higgins-Eliza romance. Higgins's overt grumpiness at the idea of Eliza having a young, foolish lover shows his own desire for her, while Eliza's suggestion that Freddy might make her happier than her "betters that bully" her again nominates Higgins as her potential lover. Yet the replacement for this exchange appears to make the union impossible. Higgins proclaims, "Oh, in short, you want me to be as infatuated about you as he is. Is that it?" (*PS*, 146), and Eliza explains in response that she entered into the experiment "not for the dresses and the taxis" but "because we were pleasant together" and because she "came to care" for him. She says that she did not want him to "make love" to her or "forget the difference" between them but to be more friendly.

In a final change, after Eliza has sung "Without You" and exits, Higgins's response was modified: *RS* has him say, "Eliza has left me! For good," while *PS* changes it to "She's gone!" (*PS*, 150). Yet again, the modification moves the script from language that implies a relationship ("left me") to something less specific ("gone"). From beginning to end, this subject was systematically deleted or obscured during the rehearsal period, so that whereas *RS* charts a conventional Broadway romance between a man and a woman, *PS* forged a bond that was scarcely less strong yet much more difficult to define. In the end, Lerner tantalizes us with the possibilities of an alliance between Eliza and Higgins, yet never quite delivers it.

STRUCTURE

The structural robustness of My Fair Lady is a major asset and it was clearly no accident. Its brilliance operates on several levels. First, the layout of the scenes takes us on a careful journey from one location to the next (see table 3.6). We meet the main protagonist, Eliza, at the very beginning of the first scene, and she is at Covent Garden market carrying a basket of flowers. The first moment of tension between her and Higgins occurs here, and it is no coincidence that the final clash between the two takes place in another sort of "artificial garden," Mrs. Higgins's conservatory. The market represents a space in which things come out into the open: Higgins's and Eliza's worldviews emerge here, in "Why Can't the English?" and "Wouldn't It Be Loverly?" respectively, and Eliza's return to the market in act 2, scene 3, is a moment of high emotion in which she realizes that she no longer belongs there. Higgins's study is also pivotal to the unfolding of the story. It is a place of learning of all kinds: in a literal sense, Eliza's lessons take place here, but this is also the place where we find out about Higgins's attitude to women (act 1, scene 3), Doolittle's background and lifestyle (act 1, scene 5), the relationship between Higgins and his household (act 1, scene 5), Higgins's newfound respect for Eliza as they depart for the ball (act 1, scene 9), his overriding conceitedness and his new awareness of her true personality (act 2, scene I), and the final resolution of the story (act 1, scene 7). One might add to this list act 2, scene 4, which takes place in the "Upstairs hall of Higgins's house" and is often staged on the same set as the study scenes. Here, Higgins learns that Eliza has bolted and realizes that she has gained complete independence from him.

Dualities are also used cleverly in the scenic structure of the piece. Act 1, scenes 6/7 (Ascot) and 10/11 (the Embassy Ball) are connected in being two pairs of scenes that take place in high society where Eliza is put to the test. In both cases the first of each pair takes place outside the main location and involves a discussion between Pickering and Mrs. Higgins about Eliza and the potential for disaster in the following scene. The second scene of each pair is the actual event—the first goes badly (Ascot), the second is a triumph (the ball). In this way Lerner cleverly replicates the format used in the Ascot scene to rebuild the tension for the Embassy Ball scene, thereby making us believe that Eliza could fail again (something that is intensified by the presence of

Table 3.6. Scenic Outline of *My Fair Lady*

Act 1	Location	Act 2	Location
Scene I	Outside the Royal Opera House, Covent Garden.	Scene I	Higgins's study.
Scene II	Tenement section— Tottenham Court Road.	Scene II	Outside Higgins's house, Wimpole Street.
Scene III	Higgins's study.	Scene III	Flower market of Covent Garden.
Scene IV	Tenement section— Tottenham Court Road.	Scene IV	Upstairs hall of Higgins' house.
Scene V	Higgins's study.	Scene V	The conservatory of Mrs. Higgins's house.
Scene VI	Near the race meeting, Ascot.	Scene VI	Outside Higgins's house, Wimpole Street.
Scene VII	Inside a club tent, Ascot.	Scene VII	Higgins's study.
Scene VIII	Outside Higgins's house, Wimpole Street.		
Scene IX	Higgins's study.		
Scene X	The promenade of the Embassy.		
Scene XI	The ballroom of the Embassy.		

Zoltan Karpathy, who threatens to reveal Eliza's background). The two remaining locations also occur in pairs. The "Tenement section" at Tottenham Court Road in act 1, scenes 2 and 4, is the place where we meet Alfred Doolittle and where he sings both the original rendition and reprise of "With a Little Bit of Luck," while the space outside Higgins's house on Wimpole Street is the location for Freddy's "On the Street Where You Live" (act 1, scene

7) and its reprise (act 2, scene 2). In both instances, we return to both a location and a song that has been heard before but experience them in a completely new light. When Doolittle's song about optimism is reprised, it comes after the news of Eliza's departure to live with Higgins, which represents a possible source of money for Doolittle. Similarly, the reprise of "On the Street" finds an "undaunted" Freddy (*PS*, 115) still singing his song in vain, but we see it in a new light when Eliza rejects his bland vision of romance and spits out the fiery "Show Me."

Strongly tied to this careful distribution of the scene locations is the musical structure of the piece (see table 3.7). Unquestionably, certain conventions determine the allocation of the numbers between the two acts, but it is striking that many of the songs from the first act either reappear or have some sort of analogue in the second act. There are several examples in addition to those discussed earlier. When Eliza hears the reprise of "Wouldn't It Be Loverly?" sung around a fire by the vegetable costermongers in act 2, it is no longer her theme, and it serves to tell her that she no longer belongs in the market. The return of "Just You Wait" has a similar function, because a song that Eliza originally sang in her Cockney accent is now sung in her refined accent, reminding her—and us—that she is no longer the person she was. It also takes on a sad irony, because the threats Eliza originally throws at the imaginary Higgins when the song first appears in act 1 are now shown to be completely empty, since he has just stormed off, leaving her crouching on the floor in tears (*PS*, 113–4).[48] In its original version, this song also shares something with "Show Me" and "Without You," two numbers that have different styles but communicate Eliza's feisty anger against men.

The trend continues with "I'm an Ordinary Man," which is strongly connected to "A Hymn to Him" in subject matter and style, since both deal with Higgins's attitudes to gender relations. Even though "I've Grown Accustomed to Her Face" has little explicit connection to the first act except for the brief reference to "I'm an Ordinary Man," we will see in chapter 5 how it contains material from the cut first-act song "Come to the Ball" and reverses the meaning of the lyric from praise to insult. This theme was also used in the cut ballet from act 1. So even if "Accustomed" was planned as a bigger summation of themes than it is in the published score, it still provides an accumulative finale to the show. In addition to its own reprise, "With a Little Bit of Luck" is obviously connected to "Get Me to the Church on Time" as a similar music hall–style song for Doolittle. There is also an irony in the fact that Doolittle's mocking rebuttal of marriage and responsibility in "Luck" has now been turned on its head as his friends bid him a poignant farewell on his wedding day. Finally, "You Did It" is briefly brought back later in act 2, when Higgins

Table 3.7.   **Outline of Musical Numbers in** *My Fair Lady*

Act 1	Title of Number	Act 2	Title of Number
Scene 1	Street Entertainers	Scene I	"You Did It" "Just You Wait" (reprise)
Scene II	"Why Can't the English?"	Scene II	"On the Street Where You Live" "Show Me"
Scene III	"Wouldn't It Be Loverly?"	Scene III	"Wouldn't It Be Loverly?" (Reprise)
Scene IV	"With a Little Bit of Luck"	Scene IV	"Get Me to the Church on Time"
Scene V	"I'm an Ordinary Man"	Scene V	"A Hymn to Him"
Scene VI	"With a Little Bit of Luck" (reprise)	Scene VI	"Without You"
Scene VII	"Just You Wait"; "The Servants' Chorus"; "The Rain in Spain"; "I Could Have Danced All Night"	Scene VII	"I've Grown Accustomed to Her Face"
Scene VIII	"The Ascot Gavotte"		
Scene IX	"On the Street Where You Live"		
Scene X	"Promenade"		
Scene XI	"The Embassy Waltz"		

interrupts Eliza's "Without You" with a short verse of "By George, I really did it." Even this brief summary of the musical contents of the show demonstrates how strongly planned the material is.

While not every number can or should be seen as functioning as part of a broader duality, there are other important aspects to the show's musical structure. In particular, both acts have a sequence of musical numbers that increase dramatic tension over a self-contained unit of time. In act 1, this happens in the fifth scene, where four musical numbers take Eliza on a journey from frustration to elation. "Just You Wait" is closely followed by the sequence of lessons that are interspersed with verses of "The Servants' Chorus." The last of these leads into the final lesson, in which Higgins teaches Eliza to pronounce "The rain in Spain stays mainly in the plain" correctly. In turn, this leads into the jubilant song, "The Rain in Spain," followed by the even more elated "I Could Have Danced All Night." This last song is the close of the sequence, which occurs over the course of a single scene and provides one of the most imaginative and effective parts of the show.[49]

Table 3.8. **Outline of Timescale of Scenes in *My Fair Lady***

Act 1	*Time*
Scene I	A cold March night.
Scene II	Immediately following.
Scene III	The following morning.
Scene IV	Three days later.
Scene V	Later that day.
Scene VI	A July afternoon.
Scene VII	Immediately following.
Scene VIII	Later that afternoon.
Scene IX	Six weeks later.
Scene X	Later that night.
Scene XI	Immediately following.
Act 2	
Scene I	3 a.m. the following morning
Scene II	Immediately following
Scene III	5 a.m. that morning
Scene IV	11 a.m. that morning
Scene V	Later that day
Scene VI	Dusk, that afternoon
Scene VII	Immediately following

The example from the second act is arguably even more special. After the concerted number "You Did It" at the opening of the act, the long scene of dialogue between Eliza and Higgins that ensues is closed by Eliza's tearful reprise of "Just You Wait." This initiates an unbroken chain of music also encompassing the reprise of "On the Street," Eliza's new song "Show Me," and the reprise of "Wouldn't It Be Loverly?" in the flower market. Even though it lasts only seven or eight minutes, this sequence of music provides just the kick that most musicals need in the middle of their second acts. The tension mounts during the first two reprises and reaches its highpoint in "Show Me," where Eliza vents her anger as never before. The vigor of this number is cleverly reduced by the "Flower Market" music, which depicts early morning at Covent Garden and segues into the gentle reprise of "Wouldn't It Be Loverly?" This complex chain of numbers is a prime example of how Lerner and Loewe's adaptation of *Pygmalion* adds an expressive dimension not found in the play.

Their third structural tool is the manipulation of time. Table 3.8 shows how the musical's timescale is specifically defined in terms of month and time of the day. Interestingly, this is in contrast to the published version of Shaw's stage play, which is comparatively vague regarding time and date (see table 3.9).[50] In light of this, Lerner's structure is especially well conceived, with the show working in three discreet periods of time. The first act is in three sequences: the meeting of Eliza and Higgins and their initial lessons during March (scenes 1–5); Ascot in July (scenes 6–8); and the Embassy Ball in late August/early September (scenes 9-11). This provides a three-part exposition in which the establishment of the bet and its early consequences (the Ascot and Embassy scenes) are depicted, leaving the second act in which to discuss the resolution of Higgins's and Eliza's problematic relationship. That makes the timescale of the second act all the more important: it takes place over the course of a single day and follows on directly from the end of act 1, with

Table 3.9. **Outline of Timescale of Acts in *Pygmalion***

Act	Time
1	11.15 p.m.
2	Next day. 11 a.m.
3	Several months later.
4	Several months later. Midnight.
5	The following morning.

scenes at 3 a.m., 5 a.m., 11 a.m., during the afternoon, and at dusk. Obviously, there is a dramatic push to this format, whereby the scenes almost occur in real time and provide a sense of continuity. By setting the action against this "cycle of the hours," Lerner ensured that the second act had just as much momentum—if not more—than the first. It is also ingenious that the day of the ball and the immediate aftermath straddles the intermission, thereby providing a "cliff-hanger" about whether the experiment has been suc-cessful—another sign of the master of the theater at work.

4

KNOWING THE SCORE

• • •

A MUSICAL PYGMALION

The fact that the likes of Rodgers and Hammerstein abandoned their adaptation of *Pygmalion* makes Lerner and Loewe's achievement in *My Fair Lady* all the more impressive. This was a show that confounded even the very best, partly because of the multifaceted challenge of writing a musical based on this particular play. Just as the evolution of Lerner's script involved a shift of focus from Shaw's determinedly unromantic view of the Higgins-Eliza relationship to something more ambiguous for the musical, a change of gesture also had to be carried through in the score. This created a semiotic problem for the composer: how to avoid writing standard types of Broadway songs but remain within the recognized bounds of the Broadway musical. Yet one of Loewe's gifts as a composer was his ability to adopt a wide range of styles. Nor was this limited to broad stylistic gestures such as the "Celtic" music in *Brigadoon* or hints of the Wild West in *Paint Your Wagon*: Loewe's musicals are written with a fine brush, allowing him to conjure up place, character, and mood within the space of a single song.

This is especially true of *My Fair Lady*. But in order to discuss the show's score, it is essential first to understand the nature of the material available. Although studies of musicals typically use published piano reductions of orchestral scores as the basis for their analyses, these commercially available scores usually represent only a retrospective snapshot of what was performed on Broadway. Rarely are all the expressive aspects of a performance represented, nor is the complexity of the compositional process normally clear from a homogenized score. Typically, the composer would write either a simple piano-vocal score or a lead sheet with chord symbols (or even just create the piece at the keyboard in the case of composers who could not notate music). This would then be adapted and expanded by an arranger according to factors such as the number of verses that appeared in the final script or the need for dance music, before the orchestrators fleshed out the material and expanded the texture for a full complement of instruments. At best, published vocal scores might partly be based on the composer's initial manuscripts, but taken as a whole they are normally extrapolated from either the full score or the conductor's short score after the event, and therefore bear a comparatively remote relationship to the stage performances.

In the case of *My Fair Lady*, the musical artifacts (mostly derived from the Frederick Loewe and Warner-Chappell Collections at the Library of Congress) can be divided into the following categories:

- Untitled melodic sketches in Loewe's hand, without lyrics, which can be identified as now-familiar songs;
- Completed melodies in Loewe's hand, without accompaniment, which may or may not have lyrics attached and may not ultimately have made it into the finished show;
- Completed piano-vocal scores wholly or partly in Loewe's hand for both familiar and cut songs; the verses may be absent or only one verse may appear, compared to multiple verses in the published vocal score;
- Vocal and choral scores of intermediate and final versions of some of the songs in unknown copyists' hands;
- Piano scores (some of them representing intermediate versions) of dance music, incidental music, vocal reprises, and instrumental numbers in the handwriting of Trude Rittmann, the dance arranger;
- Full orchestral scores in the hands of the credited orchestrators, Robert Russell Bennett and Philip J Lang, as well as the ghost orchestrator, Jack Mason;
- Instrumental performing parts and conductor's short scores in unknown copyists' hands;
- Two editions of the published vocal score: the original, edited by the show's conductor, Franz Allers (1956), and a corrected revision (1969).

In addition, lyric sheets containing versions of the texts of the songs not documented elsewhere are discussed where relevant. These come from two sources: a folder in Herman Levin's papers, and an envelope marked "Franz Allers Lyrics" hidden in the middle of a pile of instrumental parts for the show in the Warner-Chappell Collection.

No song or number is represented by a source or sources from all of these categories, nor should it be assumed that there ever were documents for each song in every category. For instance, songs such as "I Could Have Danced All

Night" were created late in the compositional process and were probably written down as relatively complete numbers first time around, so there might never have been a simple melodic sketch. Others never made it past the drafting stage and were never orchestrated. In at least one case, a score has been mislaid or separated from the collection: "Say a Prayer for Me Tonight" was performed during the initial New Haven out-of-town tryouts and then cut, but although a copyist's score and the full score have survived in the Warner-Chappell Collection, there is no autograph piano-vocal score for the song in the Loewe Collection. Nonetheless, the documents as a whole give a vivid overview of the process of creating the score of *Fair Lady* as a "performance" for Broadway.

Initial Ideas and Cut Songs

The manuscripts of the songs discussed in this section all derive from the Frederick Loewe Collection. Some of them are fully completed songs that could be performed, while others are in the form of melodic outlines and, interesting though they are, reveal little information other than the shape of the melody. There are six melodic sketches with titles but no lyrics that are known to have been intended for the show. Two of them, "What is a Woman?" and "Who is the Lady?," are almost identical and are probably different attempts to write some kind of song for Henry Higgins; "Dear Little Fool" is headed "Higgins" and is therefore presumed to be for the same character; "Over Your Head" was the original version of Eliza's "Show Me"; and "Limehouse" and "The Undeserving Poor" were planned for the original opening scenes of the show, the latter intended for Doolittle.[1]

"Dear Little Fool" is a simple melody in E-flat major with very few accidentals or chromatic inflections; its many long, sustained notes suggest that it was an attempt at a love song of the kind that Higgins does not sing in the finished show. It is difficult to tell whether "Limehouse" was intended as a solo or choral number, and indeed what its message might have been. However, there is some chromatic movement in the melody, which was probably an attempt to evoke the Chinese atmosphere of the projected opening scene at Limehouse in Outline 1 (see table 3.1). Similarly, the melody of "The Undeserving Poor" is simple, and since it was intended for Doolittle and his cronies it is probably reasonable to assume that it might have made a rousing song of the same ilk as "Get Me to the Church on Time" and "With a Little Bit of Luck."

In addition to these songs with a documented connection to *Fair Lady*, there are a few other manuscripts in the Loewe Collection, which may also be related to it. The title of "What's To Become of Me?" mirrors so closely Eliza's tortured speech after the ball—"Where am I to go? What am I to do? What's to become of me?"—that it is highly probable that it was a song for this position in the show.[2] Underneath the short melody is a note, "There's Always One," which probably refers to another sketch, "There's Always One You Can't Forget."[3] The latter is characterized by dotted rhythms and melodic leaps, but again it is difficult to infer much information from it; the same goes for "Say Hello For Me," which is on the reverse of "What's to Become of Me?" and has only a brief melodic sketch and a few chords to indicate a possible accompaniment pattern at the bottom. There is also another page of sketches for "What's to Become of Me?," the first four bars of which contain an outline harmonization.

Fascinating though these manuscripts are, they tell us only a little about the finished songs or the composer and lyricist's intentions for the characters who were to sing them. Nevertheless, some observations can be made. In the extract of "What Is a Woman?" in example 4.1,[4] for instance, we can see that part of the melody is familiar from a song that eventually made it into the show: bars 17–19 (and the similar patterns in 21–22 and 25–27) resemble the melodic line of Pickering's words "You should get a medal, / Or be even made a knight" in the second-act opener, "You Did It" (ex. 4.2). On this evidence alone, the resemblance seems curious rather than significant. All it really tells us is that when Loewe had created music that was not ultimately put to use, he thought nothing of recycling it later in a different form—a reminder of how little, sometimes, the melody of a song is bound in meaning to its lyric.

More obviously illuminating are three draft melodies with both titles and lyrics, known as "lead sheets." This time, the function, meaning, and content of all three is far more obvious here, though Loewe's exact harmonization is unknown. Lerner sheds light on one of the songs in *The Street Where I Live*: "Our first attempt to dramatize Higgins' misogyny resulted in a song called 'Please Don't Marry Me.'"[5] The song was the precursor to "I'm an Ordinary Man," but with a slightly different context (see Outlines 1 and 2 in chap. 3). The original version of the scene had Higgins responding negatively to the suggestion that he should marry someone far from his liking, so the title "Please Don't Marry Me" referred specifically to Miss Eynsford Hill as well as

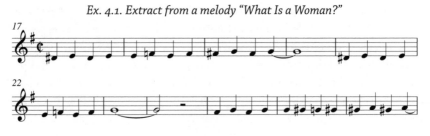

Ex. 4.1. Extract from a melody "What Is a Woman?"

You should win a med-al or be ev-en made a knight.

Ex. 4.3. Extract from the refrain of Higgins's "Please Don't Marry Me."

Please___ don't mar-ry me!___ I fer-vent-ly im-plore don't

mar-ry me!___ to love each oth-er dear-ly and dream it will re-

main_ I tell you ver-y clear-ly is real-ly in-sane! Oh please,_

being Higgins's general *credo* (see ex. 4.3).[6] By contrast, the replacement, "I'm an Ordinary Man," comes in response to Pickering's question, "Are you a man of good character where women are concerned?"[7] The focus in this song is on the perceived consequences of the repeated line, "Let a woman in your life"; although marriage is mentioned briefly, the lyric is more about relationships between men and women in general than Eliza specifically. In addition to this lead sheet, a lyric sheet in Herman Levin's papers contains the words to the second refrain, suggesting that the song was fully worked upon before Lerner and Loewe discarded it.[8]

The verse (not included in ex. 4.3) shows Loewe's freedom of form: after the simple lines of the first eight bars, the time signature briefly changes to 6/8 while he quotes the traditional song "Drink To Me Only With Thine Eyes," the romantic lyric of which Higgins mocks ("I hate that optical brew"). But again, the song is of interest because it contains material, which would later become familiar in another context. The melody in bars 36–43 is similar to that of bars 8–16 of the song "What Do the Simple Folk Do?" from *Camelot* (1960), as shown in example 4.4. The wittiness of some of the lyric writing is not entirely foreign to the way the Professor's character was ultimately sketched, for instance the couplet: "That someday you'd abhor me would torture me with fears, / But having you adore me would bore me to tears." But given the upbeat, comic character of the lyric, it seems likely that the accompaniment was quite jolly and that the tempo was fast, making "Please Don't

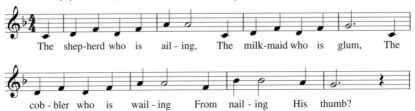

Marry Me" a glossy Broadway number that would have been incoherent with Higgins's other songs.

Similarly, the next unused song, "There's a Thing Called Love," is uncharacteristic of Eliza's completed numbers. The lyric alone tells us that this is a typical love song:

> There's a thing called love
> In the twinkling of an eye you know the meaning of.
> There's a thing called love—
> By the count of one
> The lovely deed is done!
>
> A precious thing called love—
> When it's yours you know how much it's worth.
> You can tell despair
> Farewell, despair,
> Love came in time,
> And made me glad that I'm
> On earth![9]

The number was probably intended for the position later taken by "I Could Have Danced All Night." Eliza's sentiments make sense in the context of having succeeded in pronouncing "The Rain in Spain" correctly and gained a new warmth from Higgins, with whom she now fancies herself to be in love.[10] Again, such an expression of love was probably too overt for Lerner's overall plan for the show, so it is not surprising that it was cut. However, the melody later resurfaced as "In this Wide, Wide, World" in the 1973 stage version of *Gigi*.

The next song also contains material that was subsequently reused. In his first memoir, Rex Harrison says that when Lerner and Loewe first came to talk to him about doing the show, "There was a number called 'Lady Liza', a very pushy sort of Broadway tune which Fritz later turned into a waltz and

Ex. 4.5. "Lady Liza."

used in the ballroom scene."[11] Curiously, in his second autobiography, the actor contradicts himself and says that the song "was skillfully turned into 'The Ascot Gavotte,'" but he was correct the first time.[12] As with "Please Don't Marry Me," the intended context of "Lady Liza" is apparent from Outlines 1 and 2 (see chap. 3). After Eliza's debacle at Ascot, Higgins and Pickering discover her crying on a park bench, convinced she cannot succeed. But "the men persuade her she can. They do it in a song, which they sing together to her: 'Lady Liza.'"[13]

The manuscript for the song is in two parts. On the front cover is the melody, with "Higgins/Pickering" marked to the left of the title. Inside the folded manuscript is another title, "Liza—Counter," while on two bracketed systems are the same Higgins/Pickering melody plus a counterpoint for "Jane" and "Math," presumably the maids. The start of this combined version of the piece is shown in example 4.5. As Harrison says, the melody of the first four bars was transformed into the beginning of "The Embassy Waltz," but the rest of it is different. The version of the song with the counterpoint was probably intended for a reprise after Ascot mentioned in Outlines 1 and 2, to conclude Eliza's second series of lessons ("At the end of the sequence Liza is doing everything beautifully and the chorus sings, 'Lady Liza'").[14]

Although the melody is unremarkable and the lyric full of clichés—such as "gray above once again blue"—the servants' counterpoint is notable for its wit. "Is it malaria? Or something scarier?" they ask, on seeing Eliza, Higgins, and Pickering jubilant after her transformation. In essence, this reaction was eventually replaced by two earlier reactions: first, Mrs. Pearce's lines after she has been awoken by the pounding noise made by the trio when they sing "The Rain in Spain" ("Are you feeling all right, Mr. Higgins?"); and second, the maids' interjections in Eliza's "I Could Have Danced All Night" which similarly provide a contrasting viewpoint on the main theme being heard ("You're up too late, miss, / And sure as fate, miss, / You'll catch a cold"). In the published show, of course, this material is shown before the Ascot scene rather than after it, because the final part of Eliza's transformation happens off-stage and we see only the result, not the process. The words for the remaining verses of the song are provided in the collection of lyrics in Levin's papers. This lyric sheet shows that the last line of every verse is changed from the indefinite to the personal article: "You'll be a lady" becomes "You'll be my lady" in the first two verses and "One day my lady will Liza be!" in the final one. This is yet another example of the far more explicit positing of Higgins as Eliza's lover in Lerner and Loewe's early ideas for the show.

Like "Please Don't Marry Me" and "There's a Thing Called Love," "Lady Liza" was probably dropped from the score because it simply does not fit either the style of the piece or the characterization of the main protagonists as they were ultimately evolved. These three manuscripts provide us with a window into the composer's workshop, showing how Loewe dealt with both microlevel details such as word-setting and macrolevel issues such as refitting a melody with a new lyric or developing a musical style for a character.

Advanced Ideas

In all probability, the three songs discussed in the previous section were "fully composed" in the sense that we can assume Loewe must have played them with accompaniments rather than just the melodies: Lerner reports that Loewe always composed complete songs at the piano with the lyricist in the room, and that he paid attention to the harmonic and accompaniment material.[15] But only one unused song in the Loewe and Warner-Chappell Collections exists in a completely written out piano-vocal score: "Shy." It is mentioned by Julie Andrews in her autobiography as "a very pretty song," and she adds that "originally Eliza sang it to show her feelings for Higgins. Alan Lerner realized that in Shaw's original play, the main characters never once speak of love. Therefore, he and Fritz created another song, the famous 'I Could Have Danced All Night', which conveys all the affection and emotion Eliza feels, yet never once mentions the word."[16] Andrews's explanation of the position of the song in the show is corroborated by Outline 4 (see chap. 3), which has "Shy" at the end of the montage of lessons instead of "I Could Have Danced."[17]

Two manuscripts of the song exist. The first is entirely in Loewe's hand, with the complete lyric, on three sides of the standard Chappell manuscript paper that the composer used for most of his work; there are no dynamic or expressive markings. The second document is the work of two separate parties, and the accompaniment is completely different in style.[18] The melody, title, and lyric are in Loewe's handwriting, but the clefs, key signatures, piano lines, cover title, tempo, and expressive markings are all in the hand of Trude Rittmann, the dance arranger. Of course, this does not necessarily prove divided authorship—especially since years later Rittmann confirmed that Loewe did not like to write things down but *was* concerned to have overall control of his scores—but it is striking that the accompaniment for Rittmann's version is much more fluent than Loewe's original.[19] The beginning of both versions is reproduced in examples 4.6 and 4.7.

Musically the song is particularly interesting for its employment of harmonically complex (and sometimes ambiguous) maneuvers. The tonic chord does not appear unmodified in root position until the final two bars, for example, and the song both launches on a surprising seventh chord (though there might have been an introduction, had the song made it into the show) and avoids sounding the tonic at various points where it could be expected. The minor seventh at the beginning of bar 9 is typical of Loewe's ability to

Ex. 4.6. "Shy," Loewe version.

Ex. 4.7. "Shy," Loewe-Rittmann version.

Where are the words____ I long to hear?____ And

where are the words____ I long to say?_____ Why can't I

create an unforeseen harmonization of a straightforward melody; he side-steps harmonic stability. Similarly, the accompaniment flows strongly for the first two phrases and breaks at bar 8 before continuing again in a similar vein. At bars 14–16 (not shown) Loewe employs a stepwise resolution of a strong dissonance over a vocal pedal note which is not unlike his treatment of the words "I only know [when he began to dance with me]" from "I Could Have Danced All Night"—ironically so, given that this song replaced "Shy." In both cases, the momentum of the music is stopped while the ensuing section restarts with three emphatic chords that each harmonize the repeated melody note in a different way, giving dramatic release. The two songs also share another similarity in terms of lyrics: "Why can't I open my heart and let them fly?" ("Shy") is not unlike "Why all at once my heart took flight" ("I Could Have Danced"). Amusingly, the latter line is the subject of a piece of self-criticism in Lerner's autobiography.[20]

Exactly why a second accompaniment was written for "Shy" is unknown, but it may be because, as Andrews implies, a sentimental love song was incoherent in light of the unspoken affection between Higgins and Eliza. Perhaps before discarding Lerner's lyric, which is indeed overt in its expression of love, Loewe either decided to refit the music in a new character, or he commissioned Rittmann to do so. It is clear even in the first bar of the "new" version that the melody is now matched with a beguine accompaniment, which to an extent numbs the triteness of the lyric. At the same time, the liveliness of the new accompaniment rhythms does not cohere well with the open sincerity of the words. It is little wonder, therefore, that "Shy" was not used. Even had the material been top-drawer Lerner and Loewe, the flagrant admission that Eliza is in love with Higgins is out of place in a musical where romance simmers only quietly in the background.

"SAY A PRAYER FOR ME TONIGHT," DRESS BALLET, AND "COME TO THE BALL"

One of the most intriguing aspects of the show's genesis is the sequence of numbers that originally bridged the gap between Ascot and the Embassy Ball but was later replaced by a short passage of dialogue. All sources agree that the first act of the musical was too long during its first performance in New Haven, motivating Lerner, Loewe and Moss Hart to remove "Come to the Ball," the "Dress Ballet" and "Say a Prayer for Me Tonight" and thereby excise roughly fifteen minutes from the running time.[21] The three cut numbers are at once familiar and unknown. They were performed in New Haven, "Come to the Ball" was recorded, and "Say a Prayer For Me Tonight" was reused in the film of *Gigi*. But many of the sources related to these numbers have not previously been examined or written about, and the "Dress Ballet" is especially obscure. The rest of this chapter pieces together archival material to present an appraisal of this cut scene, which was originally planned to be among the show's highlights.

"Come to the Ball"
According to Lerner, "Come to the Ball" (see ex. 4.8) was intended to be Harrison's *pièce de résistance*, but after its first performance the lyricist deemed it "a disaster in three-quarter time."[22] The piece exists in several different versions: (1) Loewe's autograph, which is in E major, contains only the first refrain and is very simply harmonized; (2) a copyist's vocal score in D major (the final key) from the Loewe Collection, lightly annotated by the composer and representing an intermediate version of the song, with different transition music between the second refrain and interlude, and a different ending; and (3) a modified version of the same copyist's score, the conductor's short score, and the orchestrator's autograph full score, all of which come from the Warner-Chappell Collection and represent the definitive version.[23]

Oh come to the ball, oh come to the ball, It would-n't be fair To the men who are there To de - ny them___ All the dreams you'll pro - vide them.

Ex. 4.9."Come to the Ball," interlude.

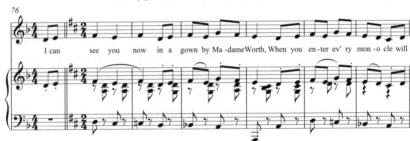

I can see you now in a gown by Ma -dame Worth, When you en -ter ev' ry mon -o cle will

The song's lyric shows an unusual side of Higgins's personality. We are used to him insulting and patronizing Eliza, declaring that she has "no feelings that we need worry about," telling Mrs. Pearce to "put her in the dustbin," and calling her a "draggle-tailed guttersnipe."[24] The only exception is in act 1, scene 3, when Eliza is on the brink of leaving before the experiment has even started and Higgins tempts her with "chocolates, and taxis, and gold, and diamonds."[25] But otherwise, the language employed in "Come to the Ball" is more overtly seductive than Higgins's normal mode of expression. He conjures up for Eliza various images of the men who await her at the ball—a dashing marquis and a bored lord—and says "it wouldn't be fair . . . to deny them all the dreams you'll provide them." For instance, the song begins:

Come to the ball! Come to the ball!
It wouldn't be fair to the men who are there
To deny them
All the dreams you'll supply them.

There even may be a dashing marquis
Who feature by feature will swear you're the creature
He always prayed for,
Single stayed for.

If you aren't there, his complete despair
Would be painful to see
So come to the ball, come to the ball
Come to the ball, come to the ball
With me.

Higgins seduces Eliza with romantic images of handsome suitors, though tantalizingly the choruses end with the phrase "Come to the ball with me." Did Lerner mean to convey a sense of the union between Eliza and Higgins by promoting the image of her accompanying *him* to the ball? There is no doubt that by removing the song, the ambiguity of the relationship between these two characters was more successfully balanced. The third verse is too flagrant a self-portrait of Higgins and his feelings for Eliza to be mistaken: it refers to a "man with a smile you could see for a mile," clearly meant to be Higgins himself. Further images of "the pride in his eyes" and "his dimensions expanding," and particularly the idea that Eliza's triumph will make him the proudest man in the world, generate a romantic intensity between the two characters, which is alien to their behavior elsewhere in the musical.

Apart from the issue of length and the problems with the depiction of romance, two other explanations for the cut are also possible. Perhaps Lerner felt there was an unintentional clash between Higgins's promise that he would be proud of Eliza if she triumphed and the events of the opening scene of act 2, when he declares that it is his triumph, not hers. Or, similarly, perhaps he felt this sequence of events would make Higgins's rejection of Eliza all the harsher and demonize him to a degree that made him too unsympathetic. Aside from this, it is also true that parts of the lyric are less effective than they could be. The stanza beginning "There even may be a dashing marquis . . ." becomes anemic toward the end, because the combination of the lines "He always prayed for" and "Single stayed for" is merely a repetition of the same (unimportant) word "for," rather than a rhyme to match those in the other stanzas. Additionally, it blurs a clause which is written as normal ("He always prayed for") with one whose words Lerner had to swap around for the sake of meter and poetry (a weak, feminine rhyme) rather than common sense ("Single stayed for" instead of "Stayed single for"). A subsequent image of a lord who is "frantically bored" and becomes "an Indian lancer" because of Eliza's failure to attend is bizarre—why would this peculiar individual motivate her to come to the ball? Farther on, a line about ladies' teeth "gnashing" is oxymoronic—a true lady would never do that—and the rhyming image of monocles "crashing" also fails to connect us with reality (how could a single lens make as loud a noise as a "crash"?). These sorts of small anomalies are probably one reason why the song failed to make an impact on the first night audience in New Haven.

Yet the middle section of the song gives us important clues about the original structure of the show and casts one of its most famous numbers in an entirely new light. Bars 76–108 are musically similar to part of the central section of "I've Grown Accustomed to Her Face," in which Higgins imagines how Eliza's life could collapse without him ("I can see her now: Missus Freddy Eynsford-Hill, in a wretched little flat above a store" and so on; see ex. 4.9). The only difference is that "Come to the Ball" does not dwell on this material for the same length of time: it omits the minor-key passage of this part of "Accustomed to Her Face." Had "Come to the Ball" not been cut from the show, the effect of this section of "Accustomed" would have been completely different. Instead of merely providing new, contrasting material to the lyrical feel of the main part of the song, the "I can see her now" section would have been a reprise of the "Come to the Ball" interlude but with a reversal of sentiment. In place of the flattering lines "I can see you now in a gown by Madame Worth [etc.]" in "Come to the Ball," Higgins sings the insulting "I can see her now . . . Not a penny in the till [etc.]." This demonstrates that each of the show's two acts were to reach a climax with a monologue by Higgins, the first seductive and flattering and sung to Eliza, the second an expression of his mixed affection for and frustration with her, sung to himself. To read this section of "Accustomed" as a reprise of earlier material also changes its gesture: the images that Higgins evokes (e.g., "the bill collector beating on the door") are obviously hyperbolic, but in the context of their relation to his previous "seduction" of Eliza they reveal a bitterness that implies a rejected lover more strongly than the song does without "Come to the Ball" in the show. Therefore, it has to be considered that by removing this romantically overt song, Lerner was making a resounding gesture about the nature of the Higgins-Eliza relationship, namely that it is not the straightforward romance that some writers assume.

The music also contributes to the song's overt romanticism: the use of a waltz signifies dancing couples, and by extension, romantic attachment. This matches the meaning of the song very well, but if a decision had been made to cut lyrics about Higgins's attraction to Eliza, it can only have been intensified by their waltz accompaniment (see ex. 4.8). On a practical level, having a waltz at this point also anticipates "The Embassy Waltz" in the following scene. Obviously, Higgins is talking about the ball, and it is natural that the music that will be played there is the musical backbone to his song. But to have first one waltz then another is perhaps too much of the same thing. Furthermore, a comparison between the dance number and the song does "Come to the Ball" no favors. No doubt to accommodate Rex Harrison's limited vocal abilities, the vocal line moves in a stepwise motion nearly all the way through, and the range is limited. In consequence, the melody is far from memorable and, in truth, sometimes monotonous. By contrast, "The Embassy Waltz" features accented leaps, both of which evoke an animated dance scene and a general smoothness of line, indicating couples skimming across the dance floor.

Dress Ballet

If "Come to the Ball" hints at a connection with "I've Grown Accustomed to Her Face," the "Dress Ballet" confirms it. Several musical sources for the ballet have survived; between them, they bring to life what was briefly the most complicated number in the show. The main source for all the manuscripts is a fourteen-page piano score written by Trude Rittmann, several photocopies of which are contained in the Warner-Chappell Collection but not the original. One copy is annotated "Freda" on the front page, indicating Freda Miller, the dance pianist; another is attached to a one-page conductor's short score titled "Intro to Dress Ballet." Another contains an insert in Rittmann's hand titled "Dress Ballet (last pages redone)"; bars 209–12 have been crossed out, and the insert shows a later version of 246–59, but the revision of bars 209–45 seems not to have survived.[26] This latter score is the closest to the final version of the ballet that exists in piano score. In addition, there is a one-page autograph score in Rittmann's hand of the new nine-bar "Intro to Dress Ballet," which is also represented by the autograph full score in Phil Lang's hand. Robert Russell Bennett's thirty-four-page full score for the ballet is also in the collection and shows the final version of the number.[27]

The idea for the ballet was present right from Lerner and Loewe's initial attempts to write the show. On May 10, 1952, Lerner wrote to Gabriel Pascal: "The end of the first act, of course, can be one of the great moments of any musical I can remember. It should be Liza's preparation for the ball, her excitement, her desire to please the Prof., her dressing, her rehearsing, her manners, etc."[28] In Outlines 1 and 2 (see chap. 3), the ballet was the centerpiece of "scene 10": "Montage of Liza's lessons, this time all done balletically in pantomime."[29] Outline 3 describes the ballet (now "scene 9") in similar terms: "We intend a short balletic pantomime of more lessons, all to take place in the study. There will be dancing teachers, those who teach her how to walk properly, hairdressers, couturieres, etc."[30] The number was also still in place in Outline 4: "Ballet: (or pantomime) The preparation of LIZA—LIZA, HIGGINS, DRESSMAKERS, DANCING TEACHERS, BEAUTY SPECIALISTS, ETC."[31]

Various documents in Hanya Holm's papers in the New York Public Library reveal her rigorous preparation for this piece, which would have been her big showcase as the choreographer of *My Fair Lady* (as the dream ballets in *Oklahoma!* and *Carousel* had been for Agnes de Mille). One sheet of paper has a brief list of numbers in her handwriting, on which she describes Higgins as "directing the dancer inside her to dance in his tempo!" Another page refers to the ballet as a "Cartoon." Of the many lists of potential characters for the ballet, the inventory of dancers, the parts they were to play in the ballet, and their proposed costumes, shown in table 4.1, seems the most likely final version.

Eleven other documents in the same folder contain additional notes on the ballet. Perhaps the most important of these is a list of the show's dance numbers in Holm's handwriting. The ballet is referred to as: "Cartoon dance [The statue comes to life]." This may be the only direct allusion in all the sources for the show to the Greek Pygmalion myth. Another intriguing description has the ballet as a "nightmare"—a more grotesque interpretation than we might expect, but nevertheless one which dominates the mood of many of the choreographer's other drafts. For instance, one set of notes includes a rather savage ending to the projected ballet: "At height of entertainment Liza breaks in[to] hysterical laughter, bringing Higgins onto balcony. He summons Pickering, who comes with Bullwhip + gun + revolver whilst wielding in air. Group vanishes every conceivable object, leaving Liza alone."[32] In addition to the hint of sadism in this account, which also contains images such as "Valse her to death" and "Liza falls exhausted" in earlier paragraphs, it is fascinating that Pickering is portrayed as such an active participant in the nastier aspect of the mime, since he is normally more sympathetic toward Eliza than Higgins is. This uncharacteristic behavior also seems briefly to have been the case in the following set of notes, where Pickering's name has been crossed out and Higgins instead has been associated with the image of the "Torturer":

Table 4.1. **Inventory of Characters and Costumes in the _Dress Ballet_**

Character	Performer	Costume
Milliner	David Evans	Black alpaca/short jacket/grey pants
Dress maker	Jimmy White	Short black jacket/striped pants
Asst dressmaker	Thatcher Clarke	Charcoal denim/square cut striped pants
Hairdresser	Gene Nettles	White jacket (no white pants)
Hairdresser	Joe Rocco	White jacket
Shoe fitter	Carl Jeffrey	Short grey jacket, striped pants
Shoe fitter	Judy Williams	Grey dress—smock type
Physical culturist	Pat Drylie	Bloomers and sweater
Beautician	Crandall Diehl	–
Beautician	Barbara Heath	White smock—head bands
Beautician	Nancy Lynch	White smock—head bands (not all white)
Maid	Imelda Demartin	Peppermint dress
Maid	Cathy Conklin	Peppermint dress
Maid	Margaret Cuddy	Grey dress
Maid	Pat Dimond	Grey dress
Butler	Barton Mumaw	–
Dance master	Fernando Schattenburg	Cutaway Ascot Tie
Dance mistress	Vera Lee	Tango dress

Eliza

Dejected
Melancholy
Upset
Determined to give up
Resentment to be worked on
~~Pickering~~ Higgins
Torturer

Teach to Eliza:

How to walk downstairs
How to curtsey
How to Valse
How to dress

The cartoon starts from reality, goes through time elapse, increases in nervous tension, all efforts are left too late, but during process of working on her, she becomes more and more twisted and when she arrives at the

Ball she is in a dream. She walks like a dreamwalker, being transported into another world.

This document is also striking for its portrayal of Eliza's emotional journey through the number on the left against the list of lessons on the right; the passage of time is vivid, and on the back of the paper Holm noted: "'Workmen' would change very simple accessories at every re-appearance to signify elapse of time." Evidently she wanted to create a dark vision in which Eliza became so mentally and physically tortured that she lost track of the boundary between dream and reality.

The following description is Holm's most detailed and final document of the choreography of the ballet:

Higgins finishes singing ["Come to the Ball"]. Lights come up full. He starts metronome and with sadistic look to Liza goes upstairs in rhythm to the tick of instrument. Entrance of first worker can blend with his exit or he can be instrumental with beginning.

[Part 1] <u>Workers in 1 part:</u> Trainer, dance master, cobbler, couturier.

Liza: Depressed, she resents all efforts done to her. Her composure falls to pieces and she has a complete fall back in her old self. She is destructive, uncooperative. Fish arrive, cockney. Speak cockney.

All efforts of "workmen" with no—if not contrary result. Trainer + the dancing master work complementary. Work themselves in a sweat over her with disheartening result. Couturier presents material to inspecting eyes. Cobbler finds unwilling feet. Utter resentment, if not illwill to accept.

She signifies defeat + depression.

After this first amount of "workmen," they retire in despair, only to return with doppeled effort.

Part 2. Liza. Mechanical acceptance. Pup[p]et-like obedience with neither understanding nor interest. Showing signs of being worked on. Trainer brings helper, couturier brings helper so does dance master + cobbler adding Milliner + make up.

Summing up: no result but more commotion + less resistance.

Part 3. "Workmen" come in greater quantities. More concerted efforts fast + furious throwing her in state of confusion + bewilderment.

Extreme + supreme effort of dancing master to perfect her in curtsey + walk + Valse. Tempo increases to whirling speed of feverish racing against time. Milliner brings head dummy, with hat on which was not finished before.

Cobbler bring finished shoes.

Couturier brings fancy negligee.

Trainer + dance master sweat over their efforts + with everybody helping in their own way, only to leave her limp and with a <u>through the will</u> feeling, an end of all resistance (kneaded like a dough to be baked).

After all have left she looks well worked over. Mrs. Pearce enters.

During this entire procedure, she speaks to herself practising speech bits like a pup[p]et with the invisible w[h]ip of Higgins above her.

This outline gives an idea of both the ballet's structure and its content. Part I is the dance's exposition: the establishment of its function, and in particular the problems Eliza still faces and which the workmen need to overcome. In the second part, Holm notes that no progress is made, but Eliza is less resistant to the workmen's efforts. Things work up into a frenzy in the final part, when Eliza is completely overcome and the lessons are completed. It is of note that the literal image of Higgins standing over Eliza with a whip mentioned above has turned into a metaphorical image in this later version.

With these choreographic notes in mind, we can approach the musical documents with some idea of the images the score had to accompany. Although it is plain which of the various scores represents the version that was orchestrated and made it to the stage at New Haven, the dance pianist's copy is also of value for the additional annotations about the dancers' movements at various points (no doubt to help Freda Miller identify which bars of music went with which parts of the dance). The ballet music started with Rittmann's eleven-bar "Intro to Dress Ballet" (see ex. 4.10); underneath the music, she wrote: "Phil, the above are orchestral exclamations in Higgins' speech before the dress ballet (no brass)."[33] The music is a simple yet attention-grabbing introduction whose pattern and style—strong accents in the first seven bars followed by the more delicate little scales (slightly reminiscent of the introduction to "I Could Have Danced All Night")—are not unlike the basic clarity of writing found in nineteenth-century ballet music. Rittmann was lucid in her instructions to the orchestrator: no brass was to be used because Higgins would still be speaking in between the orchestral statements, and the separate parts of the introduction were to be differentiated between by allotting them to alternating instrumental groups. Lang adhered to these instructions almost to the letter whilst adding a little nuance of his own: bars 1–2 and 6–7 were played by strings (and harp) as suggested, but the initial fanfare-type motive in bars 3–5 was given to clarinets, bassoon and horns while bars 8–11 were played by flute, oboe, clarinets, and bassoon (without the horns).[34]

Rittmann's score for the ballet is as fine an example of the dance arranger's art as could be found. She adheres to themes by Loewe for the majority of the number's 271 bars, yet makes a fluent composition that is fit to stand on its

Ex. 4.10. *"Intro to Dress Ballet."*

Ex. 4.11. *"Dress Ballet," bars 19–27.*

Ex. 4.12. *"Dress Ballet," bars 36–39.*

own. The ballet begins with a further eight-bar introduction (on top of "Intro to Dress Ballet") that gives way to a busy expositional passage to accompany the arrival of the Tailor to start work on Eliza. Bars 19–107 are based mostly on two motives from the central section of "Come to the Ball" (the part that returns in "Accustomed to Her Face"): example 4.11 derives from the line "I

Ex. 4.13. "Dress Ballet," bars 68–74.

can see you now in a gown by Madame Worth, when you enter ev'ry monocle will crash" in "Come to the Ball"; and example 4.12 comes from "Little chaps'll wish they were Atlas, a queen will want you for her son" (which matches the line "She'll try to teach the things I taught her, and end up selling flowers instead" in "Accustomed"). Rittmann moves freely through keys in her arrangement and goes from examples 4.11 to 4.12 and back again; this not only reflects the order in which the material appeared in the song—thereby giving the ballet music some structure—but also portrays the music as a ghostly, jumbled-up reminiscence of Higgins's coaxing words echoing in Eliza's head. Such a process adds a psychological dimension to the music's surface task of accompanying the actions of the dancers.

The hairdressers enter at bar 36, then at bar 57 Rittmann changes tack and uses two different motives in quick succession. A hint of the opening line of "Why Can't the English?" in 68–70 is immediately followed by the "I think she's got it!" theme from "The Rain in Spain" in 71–74. The effect of this is that Higgins's song about the inadequacies of education is juxtaposed with his memorable expression of delight at the success of his lessons on Eliza; now she has to aim for the same triumph in a different kind of lesson (ex. 4.13). This is repeated a tone higher, then at bar 84, example 4.12 returns, this time in a much lower register, to herald the entrance of the masseuse. Freda Miller's score is particularly helpful at this point, marking out gestures such as "prance," "roll sleeves," "clap," and "knee bends." At the beginning of a rising passage from bar 108, a book is placed on Eliza's head, presumably to teach her to walk with a better posture, and after the buildup of a repeated accompaniment pattern in double octaves by full strings, the beginning of "Wouldn't it be Loverly?" is sounded in the trumpets and flute at 120 (ex. 4.14).

Ex. 4.14. *"Dress Ballet," bars 120–125.*

Ex. 4.15. *"Dress Ballet," bars 154–159.*

Ex. 4.16. *"Dress Ballet," bars 169–172.*

The ostinato continues until bar 135, gradually calming down to *pianississimo*. There is a three-bar silence before the next part of the ballet begins. The Dance Master arrives to teach Eliza the tango, and in a piece of irony "The Rain in Spain" is heard in the underscore. What had been a spontaneous and free dance of jubilation after her success in learning how to speak properly in the middle of the act has now become yet another chore for Eliza. Again, Miller's score gives us details about the choreography, with comments such as "low jeté lunge," "double reverse turn," "tango step," "shows to Vera [Lee, the Dance Mistress]," and "curtsey." All of this is accompanied by a straight playing of the first ten bars of "The Rain in Spain," but a two-bar transition passage introduces a new episode titled "The Lesson" (ex. 4.15). Above the right-hand part, Rittmann wrote "insistent vamp!" and the music indeed takes on a strict, rigorous air. The melody in bars 156–59 (C sharp–D–F natural) is a deliberate distortion of the line "On the plain!" from "The Rain in Spain"; it follows on from the extract from the song heard in the previous section and, allotted by Bennett to a solo clarinet ("*mf* sweet"), again acts as an illustration of Eliza's mental confusion.

At 169 a faster section (marked *Più mosso*) begins. Although two-fifths of the music remains, this feels like the beginning of the end; the tension never lets up until the final bars of the ballet. The *Più mosso* section is based on a descending chromatic pattern, on top of which is floated a muted trumpet fanfare, shown in the melody line of bars 171–72 in example 4.16. The same material persists until bar 183, when example 4.12 returns once more. It is worth noting that in the full score, bars 186–89 have been rewritten by Phil Lang; the change increases the harmonic tension by adding new rising chromatic scales in the strings and tuba. This leads more dramatically into the return of example 4.12, which then continues until bar 210. At this point the music whips up into a frenzy, with the dynamic at *fortissimo* and the whole orchestra breaking into the chorus of "With a Little Bit of Luck." This develops into a free melody that adds sinister chromatic inflections to Doolittle's jaunty song. A rising sequence begins at 227, reaching its height at 245 when the same bar is repeated four times before a huge glissando into the opening of the melody of "The Servants' Chorus" ("Poor Professor Higgins," ex. 4.17). This is marked *furioso* and *fff*; Rittmann's score also has "climax" and "howling!" After the theme has been played twice *tutti*, there is a diminuendo while the cellos and trombones sound the theme one last time, and the music ends softly and mysteriously.

The harmonic complexity of the "Dress Ballet" may be considered both a strength and a weakness. Since Holm conceived it as a "nightmare," it is suitable that the music should be ghoulish both on the fundamental level of Rittmann's arrangement and the expansive surface given to it by Bennett's orchestration. Yet the number's extremity also makes it stand out from the rest of the score. None of the other numbers in the show features such a contorted palette of sounds as is found here, so much so that it might have hijacked the entire musical. By extension, the psychological extremity of the choreography was probably also ill-matched with the rest of the show. In a more general sense, the dance also repeated the image (from earlier in the act) of Eliza being taught how to do something, even if these new lessons were of a different nature. It would be fascinating if the producer of a new

Ex. 4.17. "Dress Ballet," ending.

revival of *My Fair Lady* decided to include the ballet, but the resolution to cut it in New Haven was undoubtedly born of wisdom.

"Say a Prayer for Me Tonight"

The last of the three numbers that were cut in New Haven needs the least introduction. "Say a Prayer for Me Tonight" found lasting fame as one of the title character's solos in the 1958 film of *Gigi* (though it was cut for the 1973 stage adaptation), but it was originally a song for Eliza to perform in *My Fair Lady* before she went to the ball. It is mentioned from Outline 1 on (see chap. 3), yet Lerner later confessed that he was not sorry to see it cut. "I never liked it. Fritz did. . . . It would never have found its way into *Gigi* except Fritz, that dirty dog, played it one night for Arthur [Freed, the film's producer] and Vincente [Minnelli, the director] when I was not around, and the following morning I was out-voted three to one. . . . It pains me to admit it, but I was wrong: it was one of the most touching moments in the film."[35]

The sources for "Say a Prayer for Me Tonight" are the second most extensive of any song connected with *My Fair Lady* (after "Why Can't the English?"). A lyric from Herman Levin's papers contains several revelations about the number. With the exception of the first six lines (which consist of simple verse material), Liza's opening solo (up to the entrance of the servants) is familiar from the version of the song that made it into *Gigi*. However, the rest of the lyric is completely unknown:

> SERVANTS: Have no fear, you'll be fine.
> LIZA: No, I won't.
> SERVANTS: Gracious, proud and refine.
> LIZA: No, I won't.
> SERVANTS: Stately and serene . . .
> LIZA: I won't . . .
> SERVANTS: Practically a queen . . .
> LIZA: I won't . . .
> SERVANTS: No, Miss Liza, no, you cannot fail.
> LIZA: Fail to end in Reading Gaol.
>   Oh, how I shall behave . . .
> SERVANTS: No, you won't.
> LIZA: Like I live in a cave.
> SERVANTS: No, you won't.
> LIZA: Sit when I should stand . . .
> SERVANTS: You won't . . .
> LIZA: Shake the butler's hand . . .

SERVANTS: You won't . . .
LIZA: Future history will write
  This was England's blackest night.
SERVANTS: Don't worry, Miss Liza . . . (etc.)
(spoken)

(Servants leave)

LIZA: If I were a work of art
  Would I wake his sleeping heart?
  Is perfection the only way?
  If it is—kneel down—and say

  A prayer for me tonight;
  That the night will bring
  Me ev'rything
  I've waited for.

  Say a prayer that he'll discover
  I'm his lover
  For now and evermore.
  Pray that he's lonely, a ship lost at sea;
  Searching for someone exactly like me.

  And say a prayer that he'll remember
  Long ago somewhere
  He said a prayer
  For me.[36]

The second section involves a dialogue between Eliza and the maids, split into two sections. First, they tell her four times how great she will be, and she rebuts them; then she tells them four times what a disaster she will be, and they rebut her. They comfort her once more and leave. Then begins the most interesting part. Left alone, Eliza moves on from merely worrying about her success at the ball and instead sings about why that success is so important to her. In the verse she asks whether she could "wake his sleeping heart," and the chorus is this time focused on Higgins. She hopes "that he'll discover / I'm his lover," that he is "searching for someone exactly like" her, and that "he'll remember . . . he said a prayer / for me." This adds a layer to the song and changes the focus of the show: Eliza is portrayed as going through the lessons and wanting to triumph, purely to make Higgins love her. As we saw in the case of "Shy," such an overt declaration of love is foreign to the ultimately ambiguous focus of the musical.

The musical sources for the song are the most detailed evidence in existence of the creation of a melody by Loewe. Three untitled manuscripts contain snippets of material from the song. One in particular appears to show the genesis of the melody, with three different versions of it on the same page, shown in examples 4.18, 4.19, and 4.20. The shape of the melody is already established in example 4.18, with its characteristic series of turns, then example 4.19 shows the first seven bars almost as they appear in the finished song. The only difference is that the fourth bar contains four eighth notes rather than the two quarter notes that appear in the completed melody; Loewe has bracketed and put short lines above the final two eighth notes of the bar to indicate the notes that are to become quarter notes in the final version, which is the third melody on the page (ex. 4.20, curiously transposed to E-flat major), marked "Att." ("Attention").

The latter is copied out on two other loose manuscripts in the Loewe Collection: one is in F major and reproduces the first eight bars with one small change (the two quarter notes in bar 4 changed to a dotted quarter note and an eighth note) and a small error (the first two notes are transformed from eighth notes to quarter notes, making four beats in a triple-time bar); the other contains just the first three bars in E-flat major. The two documents are quite different in nature to one another. The first is on a page consisting of four separate melodies, the third of which has been crossed out (because it is an early version of the fourth melody on the page) and all of which are slightly untidy; this feels like a true page of sketches. The E-flat major version is on a page titled "Sketches" containing three very short melodic extracts numbered 10, 11 and 12. All three are very brief, very neat, and fluently written, and the

Ex. 4.18. *"Say a Prayer for Me Tonight," sketch 1.*

Ex. 4.19. *"Say a Prayer for Me Tonight," sketch 2.*

Ex. 4.20. *"Say a Prayer for Me Tonight," sketch 3.*

first two end with "etc."; the document seems like a sort of "thematic catalogue" to remind Loewe of melodies he had invented and perhaps intended for a specific purpose. None of the other extracts on these pages is familiar as a song from another Lerner and Loewe show, so either they were very aborted attempts at writing songs for *Fair Lady* or they were related to another show altogether. Loewe could conceivably have had the melody on his desk for some years before it was used in the New Haven version of this show.

In spite of the extended lyric reproduced earlier, the version of "Say a Prayer" used in the *My Fair Lady* tryout was the same as that used in *Gigi*. Conductor Franz Allers's photocopy of a copyist's piano-vocal score shows that this document (which was presumably used to rehearse the number) is almost identical with the published sheet music for the song in its *Gigi* incarnation.[37] The orchestration of the number (by Jack Mason, the uncredited "ghost" orchestrator of *My Fair Lady*) is identical to this copyist's score, right down to the fact that the first-time bars lie empty. In the same folder as the "Say a Prayer" orchestration is a two-page manuscript in Russell Bennett's hand entitled "Bridge After Prayer," which consists of six bars of transition music based on "Say a Prayer," leading into an orchestral rendition of one verse of "I Could Have Danced All Night."[38]

It is clear from the cut lyric reproduced above that the original conception of "Say a Prayer" involved an ABA form whereby the lyric for the repeat of A had a reversed meaning. Perhaps this was Lerner's attempt to overcome what he evidently considered to be the bland nature of the song: suddenly it became more emphatic and personal in the final chorus. As it is, though, "Say a Prayer" had a similar function in *My Fair Lady* and *Gigi*: Eliza and Gigi both sing a simple song about being nervous about a forthcoming event. Nevertheless, the beauty of the melody, the subtle nuances of the harmony, and the sincerity of the lyrics show Lerner and Loewe at their best; and when Julie Andrews sang the number at a tribute concert for Loewe given in New York on March 28, 1988, a few weeks after his death, she was essentially reappropriating one of the finest songs Loewe had written for her in *My Fair Lady*.[39] "Say a Prayer for Me Tonight" is a fitting climax to this chapter, because it demonstrates how Lerner and Loewe had the confidence to cut or discard songs if they did not work in the show as a whole, even when the material was of high quality in its own terms. Likewise, the material that did eventually make it into the final version of the score was heavily scrutinized and adjusted before Lerner and Loewe were content with it. This points the way to a new interpretation of *My Fair Lady*, one which sees the piece as the result of rigorous self-criticism and discerning revision, rather than an organic act of creation from one end of the show to the other.

5

SETTLING THE SCORE
• • •
PART I

Of the songs that eventually made it into the score of *My Fair Lady*, only "The Rain in Spain" and "Show Me" were left more or less as they were originally conceived by Lerner and Loewe, and only a couple of changes were made to the lyric of "Wouldn't It Be Loverly?"[1] All the other numbers went through a considerable amount of revision and recomposition, with "Why Can't the English?" particularly notable for the existence of four completely different versions in the Library of Congress's collections. This chapter approaches the show's musical numbers through the numerous types of compositional manuscripts identified in chapter 4. Such a process helps reexamine Lerner and Loewe's approach to the show as well as the relationships between the different members of the "music department": the orchestrators (Robert Russell Bennett, Phil Lang, and Jack Mason), dance arranger (Trude Rittmann), choral arranger (Gino Smart), and various copyists. More generally, this gives an insight into the complexities of the processes that went into producing the music for Broadway shows of the period as well as a critical examination of various aspects of the definitive published text.

SETTING THE SCENE: CREATING THE OVERTURE AND OPENING

Although it was standard procedure on Broadway for orchestrators and arrangers to create the overture for a show based on themes from the main songs, Frederick Loewe seems to have played a more active role than this in the creation of the Overture for *Fair Lady*. A two-page autograph piano score from the Library of Congress's Loewe Collection shows that Loewe drafted out the opening statement, the theme from "You Did It" and the transition into "On the Street Where You Live" (only the first bar of which is included).[2] At the top of the first page, Loewe wrote an instruction to Trude Rittmann—who arranged the show's incidental music in addition to the dances—to "Have [Robert] Russell [Bennett] confirm keys." This highlights an unambiguous chain of command from composer (Loewe) to arranger (Rittmann) to orchestrator (Bennett). In addition, Loewe stated that the music should continue into a refrain of "On the Street" and "I Could Have Danced," showing how the rest of the Overture was to be filled out, and underneath this he indicated the suggested key scheme that he wanted Bennett to confirm: "'Street in C', 'Danced' in E-flat, into 'Opening' in C." Some of Loewe's articulation and dynamics were retained in the published vocal score, but basically these two pages are a set of instructions to be handed down the line to Rittmann, who then wrote out a full-length, six-page piano score.

Rittmann's score (in the Warner-Chappell Collection) reveals her contribution to the composition. Although her score is based on Loewe's, Rittmann modified the voicing or in some cases some of the counterpoint to make it less pianistic and more appropriate for the purposes of orchestration. She mapped out the entire number for Bennett, though she used shorthand to indicate where the full refrains of "On the Street" and "I Could Have Danced" were to be played. Evidently she had two attempts at creating the transition music between these two themes; the first is crossed out and an arrow points toward the replacement. Her two-bar introduction to "I Could Have Danced" (bars 118–119) is also unfamiliar, consisting of a simple vamp rather than the more smoothly forward-driving published version. Also, the sixth-to-last bar of the overture appears as an ascending scale from B flat to B flat (the dominant of the key of the passage). This was later changed to a scale of ascending minor-seventh chords with a different destination chord, but in every other respect Rittmann's score matches the published piano-vocal scores.

Clearly, it was the basis for Bennett's full score of the number, because bars 118 and 119 were amended in Bennett's score, with a new strip of manuscript paper stuck on top of the orchestration of Rittmann's version of these two bars. Bars 134–135 were amended using the same procedure. Because Rittmann simply copied out a few bars of the melody and then wrote "etc. full chorus of I Could have danced," Bennett was given no new material to increase the interest of this section and therefore orchestrated the bare song as it appears in its sung version in the show. The revision adds chromatic movement to fill in the spaces between phrases more inventively. It is impossible to know who decided that an improvement needed to be made, but it is likely that Loewe examined the score and highlighted areas for improvement such as this (not least because Bennett or Rittmann could have written them in this way in the first place).

The autograph full scores for the Overture and Opening Scene are physically bound together as if they were a single number, and the published vocal scores both list them as a single number. But though the music runs without closure from one to the other, clearly they are two separate pieces of music with disparate functions. The Overture is a conventional medley of key themes from the show, bringing the audience to attention with a fanfare; the Opening Music is mimetic and provides both a background to and an illustration of the events going on as the curtain goes up on Covent Garden market. Although George J. Ferencz implies that Bennett orchestrated both pieces, the autograph score indicates that Phil Lang was responsible for the Opening Music.[3] There is no known Loewe autograph piano score for the piece, so it is likely that Rittmann was responsible for its composition: a complete piano score in her hand has survived, and that it contains both amendments and some unfamiliar elements—suggesting an initial composition that has then been modified and improved (possibly after Loewe's intervention)–promotes her authorship. One such instance happens in bars 17–20, where Rittmann has bracketed 17–18 and 19–20 into two groups of two bars, with each group to be repeated; in the published version each is heard only once. The "Tempo di Soft Shoe" section is also twice as long in Rittmann's version—sixteen bars as opposed to eight—and it is striking that she had an additional two bars at the end, again with repeat signs around them (allowing some extra time to improvise while Eliza appeared onstage), but then struck them out to create the now-familiar version, which has a sense of interruption about it.

With the exception of the latter amendment (which Rittmann must have made before handing it over), the full score shows that Lang orchestrated Rittmann's score, and later modified it. Again, most of the revisions were made by pasting new strips of manuscript paper over the old bars. The repeat signs in bars 17–20 were scribbled out in pencil and "no repeats" written over the bars. At bar 48, she indicated with an arrow, "Phil, from here on different fill in," and in response Lang reassigned the melody from the clarinet to the flute, oboe, and violins, also fleshing out the harp and trumpet parts, and adding trombones. The ruthless editing of some passages again suggests that Loewe may have helped shape the piece, even if he did not write out the score.

Regardless of authorship, the Overture and Opening are breathtakingly crafted. The four-bar call to attention at the beginning of the Overture is followed by a snippet of "You Did It"; the procedure is repeated, but this time the theme from the song is extended to lead into a complete refrain of "On the Street Where You Live." A two-bar reference to the servants' counterpoint in "I Could Have Danced All Night" ("It's after three, now, / Don't you agree now") leads into a chorus of that number, interrupted at the end by another brass fanfare that segues into the Opening. The Overture is traditional in the sense that it contains a medley of potential "hits," but at barely three minutes' duration it is also relatively short for a show so rich in melodic invention. Evidently, Loewe wanted to push straight into the action. The Opening music is also succinct. There are three main sections: the first, in which "Crowds are milling about Covent Garden Opera House"; the second, a dainty "Tempo di Soft Shoe"; and the furious third, in which the music whips into a frenzy before being interrupted by Eliza's cry of "Aoooow!" on being knocked over by Freddy. The music for this brief piece is wonderfully free and harmonically complex, but its most obvious point of interest is in the reference to the English nursery rhyme "London Bridge Is Falling Down," which contains the line "my fair lady." Rittmann and Loewe include the music that goes with this line as a sneaky reference to the show's title. Since the musical was named only in late December 1955 (see chap. 2), the Opening music almost certainly has a late date of composition, probably during the rehearsal period, which would explain why no manuscript exists in Loewe's hand.

ELIZA'S DREAMS, ELIZA'S RAGE

Eliza's five solo songs fall into two main groups: those that express her anger ("Just You Wait," "Show Me," and "Without You") and those that express her joy or aspirations ("Wouldn't It Be Lovely?" and "I Could Have Danced All Night"). She is prone to extremes of emotion, be it elation or fury, rather than a "middle ground" position. Nor do these songs particularly convey facts to the audience. That is not to say that they tell us nothing, but rather that they are more about expression and characterization than explanation. This is especially the case with "Wouldn't it Be Lovely." In addition to the published vocal scores, there are two slightly different lyric sheets for the song, Loewe's autograph, a copyist's piano-vocal score, and Bennett's full score. Clearly, the song came easily to Lerner and Loewe—the lyricist describes how a visit to Covent Garden market in the early morning provided the inspiration for the lyric, which Loewe set to music "in one afternoon"[4]—and the sources all suggest that the song changed very little during the creative process.

Nevertheless, some ambiguities remain. The first lyric sheet (from Levin's papers) consists of the refrain with just three deviations from the familiar version: "With one gigantic [instead of 'enormous'] chair," "Lots of fire [instead of 'coal']," and "Crept over the winder sill" instead of "Crept over me winder sill."[5] The second lyric sheet (from the Warner-Chappell Collection) includes the verse and changes the refrain into its final version, with the exception of "gigantic/enormous."[6] Evidently this version was used to prepare the copyist's score in the Warner-Chappell Collection. A copy intended for Bennett is annotated throughout to show how the basic score—containing the verse and one refrain in F major—was to be developed into the whole number with dance music. Bennett's orchestral chart is almost entirely free of blemishes or corrections: the only real modification to the orchestration involves the removal of the bassoon and clarinet parts in bars 66–69 ("Lots of choc'late for me to eat . . .," second refrain).

The copy of the song in the Loewe Collection, however, is confusing. It contains the verse and one refrain, with indications for two repeats of the refrain; there are also some crossed-out bars. This would seem to identify it as an early version of the song that was passed on to the copyist and orchestrator.[7] However, it is difficult to account for the fact that this supposedly "original" composer score uses almost the final version of the lyric: of the three instances of the "pre-improvement" lyric listed earlier, only "Crept over the winder sill" (as opposed to "over me") is present here. None of this affects the authorship of the song, yet it suggests that this is not Loewe's original manuscript but rather a fair copy for the use of others. This is the case with many of the piano-vocal scores in the composer's handwriting held in the Loewe Collection that tend not to represent the actual pieces of paper on which the songs were first written. Like Richard Rodgers (more of whose sketches have survived), it seems that Loewe went about drafting his songs on a single stave before writing out a fuller piano-vocal score.[8] This serves as a reminder that placing too much importance on one source, instead of taking a larger sample and putting them into a wider context, can lead to a misunderstanding of the compositional process.

Even though "Wouldn't it be Loverly?" has a simplicity that is appropriate for its dramatic context, it is nevertheless full of interesting features. The verse begins with four arpeggiated chords to punctuate Eliza's delighted cries of "Aooow!" upon being given the money by Higgins: a seamless way for the music to segue out of the scene. This leads to the introduction, with its lazily descending melodic turns. But Loewe cuts it short with a perfect cadence as the men break into their "Quasi recitativo" a cappella verse, in which they describe their dreams. The "false" introduction then returns and drives into Eliza's F-major refrain. The latter's outward cockney charm belies its complex harmonization and chromaticism. For instance, bar 21 ("room somewhere") moves into the subdominant area, establishing the song's warmth, but although bar 23 ("cold night air") ends on the expected dominant-seventh chord, it does so via an abrupt G-major seventh at the start of the bar. Perhaps the most elegant feature is the use of contrary motion in bars 24–25

("With one enormous chair"), whose appoggiaturas come into their own when the pattern recurs in 27–28 to accent the repetition in the phrase "Warm face, warm hands, warm feet" (ex. 5.1). The bridge section ("Oh, so loverly sittin' absobloomin'lutely still") also has a fast harmonic rhythm, again featuring examples of chromatic voice-leading, while the final section is extended beyond its expected eight bars because of a prolongation of the title phrase. The second refrain features four-part choral writing alongside Eliza's line, followed by a brief dance section in A-flat major in which the men whistle the melody. The number ends as Eliza sings a final "Oh, wouldn't it be loverly?" to which the men respond by repeating the final word. What Loewe achieves in this song is an introduction to Eliza's softer side and the camaraderie of the Covent Garden workers while maintaining a richness of texture. Lerner's idiomatic lyric plays its part in establishing the social class of the characters, but so too does Loewe's melody. Its harmonization, however, is comparatively ornate, taking the song far beyond its broad allusion to the jauntiness of the English musical hall.

The same goes for "Just You Wait," Eliza's next song. It features a strong martial aspect, depicting Eliza's fury at Higgins's sadistic treatment of her, and the freedom of form Loewe uses in the number is equally striking. After the opening refrain in C minor, Loewe writes an episode in D-flat major in which Eliza dreams of fame and fortune. She imagines gaining the king's attention and requesting that Higgins be beheaded. A transition in B-flat major ("'Done,' says the King . . .") leads back into the opening material. This time it is rendered in C major, and the music portrays Higgins's march to the firing line ("Then they'll march you, 'enry 'iggins, to the wall"). Therefore, while the opening passage has the overall trappings of the 32-bar song (abbreviated to 30 due to the melodic diminution of the return of the A section at the end), the number as a whole also follows a similar form in macrocosm, namely a long opening section in which the character lays out her position, a

Ex. 5.1. "Wouldn't It Be Loverly?" bars 27–28.

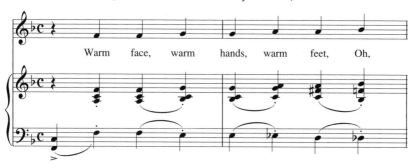

contrasting section about three-quarters of the way through, and a return to the opening material. Also, in spite of its modal contrast to the opening section, the D-flat major passage retains its links to the main "Just you wait" theme by starting each phrase with a similar three-note ascending pick-up ("One day," "One eve[ning]," "All the peo[ple]" and so on). Along with the ominously understated fermatas when Eliza declares she wants Higgins's head and the jubilant trumpet line when the king gives his order, this is one of several aspects of the number that show how Lerner and Loewe make even a short song into a complex musical scene.

Lerner states that "Just You Wait" was one of the first songs he tackled with Loewe, and names it as one of those that he played for Mary Martin during their first meeting about the show.[9] This is supported by Outline 1 (chap. 3), in which "Just You Wait" is one of the few songs referred to by title; Eliza sings it in the upstairs bathroom, "wet and shaking like a drowned rat." By Outline 3, a montage of lessons has been introduced, but the song is not explicitly referred to. Only Outline 4 confirms its final position: it takes place in Higgins's study and is the "Second Song" after a first "Song: Montage of lessons" (surely "The Servants' Chorus"). At this stage "Just You Wait" was to be preceded by a refrain of "The Servants' Chorus," but in the published show Eliza's song comes first, allowing her to vent her frustration before the servants illustrate the passage of time during the lessons. The rehearsal script shows an intermediate structure: "Just You Wait" is immediately followed by a blackout, a verse of the servants' song, another blackout, then the lesson about "The rain in Spain." The published script, however, misses out this instance of the "Chorus" and goes straight to the lesson.

This illustrates how Lerner and Loewe operated on both the local and the broader level. Originally, the song allowed Eliza to express her humiliation at being stripped of her clothes, forced to have a bath, and compelled to wear Higgins's bathrobe. But by changing it to express Eliza's frustration about her lessons rather than about being treated inhumanely, Lerner softened the dislikeable part of Higgins's personality. "Just You Wait" isolates the tension between the two so that it tells of a discouraged pupil who does not know how to fulfill the expectations of a perturbed teacher, who in turn does not know how to give his student what she needs. Language, not misogyny, is the subject of the song, even though the lyric is outwardly a hyperbolic description of Eliza's imagined retribution.

The lyric underwent one major change and one minor alteration. The major change involved the complete recasting of the third and fourth verses, which were originally as follows:

Oooooo . . . 'enry 'iggins!
Have your fun but 'enry 'iggins you beware.
Ooooo . . . 'enry 'iggins!
When the shoe is on the other foot, take care!

You won't think it such a farce
When I kick your bloomin' arse!

This version appears on a lyric sheet in Levin's papers and is also used in a copyist's score held in the Warner-Chappell Collection.[10] These sources also contain a small alteration in the lyric of the penultimate stanza of the song (the king's imaginary lines): "All the people will celebrate all over the land; / And whatever you wish and want will be my command." was modified to "All the people will celebrate the glory of you, / And whatever you wish and want I gladly will do." Though the big change was made in the rehearsal script and Bennett's orchestration, both contain the king's couplet in its original form.

However, the composer's manuscript is again difficult to place. It is certainly not Loewe's "original" score for the number, because Rittmann's hand is unmistakable in the writing of the clefs, time and key signatures, and most of the piano part. Loewe wrote out the lyric, vocal line, and tempo markings, but since Rittmann did not join the team until late 1955 (whereas we know the song was conceived much earlier), the manuscript must be a fair copy prepared for the copyist and orchestrator. On the title page, Loewe wrote "Att. Franz [Allers, the conductor]: Julie may be E flat? Please try." The copyist's score follows Loewe in every respect including the use of the key of D minor and does not make this transposition, but a note at the top reads: "1 tone lower." Since this score was intended for Bennett's use, it is no surprise that the orchestrator's full score is in the published key of C minor.[11] It is curious that Loewe's score contains the final version of the lyric throughout—unlike the original lyric used in the copyist's score, which was undoubtedly created from Loewe's manuscript—but there is some smudging around the lyric for the third stanza, suggesting a possible later amendment. In all other respects, the sources indicate very little in the way of musical changes to the song as time went on.

The next number was much slower in coming. As noted previously, the song originally intended to fill the spot after "The Rain in Spain" was called "Shy." A solo for Eliza, it speaks overtly of the character's love for Higgins and was certainly in place by the early autumn of 1955. On Outline 4, it is named as both the "Third Song" of act 1, scene 5, and the piece of music intended to end the musical. It was eventually replaced, of course, by "I Could Have

Danced All Night." A musical synopsis of the second act of the show, kept in an envelope in the Warner-Chappell Collection, refers to the reprise of a song for Eliza called "The Story of My Life," which is crossed out and replaced by "I Could Have Danced" in Loewe's hand; presumably this was an intermediate replacement for "Shy" before "Danced" was composed.[12]

Lerner admits the problems the collaborators had with this song in his autobiography. He says they had tried to give Eliza "a lyrical burst of triumph" after "The Rain in Spain," which would also reveal "her unconscious feelings for Higgins." But all their attempts "emerged with her true feelings on her sleeve."[13] Lerner goes on to explain how he managed to come up with the title of "I Could Have Danced All Night" during the final week before the start of rehearsals.[14] He says that "Fritz set it in a day" and that he finished writing the words in twenty-four hours—"but not to my satisfaction." He admired Loewe's melody, but "blushed" when singing him the line: "'And [sic] all at once my heart took flight'. I promised Fritz I would change it as soon as I could. As it turned out, I was never able to."[15] None of this confirms Marni Nixon's claim that she first heard the song in "the early spring of 1954," when it "was in 3/4 time with a very European operetta sound,"[16] but it is true that the title of the song was at one point "I Want to Dance All Night." Curiously, this was an afterthought rather than the original version. The rehearsal script, Loewe's autograph, and Bennett's full score all use the words "I Could Have Danced" as does a copyist's score in Levin's papers.[17] However, a photocopy of this copyist's score is headed "I Want to Dance All Night" in Loewe's hand,[18] and another typed script in Levin's papers replaces "Could" with "Want" in the final scene (where "I Want to Dance" is heard in the orchestra).[19] A further script also has this, and on both the list of musical numbers and the pages of the actual song (1-5-52 to 1-5-55) the title is shown as "I Want to Dance All Night."[20] Strangely, the lyric itself still reads "I could have danced." The playbills for the tryouts in New Haven and Philadelphia use the word "Want," as did early pressings of the show's Original Cast Album (though Julie Andrews sings "could" throughout).[21] It seems that Lerner briefly considered a change but finally decided to leave the lyric alone.[22]

The autograph manuscript of the song follows precedent in being a fluently written fair copy of the published version. In two respects, the score postdates the initial composition of the score. First, the verse ("Bed! Bed! I couldn't go to bed") follows the published edition in indicating "Allegro molto" as the tempo, in putting *mf* for the introduction and *p* when the voice enters, and in writing the melody and accompaniment in quaver beats. By contrast, the copyist's score (used in rehearsal) has two bars of quarter note beats for the introduction (rather than one bar of eights), has "Allegro" as the

tempo, and indicates only *mf* by way of dynamic through the whole verse. Furthermore, "Bed! Bed! I couldn't go to" (and so on) is set to quarter notes rather than eights; in other words, the copyist's score of both verse and refrain is half the speed of Loewe's score. The second difference between the scores involves the Maids' countersubject during the second refrain. The rehearsal script and full score have a bridge passage (starting "Not one word more, dear") and counterpoint for Mrs. Pearce (without the Maids). This was all replaced in the published version with a part for the Maids (who sing "It's after three, now"). They follow the original counterpoint for Mrs. Pearce for the first four lines of the counterpoint thereafter, and also take up her final four lines, but the middle of their part was replaced. Mrs. Pearce's only part in the definitive version of the show is to sing three brief lines to connect the second and third verses.[23] Perhaps Philippa Bevans's prowess as a singer was not sufficient to give her the whole of the countersubject; perhaps Lerner and Loewe wanted to make sure that the words of the countersubject could be heard by allotting more singers to it; or perhaps the intention was to create a feeling of bustle around Eliza as she continues to repeat the refrain. Whatever the case, the copy of the song in the Loewe Collection represents the final version of the lyric, rather than that shown in the rehearsal script and copyist's score. Bennett's full score confirms that the Loewe autograph was a late creation: although Bennett adopts the final version of the music in terms of rhythm (eighth notes rather than quarter notes), he uses the earlier lyric from the rehearsal script.[24]

Loewe's accomplishment in this much-heard song is easy to overlook. The verse is brief but functions brilliantly: after one bar of introduction, Eliza floats in, her notes all short in expression of her excitement. The refrain is in ABCA^1 form, with the B section a scarcely modified transposition up a tone of the A section; we feel Eliza's growing joy and her inability to contain herself. Thematically, the C part is strongly linked to A and B, too, with similar configurations of note lengths and melodic shapes, and in the first two refrains Eliza ascends to a high F before coming back down to earth to a B and C, re-energizing the music for the next refrain. Throughout, the melody floats with long notes, while the accompaniment provides the motion; in the second refrain, the maids add to this with their commonsensical counterpoint, which Eliza ignores, merely repeating the main melody. Then she is left alone, and sings a final refrain *pianissimo*, before rousing herself for the final ascent to a high G. The composer's intentions are clear: to set Lerner's gloriously overstated lyric to music that illustrates Eliza's thrill at her sense of achievement. The song is also clever in giving her a new vocal character at this point; compared to the low tessitura of her previous solos, "I Could Have Danced" shows Eliza in full lyric flow.

Musically, she goes silent at this point in the show, until her reprise of "Just You Wait" in Act 2.[25] The number is sung up a tone in D minor this time, rather than in the darker key of C minor, and the mood is fragile. Eliza sings just over six bars before crying bitterly, and the mood is less martial: there's no thudding trombone to lead into the singing this time, for instance, but lyrical clarinets and an *appassionato* violin solo instead. We then lose sight of Eliza for a couple of minutes, but the music continues straight into a reprise of Freddy's "On the Street Where You Live." His singing is interrupted upon Eliza's appearance from Higgins's house, but the music continues into the verse of "Show Me." This is in two parts: first, Freddy maintains the lyric vein of "On the Street" with the words "Speak, and the world is full of singing," then Eliza interrupts with the choppily textured "Words! Words! Words!" The emptiness of verbose language has become too much for her, be it from the adoring Freddy or the pedantic Higgins, and she cuts through Freddy's waffling—two phrases, the second repeated higher than the first—with a furious *Molto vivace* in triple time.

"Show Me" has a Latin flavor, a bit like the *huapango* that Bernstein was later to use for "America" in *West Side Story* but without any obvious intention of evoking the exotic.[26] In "Show Me," seven bars of 3/4 time are concluded with a bar of 6/8. The same procedure is followed a minor third higher, then in the bridge Loewe uses three groups of four eighths in the melody (on "Here we are to-/ ge-ther in the / mid-dle of the") to undermine the bar line and make the two bars seem like three. Eliza's fury is dazzlingly presented in this way: it is almost as if she is in such control of her world now that she can move through multiple meters without losing her way. Her fury also makes her seem to get ahead of herself. Part of this comes from the lyric, too: whereas the standard lines are only six or seven feet long, Lerner resorts to wordy, thirteen-syllable lines in the bridge, such as "Never do I ever want to hear another word." These are also colloquial and irritable in tone. Overall, the tension and fury of the piece are matched in words and music by dense harmonies and the imperative tense (such as "Don't," "Read," and "Tell").

There are no copies of the reprises of "Just You Wait" and "On the Street" in Loewe's hand because, obviously, they required no new composition other than an introduction and linking material. This new music was provided by Rittmann, and her piano-vocal score survives in the Warner-Chappell Collection.[27] "Just You Wait" is written out in full and presents the song exactly as it appears in the published score. Rittmann indicates that the first sixteen bars of "On the Street" are to be played by the orchestra, with Freddy joining in at "Are there lilac trees" and giving way to the underscoring again at "People stop and stare." This was orchestrated by Bennett, and then discarded as the

orchestral part was cut and Freddy sang from the beginning of "On the Street."[28] On a manuscript titled "Street Reprise," Rittmann wrote out Freddy's introductory verse to "Show Me" ("Speak, and the world is full of singing").[29] This was probably because Loewe's autograph—which otherwise produces the song in full—does not contain the introduction to Freddy's part. Still, it is intriguing that Bennett's orchestration of this section follows Rittmann in writing the bass part as a D-flat major arpeggio (a false relation) rather than its enharmonic, C-sharp major, as in Loewe's manuscript (again, probably a fair copy).[30] The full score contains a certain amount of revision at this point alone, where Lang seems to have orchestrated an earlier version of Freddy's opening line in F-sharp major rather than E major; this one-page score is crossed out and hidden beneath Bennett's revision.

Eliza's final number, "Without You," was partly revised during the rehearsal period—though not quite in the way Lerner later described. The lyricist claimed that during the last week of rehearsals in New York, "a major storm was gathering" because Rex Harrison refused to stand on the stage in silence while Julie Andrews sang "Without You" to his face. Lerner continues: "In preparation for the struggle over 'Without You', Fritz and I thought it might incorporate it more into the emotional action if Harrison interrupted the song at the climax with: 'I did it. I did it. I said I'd make a woman and indeed I did.'"[31] However, not only does the rehearsal script include the reprise of "You Did It," but it is also included in Outline 4, which even specifies that it is only a "short reprise." So while Harrison may well have complained about the song during rehearsals, the juxtaposition of "Without You" with a reprise of "You Did It" was planned long before then. However, the copyist's piano-vocal score and Bennett's autograph full score both contain different versions of the text to the definitive published one.[32]

The lyrics to the draft versions are reproduced in Appendix 1. Put next to the published version, they show that the lyric was both refined and reduced in length. The number contains three key pieces of musical material: the jaunty main theme, concluding in "without you" each time (A); the smoother "You dear friend" theme on the flattened submediant (B); and the "Without your pulling it" theme—a kind of "slow tease" in which the tempo broadens before a sudden acceleration—in the subdominant (C). The first version follows the formal pattern ABACABA, with the second version foreshortening the penultimate return to the A melody and the final version dropping the second AB section. This excision left the song in a nicely rounded ABACA form (allowing for the fact that the later occurrences of A are not complete). It works particularly well because the most irate and harmonically twisted section (C) comes almost at the end, allowing Eliza's anger to climax before being interrupted by Higgins; originally, the complete return to the A and B themes dissipated the anger.

It is also amusing to see Lerner's alternative suggestions for all the things that Eliza could do without Higgins. As ever, the journey to the published version involved strong self-criticism; in most cases, the original lyric could easily have stayed in the show without anyone thinking amiss of it. Still, one can see why "I can thrill to a play without you" was deemed uncompelling, and "I can still have a dream / and it's liable to seem / even more like a dream without you" is weakened by the repetition of the word "dream." Likewise, "The world without your smiling face" does not have the impact of the equivalent section in the published version (starting "You dear friend"), because the melody is drawn out into half notes rather than quarter and eighth notes, thereby slowing down the progress of the melody.

By contrast, the "You dear friend" part works brilliantly because it is topped off by a quotation from Eliza's lesson about "Hartford, Hereford and Hampshire," a strong rejection of Higgins *and* his methods. This little stanza was also in the original version, where it appeared much later on. Some of the wording was modified, again to the enhancement of the overall effect. The original has "You, dear friend, can jolly well / Plumb go straight to . . ." but the final version makes both lines start with the same word, a strong verse technique known as anaphora. It is also significant that Lerner worked the issue of language into the published version—"You . . . who talk so well"— and it was an undeniable improvement to remove the rather antiquated "Plumb" from the lyric. The part about "fog" was weak merely because it was not particularly funny, while "niche" and "itch" make a glaring half-rhyme. Conversely, most of the stanza dealing with "laughing till it hurts" is fine and was probably removed simply to shorten the song. But the excision of "[I can] Be the mother of five without you" is surely significant. Here again there is irrefutable evidence of Lerner removing a reference to Eliza as Higgins's lover—in this case, the bearer of his children, too—and therefore pushing the relationship in a deliberately ambiguous direction.

HIGGINS'S CHARM, HIGGINS'S ARROGANCE

Higgins's four solo songs also portray different aspects of his character. Yet his songs often seem more layered and ambiguous than hers, largely because he can be both charming and dislikeable at the same time. For instance, "An Ordinary Man" and "A Hymn to Him" are repulsively misogynistic but also have a charismatic element to them, perhaps because it is difficult to resist feeling amused by Higgins's unquestioning faith in himself.[33] His position is so extreme that we assume he cannot quite mean it. Loewe's musical portrayal of Higgins inclines to the elegant, too, especially in contrast to the earthier music associated with Eliza's fury or Doolittle's drunkenness. Apparently, this complexity was hard to come by. For example, no song from the show underwent as much modification during the compositional period as "Why Can't the English?" At least four distinct versions survive, offering us an unusual insight into Lerner and Loewe's thought processes, for instance, the use of a "loose" form in the verse to convey Higgins's message, the depiction of several key aspects of Higgins's character, the use of stylistic gestures to suggest location and mood, and, finally, the way in which this was achieved with relative brevity.

It comes as no surprise to learn that the song was extensively rewritten. In *The Street Where I Live*, Lerner describes how Rex Harrison was not happy with the original version, because "he said he felt he sounded like an inferior Noël Coward." Lerner put the problem down to the rhyme scheme.[34] Harrison confirms the story and specifies that it was "too reminiscent of 'Mad Dogs and Englishmen'; it needed breaking down and changing, it had a too familiar tang. Well, that song was worked on and worked on. Right through rehearsal Fritz was still playing with it."[35] The sources confirm this description of the composition period, but Lerner's explanation of the modification of the rhyme scheme does not account for several intermediate versions; nor does he mention the musical changes alluded to by Harrison.

However, he expanded on the subject of the song in a letter to Harrison on November 29, 1955. After promising to "rewrite it completely in a way that will be not only simpatico with you, but with the character of Higgins," he explained his general attitude to musical theater songs:

> There are "song songs" and "character songs." A "character song," which is basically free and is accompanied by an emotion or emotions, as in the case in "I'm An Ordinary Man," must pretty much stay within the bounds of reason. In a "song song," certain extravagances are not only permissible, but desirable. "Why Can't the English," written as it was, was definitely a "song song" and therefore contained a certain amount of satiric extravagance. The minute the same idea is written in a freer way, so that it almost seems like normal conversation set to music, those extravagances would seem definitely out of place.[36]

This reveals that he was happy to change the song because he felt it was not in keeping with Higgins's character; the lyricist himself saw the need for a transition of style—from a "song song" full of "satiric extravagance" to a "character song" with "broader scope and a longer line musically."

This fits in well with the sources for the song's four versions. The first is an early setting, with the music written out jointly by Loewe and Rittmann (mainly the latter) and the lyric by Loewe (see exx. 5.2 and 5.3 for extracts).[37] Since Rittmann's handwriting is present, this manuscript must date from late 1955 at the earliest. All the clefs, key and time signatures, dynamics, and expressive markings are in Rittmann's hand, as well as most of the notation.[38] The main piece of information to be gleaned from this is the rough date of the manuscript, rather than its authorship; it is not clear whether this is a fair copy of a previous Loewe autograph or the first time the composition was written down.

The original lyric is reproduced in Appendix 2. It is easy to see Harrison's point about its supposed resemblance to "Mad Dogs and Englishmen," which similarly contrasts the characteristics of the English with other nations. For instance:

Mad Dogs and Englishmen go out in the midday sun.
The Japanese don't care to,
The Chinese wouldn't dare to.

However, it is also surely true that the revised lyric is not dramatically different in this respect. Nor does Lerner's reasoning fit all of the revisions. For example, changing the couplet "Daily her barbaric tribe increases, / Grinding our language into pieces" into "This is what the British population /

Ex. 5.2. "Why Can't the English?" version 1 (excerpt).

Ex. 5.3. "Why Can't the English?" version 1 (excerpt).

Calls an elementary education" surely defines Higgins's character more directly by giving his statement substance, rather than obliterating a Cowardesque element. If anything, one can sense Shaw's socialist outlook in the new couplet, which attacks the institution of elementary education as the reason behind Eliza's woeful accent and use of the English language, and by extension her meager lifestyle. The change from "Hear a Yorkshireman converse, / Cornishmen are even worse" to "Hear a Yorkshireman, or worse, / Hear a Cornishman converse" is another example of an enhancement process: the original is adequate, but the change propels the song forward more effectively because the "or" tells us that the next phrase will add something to the initial thought. The use of anaphora ("Hear" to start both lines) is also a stylistic improvement. Similarly, the change from "A national ensemble singing flat" to "I'd rather hear a choir singing flat!" clarifies the motivation of the line (flat singing is not Higgins's focus, even though he detests it).

The refrain is more obviously similar to "Mad Dogs and Englishmen." In particular, Lerner's "Canadians pulverise it / In Ireland they despise it" has an air of Coward's "The Japanese don't care to / The Chinese wouldn't dare to." Yet the couplet cited by Lerner to explain why the original version was too similar to Coward's song in truth seems only loosely related to it: "In Norway there are legions / Of literate Norwegians."[39] So aside from a few similarities, there is little to link the songs.

Ex. 5.4. "Why Can't the English?" early version.

Why can't the Eng-lish teach their chil-dren how to speak? In

ev - 'ry oth - er na - tion they stress pro-nun - ci - a - tion.

Ex. 5.5. "Why Can't the English?" published version.

Why can't the Eng-lish teach their chil-dren how to speak? This

ver - bal class dis - tinc-tion By now should be an - tique. If

Ultimately, the main reason for the revisions was Lerner and Loewe's ambition to make the number as effective as possible. To this end, both the lyric *and* the music were changed for the final version. The musical adjustments were small but significant, and suggest that the reason for the rejection of the early version was that the verse form did not suit the form of the music. Whereas the opening line of the refrain ("Why can't the English teach their children how to speak?") did not rhyme with the ensuing line ("In Norway there are legions"), in the revised version it makes a couplet with the second line ("This verbal class distinction by now should be antique"). This is much more coherent with the construction of the music. As example 5.4 shows, the antecedent-consequent phrase structure of the music is at odds with the original lyric. Three lines of text are set to two well-balanced musical phrases—the first arriving on the dominant, the second returning to the tonic. The first line of text is twice the length of the other two, which are set to the second phrase of music. The word "speak" does not rhyme with the word "pronunciation," even though they are related musically by their appearances at the ends of the two phrases. Stylistically, the original lyric is awkward, and the rhyme of "In every other nation, they stress pronunciation" is laborious.

The final version (ex. 5.5) overcomes these problems: rhyming the first two lines makes them reflect the musical structure more neatly, and the replacement second line again intensifies the social aspect of Higgins's argument with the reference to a "verbal class distinction." The music is also strengthened by having one less syllable in the replacement second line, resulting in a quarter note at the end of the phrase rather than two eighth notes; and "[pronunci-]a-tion" is undoubtedly weaker than "antique." In all, the issue is not whether the song resembled "Mad Dogs and Englishmen" but rather one of relative inferiority. The original does not serve the show as well as the final version, often because the initial lyric is about linguistic fastidiousness where the final lyric deals with a social concern.

A copyist's score based on the original version also exists in the Warner-Chappell Collection.[40] The verse by this point had almost taken on its definitive form, with a few exceptions: Higgins says "Heavens, what a sound!" (rather than "noise!") and "Take a Yorkshireman" rather than "Hear a Yorkshireman." The couplet about the "writing on the wall" was completely removed (including the music) so that the verse goes straight from Higgins's "I ask you sir, what sort of word is that?" to the chorus via a new two-bar introduction. The refrain, however, still retained its original poetical structure, with some amendments to the lyric. The couplet dealing with the Germans was expanded slightly and brought forward to replace the weak lines about the French.[41] Lerner also worked on the image of the Irish, taking the lyric closer to its final form and removing the Canadians from the picture: "The Scotch and the Irish do some / Pronouncing that is gruesome." The Norwegians have gone, and in their place Lerner alludes to the Orient and introduces the joke about the French with the musical *tacet*: "With ev'ry Oriental good speech is fundamental. / In France make a slight mistake; they regard you as a freak . . . (*Spoken:*) The French never care what you do, as long as you pronounce it properly." The last verse also comes very close to its ultimate setting, with only three variations.[42]

Lerner had started to move in the right direction with the number in the version contained in this copyist's score. But he and Loewe then briefly changed track completely and shifted the focus of the number more onto national identity and less onto language. This third version of the song is the most surprising. Loewe took the first four pages (which contain the verse only) of the copyist's score of the second version and appended to them a new six-page autograph. Following precedent, this contains the lyric in his hand and the music in a combination of his handwriting and Rittmann's. On the front cover, Loewe crossed out the title and replaced it with "The English."[43] Here, Higgins rants about the way that the English "will go to any limit for the King," "rally like a puppet on a string" and "fight without a whimper or a whine" but will not learn their language properly. Part of the refrain of the song is reproduced in example 5.6.

Ex. 5.6. "The English."

Starting at bar 56, this version is almost completely different from the others, but it is inferior in most respects. The harmonically static first phrase is repeated note-for-note to form the second phrase; in itself, this is a redundant gesture. Bars 64–68 are more interesting, with minor-key inflections, but 72–80 are again repetitive and harmonically awkward. However, after a restatement of the opening material (80–95), from 96 to the first beat of bar 111 the music adopts almost the version that appears in the published score. The significant part is bars 102–111 ("The Scotch and Irish leave you close to tears"), in which both the music and lyric are practically in their final form for the first time.[44] This helps to place the song roughly between the production of the copyist's score and Loewe's autograph for the final version.

Perhaps Harrison's insistence that the number sounded like Coward had finally driven Lerner and Loewe almost to ditch the original premise of the song. Until the modulation at bar 96, there is not the slightest mention of a nation other than the English. Rather than setting the character of the English as an explanation for their sloppy linguistic habits in relief with the strict education of other nations, this lyric lists the positive aspects of the English, and in particular, how they display courage ("The English will fight without a whimper or a whine") or rigor ("The English will go to any limit for the King"), in many respects other than language. This is not one of Lerner's happier creations, however, and aside from the development of the middle section, Loewe's setting diverges almost pedantically from the original music. Compared to the fluidity of "Why Can't the English?" even in its initial form, "The English" has a choppy texture and the melodic line is constantly broken by rests.

The definitive version of the song exists not only in Loewe's autograph, the published vocal scores, and full score, but there is also a copy of the same copyist's score referred to earlier, annotated throughout to indicate the musical changes required to bring the score into line with the final version of the lyric (which is not, however, included).[45] In addition, a lyric sheet dated January 27, 1956, gives almost the final version of the song, with the exception of the lines about the Americans (which is still sung rather than a spoken aside), the French (which is in the second person rather than the third, i.e., "The French never care what you do" rather than " . . . they do"), and the penultimate line of the song is sung ("Use decent English?") rather than left up to the orchestra.[46] The differences between Loewe's score and the published edition are minimal, involving mainly some disagreements between the placing and type of articulative gestures (for instance, accents instead of staccato dots) and Italian terms (Loewe has "Vivace" at "Hear them down in Soho Square"; the published score has "Vivo"). A couple of bars also lack their final accompaniment pattern, but the score largely represents a version that could be put into print. Interestingly, the manuscript paper on which the joke about the Americans appears is of a different brand to the previous two pages (Chappell rather than Passantino), while the final syllable of the word "disappears"—which begins the new page and is followed in the next bar by the spoken line about the Americans— is not in fact written down. Furthermore, the two bars of accompaniment that follow the musical tacet have clearly been erased and rewritten, and there is also evidence of the joke about the French (squeezed into the last bar on the page) having being rubbed out and replaced (though Loewe omits the word "actually" from the revised version—probably due to a lack of space on the page). This all fits in with the evidence about final revisions to the song and shows that Loewe revised his personal manuscript to document the changes.

As before, the full score of the number is a complicated document rather than a consecutively written, neatly produced manuscript. It is the work of both Lang and Bennett and contains numerous modifications. Broadly speaking, bars 1–95 (up to "Oh, why can't the English learn to") are Bennett's orchestration, and 96 (from the key change at "set a good example") to the end are by Lang. The introduction seems to have caused a few problems: the original orchestration consisted of a solo clarinet giving Higgins his opening pitch (A) and the harp playing a D-major scale from A to A to strengthen the lead-in. This was rejected, and instead Bennett wrote a short A-major chord on all the instruments, perhaps to act as a more assertive introduction for Higgins. That in turn was crossed out, however, and the two-bar bassoon introduction that appears in the published score was added. Curiously, this, too, was crossed out, but was later reinstated for the published show. The first three pages of score contain significant alterations, usually with lines being taken away from one instrument and given to another or the harmony being filled out. There are also places where changes were indicated but went unused in the definitive version. An example is in bars 14 and 15, where Bennett added trumpet parts to accompany Eliza's cry of "Aooow," but the final orchestration does not include them. Another case is in bars 34–39, where the original orchestration was saturated with busy sixteenth notes in the flute and oboe parts; Bennett replaced them with a eighth-note motif on the trumpets' staves, indicating with arrows that they are for flute and oboe. Such examples are to be found throughout the score. Lang's part of the orchestration can be dated fairly accurately, because he clearly orchestrated the version shown on the lyric sheet from January 27 (i.e., almost the final version, but not quite). The line about the Americans is written in its sung version but crossed out and changed to allow for the new spoken line; the comment about the French is spoken but in the second person rather than the third; and the line "Use decent English" still appears. Aside from this, the final two bars have been crossed out and replaced with a new version on the subsequent page, proving that, no less than Lerner and Loewe, the meticulousness of the orchestrators knew no bounds.

In his autobiography, Lerner describes how the composition of both "Why Can't the English?" and "I'm an Ordinary Man" was the result of having met Harrison and evolved a style of music for him. Supposedly, the two songs took "about six weeks in all to complete."[47] "I'm an Ordinary Man" replaced "the totally inadequate" "Please Don't Marry Me" and was greeted with enthusiasm by Hart and Harrison.[48] The few surviving sources for the song uphold this image of a smooth creative process. Levin's papers contain the earliest version of the lyric, both as a loose lyric sheet and as part of the rehearsal script. The words are almost the same as in the published version, with a few minor edits.[49] Lerner's only substantial change improved one of his images: "I'm a quiet living man / Who's contented when he's reading / By the fire in his room" became "I'm a quiet living man / Who prefers to spend his evenings / In the silence of his room." Whereas the original picture merely portrayed Higgins as bookish, the replacement promotes the stony "silence of his room"; the point was not to show his scholastic side but his solitary, unsociable nature.[50]

Not surprisingly, the autograph score of "I'm an Ordinary Man" in the Loewe Collection is a fair copy. Although it does not match the published vocal score, it contains only one major difference.[51] The passage "Let them buy their wedding bands / For those anxious little hands" was originally punctuated by two imitative gestures in the music. These are crossed out but are still legible. The material in the second half of the song that repeats the earlier music is written out in shorthand with the melody alone; Loewe indicated with numbers where the piano part was to be copied from the first half of the song, suggesting the score was written for the use of the copyist. This is corroborated by the fact that Bennett's autograph full score uses the same earlier version of the lyric as Loewe's autograph. The orchestration is largely free of corrections and modifications: the one-bar flute melody following the line "free of humanity's mad inhuman noise" was cut, as was the nine-bar harp part after the thrice-repeated "Let a woman in your life" near the end, and there are some small additions of expressive markings and string bowings in pencil. Otherwise, the number does indeed seem to have been written with ease, as Lerner suggested.[52]

Like Eliza's "Just You Wait," Higgins's "Ordinary Man" is constructed with a freedom that helped to portray the two sides of Higgins—charm and arrogance—within the same number. The verse is roughly twelve bars long, and the gracefulness of the dotted rhythms, gently descending harmonic lines and flexed, rather than strict, triplets add to Higgins's charm, even if he is arrogant in his idealized description of himself. With the refrain comes a shift to the subdominant, E-flat major. A typical rising-and-falling Broadway thumb-line creates unrest while Higgins sings "But let a woman in your life," and many of his lines are punctuated by chromatic scales in the woodwinds. A sinister edge is added by the use of the subdominant minor on the lines "Then get on to the enthralling / fun of overhauling you." The larger gesture is that Loewe paints Higgins's description of himself in a tranquil light and his description of life with a woman as—literally—a nightmare: everything about the verses is relaxed, but the refrains are uneasy throughout, complete with howling high woodwind scales. This contrast is brought to a head at the end of the song, when Higgins turns on several phonographs with "gibberish voices" playing on them, while the music whips itself into a frenzy until Higgins suddenly turns them off and makes his final statement: "I shall never let a woman in my life." No less than in the Soliloquy from Rodgers and Hammerstein's *Carousel*, which has long been held up as the outstanding example of a musical monologue in loose form, Loewe is capable of tying together disparate musical strands to create an insight into a character's psyche.

Likewise, there are several different types of material in "A Hymn to Him," rather than a regular structure. The song begins without introduction, and the declamatory manner of the lyric for the verse is matched by a simple vamp accompaniment. A transition passage, during which Pickering calls the Home Office to get help in tracking down Eliza after she has bolted, takes us into D major, and the same material is repeated with a slight melodic variation. The refrain is a self-righteous march in 6/8 time (from bar 59). The use of compound duple time here is clever, because it allows the composer to mix a martial character with Higgins's characteristic elegance, whereas a straight common-time march could have been heavier. At bar 79, Loewe turns the ascending "Why can't a woman" theme on its head and writes a descending melody for "Why does ev'ry one do what the others do?" Then at bar 90, the music briefly moves into cut time as Higgins delivers his punch line ("Why don't they grow up like their father instead?"). This alternation of time signatures continues throughout the song, then in the final refrain Higgins finally comes clean and says what he has been thinking all along: "Why can't a woman be like me?"

"A Hymn to Him" was one of the final songs to be completed. Lerner explains that it was added after Harrison's worried reaction to the show during its first rehearsal: "His face grew longer and longer and his voice softer and softer. . . . Somehow Higgins had gotten lost in the second act and because this is the central story, I felt his concern was justified . . . I turned to Fritz and Moss and said that I thought Higgins needed another song in the second act."[53] Harrison confirms this chronology and motivation in his autobiography, adding that Lerner's wife invented the title "Why Can't a Woman Be More Like a Man?" and that the song did not reach him "until almost the last week of rehearsals."[54]

None of the pre-rehearsal outlines of the show contain a reference to the song nor does the rehearsal script, and there are no lyric sheets for the piece among the others in the Levin or Warner-Chappell materials. All of this confirms a late composition. However, the latter collection does contain an autograph piano-vocal score for the number.[55] The lyric, title, and vocal line are in Loewe's hand, while Rittmann is responsible for the rest of the material (accompaniment, expressive markings, etc.). She probably completed the score on the basis of Loewe's melody, perhaps with the accompaniment taken down by ear on hearing him play it on the piano. There are a couple of changes of lyric in this version of the song.[56] In two places, fragments of lyric dangle out of context, saying "Ready to see you" and "We're cold in the winter." Another small difference is that both the Rittmann/Loewe score and Lang's full score have "But by and large they [rather than 'we'] are a marvellous sex."[57] Otherwise, the lyric is familiar from the published version. The composer autograph in the Loewe Collection contains neither the introduction nor any sign that the original version of the lyric was ever present, so again this was probably written out later, perhaps for publishing purposes.

The Rittmann/Loewe autograph does contain a tantalizing musical difference, though. Whereas the published song begins without an introduction because Higgins speaks the first few words ("What in all of heaven"), this manuscript shows an extended introduction of nine bars (as shown in ex. 5.7), quoting five bars of "The Rain in Spain," followed by an echo of the introduction of "I Could Have Danced All Night." This creates an allusion to Eliza's two songs of triumph on learning how to speak properly, and makes it more obvious to the audience that the music of Higgins's "What in all of heaven . . ." is based on the introduction and verse to Eliza's "Danced." This makes new connections between both the characters (Higgins and Eliza sharing the same music) and the two acts (music from act 1 comes back in act 2 to link the two)—another instance of Loewe acting on both micro and macro levels.

One of Lerner and Loewe's golden moves in the show is the positioning of "I've Grown Accustomed to Her Face." By delivering it at the last moment they kept the tension high right through to the end of the story. On

Ex. 5.7. "A Hymn to Him," original introduction.

November 29, 1955, Lerner wrote to Harrison in the wake of having composed the number, telling him about the character of the song ("funny, touching") and its structure (a reprise soliloquy framed by new material):

> The big news of the letter is that we are practically finished with your second act number and our collective enthusiasm is boundless. I think it's going to be one of the most important things you'll do in the show— funny, touching in an odd way, and "Higgins" to a tee. We wrote a new song, which frames an entire interlude of a soliloquy that contains bits of "I Can See Her Now" and "I'm an Ordinary Man," all with new lyrics, of course. We want to let it marinate for a few days after it's finished, which is our custom . . . [T]he melody itself is very simple (only twenty bars).[58]

Lerner later claimed that "By the first week in December, Fritz and I had . . . begun work on what was eventually to become 'I've Grown Accustomed to Her Face.' . . . We finished 'Accustomed' a few days before Christmas."[59] Clearly this is not completely accurate, since Lerner's letter is explicit in both having found the "Accustomed" theme (lasting "only twenty bars") and having decided to return to existing themes. They must have begun work in mid-October or November.

That fits in well with Outline 4 (from around September 1955). Scene 6 of act 2 is set on the Embankment of the Thames at sunset, with Higgins and "Passersby (number to be determined)." The reference to the "Passersby" becomes clear in the rehearsal script. Between the sixth and seventh scenes of the second act is a page describing the scene change:

> (In the darkness the female voices of the Ensemble are heard singing
>   gaily)
>
> GAY FEMALES
> There'll be spring every year without you.
> England still will be here without you.
> I can still have a dream
> And it's liable to seem
> Even more like a dream
> Without you.
>
> I can do . . . I can do . . . (repeat)
> Without you . . . (repeat three times)
>
> (The voices trail off, as the next scene begins)

This was rather an odd transition—anonymous voices floating out of nowhere—though psychologically it illustrated how Eliza's song was echoing round Higgins's head. This little reprise was kept in the show until a fairly late stage: it is included in the copyist's piano-vocal score of "Accustomed to Her Face" used in rehearsals (several copies survive in the Warner-Chappell Collection), and there is also a five-part choral score (SSSAA) for the number, consisting of the "Without You" reprise.[60] The original version of the song began with the same two-bar flourish that the published version begins with; but instead of going to "Accustomed" via a short orchestral blast of the "Let a woman in your life" theme, the original had the "Without You" reprise, in G major (ex. 5.8). The repeated cries of "without you" at the end were written *a cappella* and ended on a G-major chord followed by a fermata. From there, Higgins was to launch into "Accustomed" without further introduction or transition.

Notably, the original version does not contain Higgins's opening words from the definitive version: "Damn! Damn! Damn! Damn!" A photocopy of a copyist's score marked up by Rittmann for Bennett's use shows that initially, although the "Without You" reprise was to be removed, it was not yet replaced by the thirteen-bar orchestral passage and Higgins's cries of "Damn!" (lasting three bars, making a total of sixteen). Rittmann simply crossed out the "Without You" material and above the first bar of the melody of "Accustomed" wrote: "orch. alone, *rich* but *mellow*." This brings the bar into line with the published version, in which Higgins says "I've grown accustomed to her face!" during a tacet, before the orchestra plays the first bar of music; then Higgins sings the next line (which Rittmann also indicates with "He sings:").[61] A separate two-page score, with "Intro to 'Accustomed'" on the front in Loewe's hand and the music in Rittmann's, gives the entire revised introduction including Higgins's opening blasts of "Damn!"[62]

Ex. 5.8. *"I've Grown Accustomed to Her Face," original introduction.*

The copyist's score contains even more unfamiliar material. Originally, Higgins's mid-song speech in which he introduces the idea of Eliza marrying Freddy was delivered over thirty-two bars of orchestral music that anticipated the "I can see her now, Missus Freddy Eynsford-Hill" section, which immediately follows (and which had also appeared in the cut "Come to the Ball"), rather than during an orchestral tacet.[63] Perhaps the most significant excision occurred to the reference to "I'm an Ordinary Man." Originally, Lerner and Loewe used a whole verse of the song:

I'm a most forgiving man:
Not inclined to be vindictive
Or to harbour any spite;
The sort of chap who when he's needed
Will come through with all his might.
A lenient man am I,
Who never bears a grudge;
The sort who never could,
Ever would,
Take a position and staunchly never budge.
Just a most forgiving man.

In the final version, lines two to seven (in italics) are cut, leaving a brief, five-line reminiscence. This allows the song to wear its looseness of form more lightly: by connecting the material more smoothly and lingering less on the "Ordinary Man" theme, it does not stand out so obviously and gains its own character rather than seeming too flagrantly pasted in from elsewhere.

There was one additional small change to the lyric, but otherwise the copyist's score runs in line with the published version up to the end of the sung section.[64] It does not, however, include the orchestral verse of "Accustomed" or the underscored reprise of "I Could Have Danced" that heralds Eliza's return. This material was provided by Rittmann in a handwritten piano score.[65] She addressed Bennett in a couple of sentences at the start: "Russell: At end of Soliloquy: one full chorus of "Accustomed" in F (strict Tempo di Rodgers—ma molto espressivo!!) for scene change into study (last scene of show)."[66] She then wrote out the last two bars of this full chorus and moved onto "I Could Have Danced," which is roughly in its final state. Below this, she wrote the familiar "Higgins: 'Eliza, where the devil are my slippers,'" but the final six bars of the show remain in B-flat major rather than moving to the definitive key, E flat. In Bennett's orchestration, however, the final phrase has already been changed to this key, so Rittmann or Loewe must have told him separately to do this. The orchestral score follows the copyist's score in terms of the lyric anomalies,[67] but there is no sign of the "Without You" reprise having been orchestrated. The only modification made to the orchestration itself is the removal of the flute in a couple of places during the refrain, where Bennett had originally written a doubling but later removed it.

At the very end of Rittmann's "Finale Ultimo" score are two notes written on top of each other. One, in the arranger's handwriting, says "Fine, grâce a dieu!" Underneath, Loewe added: "Moi aussi, Ami Fritz." Appropriately, this document—the very final page of the score—represents more clearly than any other the relationship that existed between Loewe, Rittmann, and Bennett. We know that Rittmann wrote out the music, because it is in her handwriting; we know that it was intended for and used by Bennett, because his name is on the front and he followed the score in his orchestration; and we know that Loewe saw the manuscript before it went to Bennett because he signed off on it at the bottom. If it seems surprising that some of Rittmann's piano-vocal scores predate some of Loewe's, here is ample evidence that the two worked in such close proximity that it did not really matter whose hand was holding the pencil; the overall authorial control was Loewe's. It is important to differentiate between the manuscripts and to understand where Loewe's hand is not present, but we can see from these notes at the bottom of the finale autograph that the interaction between Loewe, Rittmann, and Bennett was extremely close, and that their respect for each other was deep. Like all music theater, *My Fair Lady* was the result of collaboration.

"I've Grown Accustomed" is certainly the most complex piece of music in the show, at least from the point of view of structure; originally, it was an even greater summation of themes from the musical as a whole. The "Accustomed" theme acts as an outer structure heard at the beginning and end, in between which Loewe slots the "I can see her now," "Let a woman in your life" and "I'm an ordinary man" ideas from previous songs. The themes overlap and move at breakneck speed from one to the next, which is Loewe's way of increasing dramatic pressure at the end of the show. What makes the "Accustomed" theme particularly moving is its short melodic fragments, which almost give the impression of sobbing. It is also Higgins's slowest song. Overall, the number is engaging because of the way Higgins's neurotic thought processes are so vividly portrayed, and in particular the sense of loss he feels at Eliza's rejection. Her intention to marry Freddy heightens his anger, since Higgins considers this an inappropriate match. The use of voice in the final scene is also hugely effective: we hear Eliza on the gramophone before she returns physically, which makes the contrast between Higgins's despair (represented by having to switch on an artificial "version" of her) and his relief (at her return, when her real voice is present) all the starker. By hearing Eliza speak her final line—"I washed my face and hands before I came, I did"—live, in her post-training accent, we are also reminded of the education she has received from Higgins. This reference to the early stages of their relationship might be read as Eliza's capitulation to Higgins's authority because she has remembered what he gave her, in spite of his disrespectful treatment, rather than as a sign of the characters' romantic union.

6

SETTLING THE SCORE
• • •
PART II

THE UNDESERVING DOOLITTLE

One aspect of the show with which Shaw scholars have been particularly dissatisfied is the abbreviation of Doolittle's role and characterization. Yet this is to ignore the vitality he gains through his two songs, "With a Little Bit of Luck" and "Get Me to the Church on Time." The former is especially philosophical, with its rather cynical outlook, but the latter is arguably the more moving song, depicting with ruthless abruptness Doolittle's severance from the company he has kept all his life upon entering the respectable middle class. The composition of "With a Little Bit of Luck" is easy to document.[1] An early version of the lyric survives and is largely familiar. But there is a single verse, preceding the refrain, to which no music remains:

> It's a long and weary road we're on, old pal.
> It's a struggle all the way, a bitter fight.
> But keep your eye on your goal
> And with hope in your soul
> Everything will turn out right.[2]

There are also some deviations from the published text. For instance, "When you're tempted you will give right in" later became "When temptation comes you'll give right in."[3] There was also an extra chorus:

> The Lord above made man to be a dreamer;
> Gave him a bold, ambitious sort of mind.
> The Lord above made man to be a dreamer—but
> With a little bit of luck,
> With a little bit of luck,
> You will only dream the naughty kind.

As ever, Lerner's amendments represent a high level of self-criticism, while the cutting of the verse may have been motivated by shortening the song or avoiding the risqué image of the "naughty dream."[4]

Loewe's piano-vocal score is difficult to date, because it does not fit in with the other sources.[5] It contains the first verse, goes straight to the bridge, and ends with the final verse. The lyric follows the published version, though the place where there is a discrepancy between the rehearsal script and the published lyric shows signs of erasure. On the other hand, some of the rubbed-out letters are still legible, and it is clear that "to share his nest" did not originally say "to tend his needs" (as in the rehearsal script).[6] The score is very neat, and in spite of the absence of the repeat signs and first-time bar to allow for the second verse, the piano part is almost exactly the same as in the published vocal score, right down to details of articulation and dynamics. Loewe also uses the cue from the published script—"[It's just Faith,] hope and a little bit of luck!"—rather than the one in the rehearsal script ("It's just faith, hope and luck, boy. Faith, hope and luck."). The score shows no indication of any attempt to set the unfamiliar verse cited above, nor is there any sign of the cut "naughty dreams" verse. Confusingly, Loewe refers to Doolittle's friend as "Jimmy" rather than "Jamie," but in all other respects, it seems that this document dates from after rehearsals had started. Again, we can see that relying on the composer's manuscript alone can be problematic.

Most of the "Luck" full score is in the hand of Jack Mason. It contains a two-bar introduction, which was crossed out. This brings it into line with the published version, which starts with Doolittle speaking the first three syllables of the first verse while the orchestra joins in at the start of the first full bar.[7] Mason's score blocks out the song over sixteen pages, indicating the different verses (including the cut verse about "naughty dreams") with repeat signs. However, the third and fourth verses of the published song are separated by dialogue between Doolittle and some angry neighbors. This necessitates not only a repeat but two different endings to the song: one before the dialogue, and one at the end of the final verse. Since the song closes the scene, Bennett concocted a more conclusive ending for the final verse. As ever, the master orchestrator knew how best to serve the show.[8]

In his memoir, Lerner says that "Get Me to the Church on Time" was one of the last numbers to be composed. He claims it was finished "by the first week in December," corroborated by the fact that the title of the song is not included in Outlines 1–4 (see chap. 3).[9] The outlines do include a song at this point in the show, though—specifically, in Outline 4, a "rousing number by Doolittle and Ensemble." Mention is also made of an important sartorial issue, signifying the oncoming matrimony and thereby Doolittle's new social division from his former friends: "Doolittle will be in his striped trousers. Everybody else in Cockney garb, except, of course, Liza." The song seems to have stayed almost in its original form from composition to performance, with the exception of the opening verse material. The published song has a stanza sung by Doolittle's friends, Jamie and Harry, beginning "There's just a few more hours." The rehearsal script and a lyric sheet in the Warner-Chappell Collection, however, both follow this with two stanzas for Doolittle:

> If I had stayed a bachelor all my life,
> I could have had a beer in ev'ry pub in town;
> I would have met a dozen different girls a week;
> And every night put half a pint of whiskey down.

> There's just a few more hours
> That's left to have some fun;
> A few more hours
> For doing everything
> I would have done.

The lyric sheet has these verses crossed out, and no musical setting of the first of them has survived.[10] The autograph manuscript in the Loewe Collection might be taken to back up the view that these verses were originally set and then discarded; because the refrain is written on pages numbered 1 to 4 while the verse is marked "A" and seems to have been added to the front later, it is possible that all three stanzas of the original verse were set to music and then replaced by the single page in the Loewe Collection. On the other hand, the fact that the refrain starts on page 1 could mean that Loewe did not get round to setting the verse at all until it had been reduced to one stanza.

The autograph gives no more than a basic piano-vocal score of a single refrain. Following standard procedure, it was left to Rittmann to draft the dance music—no mean feat at over three hundred bars in length. Both Rittmann's autograph of this music and the photocopy of it used by the dance pianist have survived.[11] Rittmann's score is fluently written and contains various suggestions for orchestration, as well as some of the choreographic gestures; Miller's copy contains even more of these, presumably to orientate her during rehearsals. The climax of the dance is a return to the main theme of "Get Me to the Church" in double time, and Rittmann indicates it in shorthand, adding a note to Bennett: "Russell: follow song copy, as indicated, prego. For Coda, see pg.8." As promised, the following page contains the end of the dance, with a further message at the end: "or notes to that effect!"

Rittmann also provides the introduction to the chorale version of the final verse (when Doolittle's friends bid him farewell), but the vocal arrangement by Gino Smart is on a separate manuscript, showing the division of labor.[12] Two different orchestrations of the number survive: the original, and the final version. Both are by Lang, but although there are numerous small changes throughout, the main difference is that the revision is kinder on Doolittle's voice. Originally, Lang had the violins *divisi* doubling the melody in thirds, an octave higher than the vocal line; in the final orchestration, the violins double the vocal line in unison. The other big change is that the caesuras in the melody were punctuated by more assertive and aggressive fills from the brass and winds than is the case in the final version. To complete the texture, Lang went from having the brass play *pianissimo* and with mutes in the original to *mezzo forte* and open in the revision. There are changes in the dance section, too, but the majority concern coloristic nuance (the addition of a flute line doubling the melody, for instance); and the orchestration of the final version was simplified, removing scales and flourishes in favor of strong chords in contrary motion. Other than these, the decision to rewrite the whole orchestration seems to have been a matter of perfectionism rather than necessity, since much of it remained the same.

On one level, the song is absolutely tragic, ample evidence that Lerner and Loewe understood the depth of Doolittle's character. It is not merely an embellishment or divertissement but represents passage of time and depicts action. A breathtaking process of *chiaroscuro* (a contrast between light and dark) takes place during the course of the number. Most of the song is humorous: the beer-loving dustman ruefully drinks his way around London in the final hours before his wedding. Although the material is simple, Loewe puts in witty little touches such as the appoggiaturas on "married in the" to suggest Doolittle's "comfortable" nature. But suddenly, after the main part of the song and Rittmann's imaginative jig, "Dawn breaks over the Flower Market" and the revelry must end. To the music of the main refrain, Doolittle's friends suddenly adopt a hushed tone and provide their own harmonies (with only occasional horn and harp notes to maintain the pitch) in an unexpected farewell stanza, ending with "Good luck, old chum. / Good health, goodbye." The final four lines of the refrain are alternately marked *mezzo forte* and *pianissimo*, so that the actual "goodbye" is almost whispered. Doolittle's journey from obscurity to fortune is now over, and he departs from the show. Like Eliza, he has been both bruised and helped by Higgins's intervention, but in his case it is money, not education, that has caused this outcome. Through "Get Me to the Church" in particular, Lerner and Loewe make Doolittle into a figure of pathos, and they do so through both words *and* music.

The supposed inspiration for the creation of "On the Street Where You Live" is the subject of a romanticized anecdote in Lerner's memoir. He says that "When I was ten years old I had been sent to a dancing class on Sunday afternoons, white gloves and all. The prettiest girl was, of course, the most popular, but I was too shy to make my presence felt."[13] He goes on to describe how he sat outside what he believed to be her house every Saturday, only later to discover that she lived somewhere else. But in truth, other than its reference to a boy waiting outside the house of the girl he loves, Lerner's story bears little resemblance to the scene from *Fair Lady*—especially in the sense that Freddy Eynsford-Hill is not exactly shy in his advances. Outline 1 shows that the number was to have been sung in a scene where the spectators are shown leaving Ascot, and its purpose was always clear: "Freddy is absolutely smitten with Liza. (He may have a song about it.)"[14] This could be taken to disprove Lerner's story, because the song had been imagined in a setting that bore no resemblance to the tale; or it could be taken to corroborate it, because its title and final conception are very much bound to the idea of a boy waiting for his beloved on a street. Outline 4 mentions the song with the name by which it was known throughout rehearsals: "On the Street Where She Lives."[15]

Later in his book, Lerner elaborates on the development of the song during the New Haven previews, describing how the whole creative team, apart from Lerner himself, wanted to cut it. It even had a lukewarm reception from preview audiences. But Lerner became conscious that "perhaps the audience did not realize [Freddy] was the same boy who had been sitting next to Eliza and talking to her during the [Ascot] scene. . . . So as a last-ditch effort to save the song, we changed the verse . . . and replaced the flowery, romantic one he was then singing with one that echoed Eliza at Ascot, beginning with: "When she mentioned how her aunt bit off the spoon / She completely done me in, etc." Fritz changed the music accordingly and the new verse went in on Thursday night." The number "almost required an encore," Lerner concludes.[16]

He told the same story during a concert presentation in 1971, and what he referred to as the "original version" of the verse of "On the Street" was performed.[17] However, the performance was based on the published song sheet (from 1956), which contains just a section of the original verse, and in fact the number was originally more extensive than even this score suggests. The original lyric is shown in appendix 3 (with the cut passages in bold text). The second and third stanzas in this original version are what was printed in the published song sheet; the only difference is that the published version changes the tense from the third person to the second (so it becomes "Darling, there's the tree *you* run to," and so on). A copyist's piano-vocal score shows the number in its original form, complete with full verse (an extract is reproduced in exx. 6.1 and 6.2) and the whole refrain.

It is difficult not to conclude—more straightforwardly than Lerner—that these sections were discarded simply because they were insipid. The lyricist would have us believe that the verse was changed because people might not connect the character singing the number with the character having the dialogue with Eliza at the races, but the original lyric already referred to the Ascot scene ("Love attacked me while I was at the races"). The new verse ("When she mentioned how her aunt bit off the spoon . . .") also brought about an endearing comic moment in which Freddy strings together phrases

Ex. 6.1. "On the Street Where She Lives," original verse.

Ex. 6.2. "On the Street Where She Lives," original verse.

from Eliza's conversation at Ascot, leaving the audience to fill in the final word—"[move your bloomin'] arse" as a rhyme for "[a more enchanting] farce"—when Mrs. Pearce conveniently opens the front door of Higgins's house to interrupt him. The humor is pointed in the musical word-setting with pauses after "aunt" and "father," gentle prods in the audience's ribs to milk the laughs.

Lerner also makes no reference to the fact that sixteen bars were cut from the middle of the song (part of which is shown in ex. 6.3), reducing the refrain to its familiar sixty-six bars (AABA, each section consisting of sixteen bars, with an extension at the end). In itself, this evidently makes the song more rounded in form, which would have been AABCA. Furthermore, the melodic contours, harmony, and accompaniment style of this cut section do not sit easily with the rest of the song. But there is another possible reason for the cut. The section starting "Some men hate to wait and wait" bears a resemblance to the B section of Higgins's cut song "Please Don't Marry Me": "Some chaps see their lady fair / Always as she looked their wedding day. / Some chaps do but this I swear: / When you're old and ashen gray, I will see you just that way." Higgins's song is a declaration that he has no sympathy with women, whereas this section of Freddy's song states the reverse. The similarity between the constructions "Some men" and "Some chaps," and the subject in question, draws an automatic comparison between the numbers, while the messages they deliver are diametrically opposed. Had all this material remained in the show, it could have posited Freddy and Higgins more overtly as rival suitors for Eliza's affection.

The full score of the number reflects the changes made during rehearsals. Most of it is by Lang, and it gives the original version of the verse, but the original middle section of the refrain was cut before the song was orchestrated.[18] Attached to the back of the score is an orchestration for the final version of the verse in Bennett's hand; it also includes a revision of the orchestration of the four bars before the words "And oh, the towering feeling,"

Ex. 6.3. "On the Street Where She Lives," extract from cut section of original refrain.

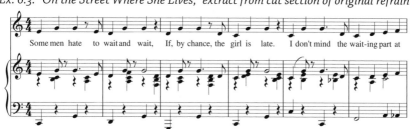

as well as the final four bars of the number.[19] Lang's part of the orchestration contains a couple of places where the harmonization has been slightly amended, but on the whole it was left as he originally wrote it. The composer's manuscript of the song in the Loewe Collection represents a post-composition document; it is fluently written and uses the published verse, as well as completely omitting the original middle section of the refrain.

Of the four key players in the drama, Freddy is the only one who does not undergo any kind of transformation.[20] The emotions of Eliza and Higgins veer throughout and Doolittle's change of social class affects his life (if not his personality), but Freddy is the constant, foolish romantic. This is best represented by the fact that when his first-act song returns in act 2, it does so without modification. Freddy is silly: he sings in rhyming couplets and romantic clichés, and, with Eliza's "I Could Have Danced," his song is one of only two based on a conventional lyric arch. But if his constancy is comically extreme—all he wants is to stand in the street where Eliza lives—it is also the crucial representation of Shaw's insistence that Freddy and Eliza marry after the story's conclusion. By making sure that Freddy stays in the story and looks after Eliza in her journey from Higgins's house to Mrs. Higgins's, Lerner and Loewe guarantee that we know that an Eliza-Higgins union is not inevitable, even if that is where the plot's main point of tension lies.

SERVANTS AND LESSONS

"The Servants' Chorus" is one of the show's most ingenious numbers. It allows Lerner and Loewe to give momentum to the series of lessons for Eliza—each lesson is punctuated by a single refrain, played a semitone higher and faster each time. The relationship between song and dialogue is at its most fluid here: the verses begin with one bar of introduction to give the servants their pitches, and the music fades out in every case to the middle of Higgins's next lesson, without musical closure. This was planned from the beginning: Outlines 1–4 all mention a montage of lessons. In Outline 4, the chorus appears both before and after "Just You Wait"; it is surely better that in the published version it comes afterwards only and propels us without interruption to "The Rain in Spain."

The content and number of verses were decided late in the day. The rehearsal script indicates five places during the scene where the chorus was to be sung, but no lyrics for the number are included. Unusually, there are two copies of the number in Loewe's hand: one in the Loewe Collection, and one in the Warner-Chappell Collection. Both plot out the first verse, though only the first page of the Warner-Chappell manuscript is in Loewe's hand, and even then, Rittmann wrote both the "Moderato" tempo marking and the whole of the second page. The Loewe Collection version is in G minor—the key in which it was orchestrated and published—and is fluently written. At the top of the first page, Loewe wrote "Alan—Call Moss: How many verses?" while at the bottom of the final page he has indicated: "Each verse ½ tone higher into 'Rain in Spain.'" That the lyric was written in pen (uniquely among the Loewe manuscripts) might, as Geoffrey Block has proposed, suggest that it was therefore a late addition, because the use of ink is a more final gesture than the more normal pencil.[21]

On the other hand, it is unclear which of the two manuscripts came first. After all, the Warner-Chappell version is in A minor, whereas the composer appears to have known that the final key would be G minor when writing the Loewe Collection version. Then again, that the Loewe Collection manuscript is entirely in the composer's hand and the Warner-Chappell one is in a mixture of both his and Rittmann's could point toward the latter being a subsequent version. At the bottom of the second page of the Warner-Chappell score is a message in an unknown hand indicating the verses and the keys they were to be written in next to them.[22] On the reverse, Loewe himself wrote more specific directions:

(1). As is (Cup of tea) G min
    (2). 3 (blackout) Higgins continues 4-5-6 A flat min
    (3). As is. 11th bar "How kind of you" (Orch.) blend to Higg.
    (4). As is (Rain in Spain) A min.

These slightly cryptic fragments indicate what dialogue the verses are to fade into, with a special case of enjambment in the second chorus where the servants end by counting the hours of the morning at which Higgins is working ("One a.m., / Two a.m. / Three . . .") followed by a quick blackout, after which Higgins continues the numbers by counting marbles into Eliza's mouth ("Four, five, six marbles").

Inserted into the score is a typed lyric sheet with four verses of the song. The published version has only three, but originally the following was the penultimate verse:

Stop, Professor Higgins!
Stop, Professor Higgins!
Stop we pray
Or any day
You'll drop, Professor Higgins!
Hours fly!
Weeks go by . . . !

Keith Garebian writes that the servants "sympathise with Higgins rather than Eliza" in this number, but this early lyric (which is also used in the copyist's piano-vocal score and Bennett's orchestration) shows that it was originally more sympathetic to him than it is in its published form.[23] In the cut verse, the servants encourage Higgins to "stop before he drops"; but Lerner and Loewe left in the far-from-sympathetic final verse, which tells him to "quit" before the servants do.

The climax of the lessons sequence is, of course, "The Rain in Spain." As Geoffrey Block has noted, there is a discrepancy between Lerner's account of when it was written and Harrison's autobiography, which names the song as one of those played by Lerner and Loewe for him at their initial meeting.[24] The actor claimed that at the time this was "the only number that really whizzed along," adding that it was "about all they had in the way of show tunes, and it was obviously a great one." Lerner, by contrast, says that the song was written later, during auditions in the summer of 1955. It was supposedly their only "unexpected visitation from the muses" and came as the result of Lerner's idea to write a song in which Eliza can now speak correctly all the things she has done wrong before. Since her main problem is with the letter A, Lerner suggested calling it "The Rain in Spain." This inspired Loewe to write a tango, taking only ten minutes to finish it. Since Outline 1 mentions both the song and its function in quite a lot of detail—"In the joy of the moment the line turns into a song, a Spanish one-step, which the three sing and dance jubilantly"—Lerner's chronology is clearly inaccurate. Furthermore, he obscures the chronological relationship between "The Servants' Chorus" and "The Rain in Spain," even though the latter was clearly one of the earliest songs and the former was one of the last to be finished.

Still, the ease that Lerner associates with its creation is upheld by the sources. Loewe's autograph score reproduces the vocal section of the song in its final version, though the dance music is not included, and as before, it is a fair copy, not an "original" manuscript. Although there are lines on the second and fourth pages where the music has been crossed out, these are the result of a slip of the pencil (p. 2) and perhaps the need to reuse manuscript paper that already had a small sketch of a different piece of music on it (p. 4, which has two-and-a-half bars of unrelated material crossed out at the top) rather than showing Loewe's evolving ideas. In most respects, the voicing is too well worked out and the writing too neat and fluent to allow us to consider this the initial result of Loewe's thought patterns. Once more, Rittmann composed the dance music. A negative photocopy of her piano score for the dance has survived, though the original pencil copy has not.[25] She indicates the righthand part only for the first fifteen bars, which are a continuation of the "Rain in Spain" music, but from bar 16 on (the "Jota" section from the change to triple time) she writes out the whole thing, including the final shout of "Olé" from Higgins, Eliza, and Pickering. Together, Loewe and Rittmann provided Bennett with all the information he needed to orchestrate the number, and his autograph score is clear of changes.

ELIZA ON SHOW: ASCOT AND THE BALL

Brief mention is due to the scene change music (No. 10a) that follows "I Could Have Danced" and leads quickly into "The Ascot Gavotte." This little snatch of music for solo trumpet takes up only two bars and eight notes (ex. 6.4) and was written by Lang on a blank system in the middle of Bennett's "I Could Have Danced" full score (in line with the final bars of that song). But there can be no doubt that Loewe is responsible for the theme, because it is an exact copy of the first two bars of the introduction of his 1941 song "The Son of the Wooden Soldier," written with lyricist John W. Bratton (ex. 6.5).[26]

Piecing together the score for the Ascot scene was complicated. The autograph score contained in the Loewe Collection is so brief that it does indeed seem to be the basis for the copyist's arrangements.[27] Loewe provided a three-page score containing a full verse of the song, completely harmonized. However, Rittmann stepped in to flesh out the number to its familiar proportions, and there are surviving fragments of her manuscripts for the dance section, the introduction, and the music that closes the scene (including the brief reprise).[28] Dance pianist Freda Miller's copy of the copyist's score is fully annotated to show how Rittmann's "Gavotte Dance" music was to be fitted into

Ex. 6.4. No. 10a, Scene Change.

Ex. 6.5. "The Son of the Wooden Soldier."

the middle of the sung verses. A separate photocopy of Rittmann's "Intro to Gavotte" manuscript, marked "Freda" at the top, shows a new, longer introduction for the final version,[29] as well as the original lyric, which had an extra verse and different words for the reprise (see appendix 4).[30] A lyric sheet from the Warner-Chappell Collection also indicates that originally, Eliza's shocking cry to close the scene was "Come on, Dover! Get the bloody lead out!"[31] This seems to have been kept into the rehearsal period: the copyist's choral score and conductor's score both contain two verses of the song, even after the new introduction and dance section had been added.[32] Bennett's full score also follows this version, but Lang intervened by adding two pages to end the first sounding of the song and thereby complete the number.

The end of the scene caused difficulties. In every extant version of the song, the chorus resumes with the "There they are again" section. However, Rittmann composed an original piece of "Fainting Music" (to follow Eliza's *faux pas*), which must have been rejected after it was first played. Rittmann's autograph contains a message that illustrates her collegiality toward Bennett: "Russell, mon cher, this is the end of the Ascot Gavotte. It would be loverly, if the orchestra could have a GEGENBEWEGUNG [counter-movement] from the bass up. Love Trude." Although her manuscript contains a chromatic scale descending two octaves, Rittmann requests a contrary motion gesture from the orchestrator; her sketch of the piece survives on the bottom of a photocopy of her "Gavotte Reprise" autograph.[33] Orchestra parts titled "Fainting Music" have survived, presumably representing Bennett's loose interpretation of Rittmann's score.[34] Bennett's autograph full score for the scene contains its now-familiar ending, however, and there is no sign of the "Fainting Music." Since there is no surviving autograph piano score of the final version of the section, we will probably never know who wrote it. But the first four bars of the music that follows Eliza's cry of "Move your bloomin' arse" were clearly added after the rest and were written on a separate page with its own title ("Intro to End of Gavotte"), suggesting this was a late addition.

The only drastic change made to the show during its out-of-town tryouts was the excision of "Come to the Ball," the "Dress Ballet," and "Say a Prayer for Me Tonight" in the penultimate scene of act 1. These numbers were replaced by a short scene between Higgins and Pickering, after which Eliza enters the hallway underscored by "I Could Have Danced All Night" before moving straight to the Ball scene. This excision had an impact on other numbers, too. Various stages were gone through between the deletion of "Say a Prayer" and the definitive version of the show. There are at least sixteen different sources for this part of the show, including piano scores in the hands of Loewe, Rittmann, Bennett, and an unknown copyist; orchestral parts; and Bennett and Lang's full scores. Together, these sources amount to more than a hundred pieces of paper, many of which are fragments and in some cases may not have been used in any form.

The genesis of the waltz music was as much a question of arrangement as of composition. Here, Rittmann came into her own as the dance arranger. Five of the sources for the music of the end of act 1 contain her handwriting, either entirely or as annotations of others' work. One piano score is in Bennett's hand, and another is in Lang's. Originally, the end of "Say a Prayer" segued straight into a piece of music called "Ballroom Intro" and from there into "The Embassy Waltz" via the "Processional." The conductor's piano scores of "Ballroom Intro" and "Processional" (which are bound together) are in two hands; Bennett's is recognizable on the front page, but the other is of an unknown copyist.[35] The "Intro" is a clever reworking of "Say a Prayer" into a Viennese waltz (first in D major, then E-flat major). At that point, it runs into the "Processional" in A-flat major, which is a four-bar version of the ten-bar published introduction to "The Embassy Waltz." Geoffrey Block has noted that this piece of music—later retitled "Introduction to Promenade"—is derived from "Say a Prayer," and now it becomes more apparent why: it is a continuation of the gradual dissolution of the "Say a Prayer" music into "The Embassy Waltz."[36] Consequently, the "Introduction" music was better integrated into the musical canvas when "Say a Prayer" was still in the show, since it alluded to Eliza's nerves when she arrived at the ball, albeit transformed into a guise that was appropriate to the grand setting. When it was removed, there was no motivation for invoking the theme, a redundancy of meaning caused by musicians working at top speed during an intense period of creativity. It is only on this very pedantic level that one can find flaws in the show.

Of the numerous sources for this number, there are two main versions. The basis for the first is a score titled "The Pygmalion Waltzes," which exists in two different versions in the Loewe and Warner-Chappell Collections. Both start off with two pages of photocopies, which have been annotated and then added to. The title on the front page is in Rittmann's hand, but the two photocopied pages of music are in Loewe's hand. The remaining five pages in the Loewe Collection version are in Rittmann's writing, and consist of photocopies with pencil annotations (also by Rittmann); the Warner-Chappell version has those five pages plus another two, again photocopies rather than originals. Corresponding almost exactly to the Warner-Chappell version is a complete set of instrumental parts in the same collection.[37] Interestingly, this version does not contain the main theme of the published "Embassy Waltz," even though the orchestral parts are given that title. Instead, the main theme of this earlier waltz (shown in ex. 6.6) was totally discarded. It resurfaced in the 1964 film version of the show, when it underscores the part of the Ball scene when Higgins and Pickering observe Eliza being the attention of the room, following her commendation from the Queen of Transylvania. As with the "Dress Ballet," Rittmann mapped out the entire number, and it was orchestrated, without major amendment, by Bennett.[38] The orchestration of the preceding "Intro to Ball" is by Lang, with the exception of the first page, which is in Bennett's hand.[39]

Why this original waltz was discarded is unclear. The excision of the two songs and the ballet automatically changed the nature of the closing of the act, but that does not explain why the waltz theme was changed. It might be that Loewe felt that with its numerous accidentals and harmonic clashes, the music was a little too sardonic, almost sinister, for the romantic scene that was to unfold. The replacement, after all, is smoother and more fluent; it glides but does not draw attention to itself. There are several sources for the published "Embassy Waltz," and yet again the Loewe autograph is not the "original" manuscript. It was clearly created after a score titled "New Waltz," which is in Rittmann's hand and contains corrections where she considered different possibilities. This is a draft that actually bears a direct relationship to the performance, because it is full of directions to Bennett about the orchestration. By contrast, Loewe's manuscript is so fluent and free of errors that it is obviously a later creation. Nevertheless, the presence of notes on the front cover about a rehearsal venue makes it likely that it was produced sometime during the rehearsals or tryouts (rather than being a fair copy for use in the production of the vocal score, for instance). No copy of "Eliza's Entrance" has survived among the Warner-Chappell materials, and there is no Loewe manuscript for it. Presumably, the fact that it is the music of "I Could Have Danced All Night," re-orchestrated for its dramatic purpose, meant that Lang was simply told to base his orchestration on a straight copy of the song. However, an earlier version of the entrance has survived; it consists of the same thematic material, orchestrated for *tutti* rather than just the strings (as in the final version). It is also in A major rather than the definitive G major. Lang orchestrated the final version, but Bennett took over for the "Intro to Promenade" and the whole of "The Embassy Waltz," leading to the end of act 1.

Ex. 6.6. "The Pygmalion Waltzes," original ball music.

Once again, four different sources for the Entr'acte highlight the composer-arranger-orchestrator relationship: a piano score in Loewe's hand, another in Rittmann's hand, the full score, and an early or alternative orchestration of the end of the Entr'acte. Rittmann's autograph piano score is the earliest of these.[40] As the number follows conventional musical theater entr'acte medley form, Rittmann writes out the introduction and transition passages but only indicates the beginning and end of each of the statements of the three songs sounded in the number ("I've Grown Accustomed," "I Could Have Danced," and "Little Bit of Luck"). However, she provides no conclusion. The manuscript introduces three bars of the "Little Bit of Luck" theme, and then underneath indicates: "And a big glorious Russell Bennett finish!!" Bennett's full score follows Rittmann's outline up to bar 110 (the middle of the chorus of "With a Little Bit"); the second half of the chorus has been crossed out, then the melody of the song picks up again. Bennett seems to have written out more of "Luck" than was desired, so several pages have been crossed out.

The original ending of the Entr'acte was also discarded completely, and extra music was added to the end, orchestrated by Lang and stuck onto the rest of the score.[41] Appended to the full score is a manuscript called "End of Temp[orary] Entr'acte" in Bennett's hand. The word "Out" has been written across the middle, indicating that it was cut, though this music later became the final sixteen bars of the show's "Exit Music." There is another score in Lang's hand titled "Finish of Entr'acte," which brings the tally of endings to the number to three; clearly, the piece was more difficult to write than might be expected.[42] That leaves the difficult task of placing Loewe's autograph score in the process. Like Rittmann, Loewe indicates the sections where "Accustomed" and "Danced" are to be sounded, but he writes out the final abbreviated version of "Luck" and continues straight to the end. The fact that he reproduces the completed version of the number suggests he wrote it out for his own reference, or perhaps for the vocal score.

Lerner tells us little about the genesis of "You Did It." He mentions that it was written during the middle of 1955, and recounts a story about the supposed meeting between Lerner, Levin, Loewe, and Michael Kidd, when the latter was approached to be the choreographer of *My Fair Lady*; Lerner claims that Kidd said "You Did It" was "wrong" because "it's describing offstage action" and that as a result, Moss Hart refused to have Kidd on the show.[43] However, as we saw in chapter 2, Hart was certainly not part of the creative team at the time when the meeting with Kidd took place, so at least part of the story must be inaccurate. Lerner's only other mention of the song is in a passage about the Philadelphia tryout. He says that he and Loewe tried to improve the song one night by adding a "proper climax" to a section in the middle with the words "I know each language on the map, said he, / And she's Hungarian as the first Hungarian rhapsody." According to Lerner, Harrison "loved" the new lines, but "the night they went in he forgot every lyric in the entire show," whereupon they were removed.[44]

Lerner's story is confirmed by the compositional sources for the show, but he does not mention that the song was partly cut as well as added to. A lyric sheet from the Levin Collection, various copyist's scores from the Warner-Chappell Collection, Bennett's full score, and Loewe's piano-vocal score all indicate two extra sections that are not included in the published vocal score.[45] None of these contains the section Lerner refers to as having been added late in the day (though he misleads us slightly by suggesting that only two lines were added; it was in fact a stanza of four lines, beginning "'Her blood,' he said, 'is bluer than the Danube is or ever was!'").[46] The first excision involved condensing the first return of the opening theme. Pickering sings three sections, starting "Tonight, old man, you did it" (A), "I must have aged a year tonight" (B) and "I said to him, 'You did it!'" (A), respectively. Originally, the return of A was as long as its original statement:

Pickering

I said to him, 'You did it!
You did it! You did it!
I didn't think it possible
But there she is!

I told you to forget it;
I warned you'd regret it.
And now a prince is telling her
How fair she is.

I was as excited
And agog as I could be.

Higgins

It was nonsense. Silly nonsense.[47]

Pickering

I was more uneasy,
More afraid than even she.

Higgins

Of course. Of course.
Dear chap, of course you were.
It didn't mean half as much to her.

Pickering

You absolutely did it!
You did it! You did it!
They thought she was ecstatic
And so damned aristocratic,
And they never knew that
You did it!

Eventually, the first two lines of Pickering's first stanza and the last four of his final stanza were welded together and the rest discarded. The change shortened the number and thereby increased its musical pressure, and also removed the comments made by Higgins and Pickering that vigorously insult Eliza. Pickering asserts that he was more afraid about the ball than Eliza was, while Higgins agrees that the episode did not mean "half as much to her" as it did to the Colonel. This represents something of a turn of character for Pickering: though the entire song finds him less sympathetic than normal toward Eliza, the point is that the men ignore her after her triumph, rather than being actively insulting.[48] Likewise, for Higgins to say "It didn't mean half as much to her" demonizes him in a way that the rest of the song does not.

The other change was probably for musical rather than dramatic considerations. Originally, the final section of the song—when Pickering and the servants sing a contrapuntal passage following "Congratulations, Professor Higgins!"—was more extensive (see appendix 5). The published version contains only the first and last stanzas of this initial lyric (with a couple of minor changes), and the majority of the material at this point was cut. Interestingly, this music contains a different gesture to anything else in the show (partly quoted in ex. 6.7). Although the "Congratulations!" passage is contrapuntal even in its published form, the antiphonal effects between Pickering and the servants in the original version made the number stiffer, more like an operetta ensemble, and thereby more old-fashioned. In spite of William Zinsser's insistence that Lerner and Loewe "were a throwback to the earlier generic team of Gilbert and Sullivan" and that Loewe's music "continued to sound Viennese," the composer in fact removed the passage of music that most connected the show to these styles of composition.[49]

Ex. 6.7. *"You Did It," cut passage.*

This cut also represents an act of compression: it drives the piece home more quickly, more smoothly, and more breathtakingly. One notable aspect of the passage was the return of a second earlier theme ("I must confess without undue conceit," deriving from "Now wait, now wait, give credit where it's due") in addition to the "You did it!" theme. The latter remained in the published version but only as a contrapuntal underpinning of the new "Congratulations!" theme; the barer "I must confess" part and the antiphonal section as a whole draw attention to themselves more assertively. By removing them, Loewe gave the closing section the air and function of an operatic *stretta* but foreshortened it to avoid direct allusion.

Loewe's triumph in *My Fair Lady* was to create a score that truly enhances the potential of *Pygmalion* yet without overwhelming or undermining that text with extraneous musical numbers. Surely "Why Can't the English?" depicts Higgins's character better than any dialogue could, while the lessons sequence is a series of musical scenes with little precedence in the musical theater repertoire. This also represents a clear enhancement of Shaw's text. Furthermore, theatrical technique is apparent throughout the score; for instance, "The Embassy Waltz" is a compelling use of musical diegesis, where the music is both part of the onstage action and expressive of the emotion of the scene. As for musical technique, the range of compositional approaches is brilliant, whether in the use of dance forms in the creation of songs like "Show Me" and "Just You Wait" or large-scale forms as in "You Did It," as is the no less impressive way in which Loewe binds it all together. In this, he shares the credit with his colleagues: Rittmann's arrangements and the orchestrations of Bennett, Lang, and Mason helped make the score contrapuntally taut and gave it its magical palette of sonorities.

But in the end, Lerner and Loewe's most impressive achievement was the way in which they eventually balanced the Higgins-Eliza relationship in their songs. We have seen numerous examples of songs discarded as inappropriate ("There's a Thing Called Love"), replaced by better numbers ("Please Don't Marry Me" into "An Ordinary Man"), replaced by songs with a completely different subtext ("Shy" into "I Could Have Danced All Night"), or refined to remove gestures of conventional romance ("You Did It"). Although it is relatively commonplace for large numbers of songs from Broadway shows to be discarded before completion or cut before opening night, it is rare to find quite such a clear motivation for their removal as in *My Fair Lady*.

7
PERFORMANCE HISTORY
● ● ●
MY FAIR LADY ON STAGE

The performance history of *My Fair Lady* has been characterized by long runs and critical success. The original Broadway production ran for more than six years and 2,717 performances, and in so doing overtook Rodgers and Hammerstein's *Oklahoma!* to become the longest-running Broadway show to date; it maintained this record for nearly a decade. The original cast won almost universal raves, both on Broadway and in London, and in 1964 the show went on to be adapted into one of the most successful movie musicals of all time, winning eight Academy Awards. The show was also seen internationally, including a tour to Russia at the height of the Cold War as part of a goodwill exchange with America. Broadway revivals in 1976 and 1981 returned to the original designs, choreography, and direction for inspiration, and three of the original 1956 cast members returned to their original roles. A further revival in 1993 continued this pattern, as Stanley Holloway's son, Julian, took on his father's role of Alfred Doolittle. Trevor Nunn's 2001 production at London's National Theatre quickly transferred to the West End, where it ran for 1,000 performances before touring first the UK and then the United States to mark the musical's fiftieth anniversary. A new film version is currently in pre-production, which will make it one of the few musicals from Broadway's golden age to enjoy two big-screen adaptations. Clearly, the show has a special place in the repertoire. This chapter explores its legacy in the theater, both in terms of trends and gestures in productions of the piece and how it was received by critics.

ORIGINAL BROADWAY PRODUCTION (1956)

Variety was one of the first publications to review the show. Its critic saw the premiere at the Shubert Theatre in New Haven on January 4 and reported: "[The show] has so much to recommend it that only a radical (and highly improbable) slipup in the simonizing process can keep it out of the solid click class."[1] This was the first of many ecstatic responses that the work would receive and is littered with gushing statements such as "George Bernard Shaw . . . never had it so good as with this lavish production," "a glove-fitting score," "stellar direction," and "a general aura of quality." A week later, *Variety* published a short article stating that fifteen minutes of the show's running time was cut during the New Haven run (which ended on February 11), largely consisting of the "Come to the Ball" number. "Say a Prayer for Me Tonight" and the "Decorating Eliza" ballet were reported to have been cut after the New Haven closure but before the start of the Philadelphia tryouts on February 15. The article also said that "Local reaction to the musical set a new high for the last six years, rivaling that for the break-in stand of *South Pacific* at the same house in the spring of 1949."[2]

This critical and popular success was to be more than matched when the show reached Broadway. The early reviews underline certain elements of the work that continue to inform its critical reception to this day. The first is the musical's Shavian precedent, which was mentioned by all the reviewers. This is one of the points on which they were most divided. Some were highly complimentary of Lerner and Loewe's work; for instance, Robert Coleman in the *Daily Mirror* said that Lerner's lyrics had "kept the essence of the original" and that they "beautifully complement the Shavian dialogue."[3] Similarly, William Hawkins in the *New York World-Telegram* claimed that *Pygmalion* "has been used with such artfulness and taste, such vigorous reverence, that it springs freshly to life all over again."

Most of the other leading critics made a point of attributing much of the musical's success to Shaw. John Chapman's review for the *Daily News* described *My Fair Lady* as a "musical embellishment of Bernard Shaw's romantic comedy," and went on to say that Lerner and Loewe "have written much the way Shaw must have done had he been a musician instead of a music critic." The word "embellishment" here seems pointed; though not entirely pejorative, it portrays the composer and lyricist as having merely decorated something that was already there, rather than adapting the play as radically as they did. Similarly, Chapman's comment about composing "as Shaw must have done" to some extent denies the imagination of Lerner and Loewe's approach: it is as if their creation was pastiche rather than original. Three of the other reviewers were even more direct on the subject. John McClain's *Journal American* review refers to the fact that Shaw's text had not been "tamp[ered with] too much," while Richard Watts Jr. in the *New York Post* wrote: "In handing out the allotments of praise, I suppose it would be a good idea to begin with Bernard Shaw. As a librettist, he is immense." The latter comment apparently puts Lerner out of the picture as the show's book writer. Along similar lines, Brooks Atkinson's review in the *New York Times* contained the comment, "Shaw's crackling mind is still the genius of *My Fair Lady*."

In sum, although all the critics seemed to have hugely enjoyed the musical, they were almost united in denying Lerner and Loewe credit for its success, in spite of Lerner's large number of departures from Shaw in his book. Of course, they did have a point, since more of Shaw's play remains in the musical than would normally be the case, but one of the reasons for their stance is probably that they were drama specialists who all revered *Pygmalion*, rather than music specialists with an interest in the process of making it into a musical. The comments on the music almost speak for themselves: "Unpretentious and pleasantly periodic" was McClain's description; "robust" was Atkinson's adjective for the score; "they certainly are clever" said Hawkins of the songs.

In addition to overemphasizing Shaw's contribution and lacking the space (or knowledge) to do justice to Loewe's music, the critics' comments on the Eliza-Higgins relationship are fascinating, not the least because there is no consensus. Atkinson refers to "love music" and describes Higgins as "a bright young man in love with fair lady." Coleman is likewise certain that Harrison is "the Pygmalion who falls in love with his creation," and McClain mentions Higgins's "revelation," hinting at a "Cinderella" romance. John Beaufort agrees, stating that Higgins's "single-minded preoccupation with Eliza's education makes him almost overlook Eliza until it is too late." On the other hand, Hawkins makes no comment on the subject, focusing on "the effort to make the lady of Eliza," and the same goes for Chapman, Kerr, and Watts; none of these critics say that the characters are in love, or even seem to hint at it. This is a useful point of reference for subsequent interpretations of the piece: from the very start, the nature of Higgins and Eliza's relationship was never absolutely defined.

This point was continued on March 25, when Brooks Atkinson returned to the show and wrote another article, headed: "Shaw's *Pygmalion* Turns into One of the Best Musicals of the Century."[4] The beginning and end of the new review refer to romance but hint that Atkinson is trying to backtrack from his firm portrayal of the supposed love between Eliza and Higgins. He admits that one of the other critics had pointed out that "the hero and heroine never kiss," and that *My Fair Lady* "reflects Shaw's lack of interest in the stage ritual of sex." Significantly, Atkinson also discusses Shaw's decidedly unromantic epilogue to *Pygmalion*, and in the phrase "Eliza's life in an imagined future is beside the point" underlines a major issue: since these are characters rather than real people, they do not have "life" beyond the final curtain and cannot be assumed to be joined in matrimony. Aside from this,

Atkinson's overwhelming message is simple: "*My Fair Lady* is the finest musical play in years."

RECORDING THE ORIGINAL BROADWAY CAST ALBUM (MARCH 25, 1956)

CBS's financing of the original production was not merely a good investment because of the outstanding ticket sales. That their record label, Columbia Records, could put out the original cast album ultimately earned them a huge amount of money. On October 2, 1957, the *New York Times* reported that the album had sold over a million copies already. By March 3, 1962, *Billboard Music Week* was able to confirm that the LP had sold over 3.5 million copies to date; it was also the first album in history to exceed both two and three million sales. In the same article, it was estimated that the sales of the Broadway and London cast recordings had grossed over $15 million, on an investment of roughly $40,000.[5] These figures attest to the fact that the album was a phenomenon in itself; as a way of disseminating the content of the show to society in general, it had even greater impact than the stage production.

Goddard Lieberson, who was the producer of many Broadway albums for Columbia in this period, took the cast into the Columbia Thirtieth Street Studios on March 25 to record the show. As was usually the case, the album was to be recorded within a single day and released as soon as possible to maximize sales. (Symptomatic of the speed of turnaround is an error on the initial batch of albums, which retained the early title of "I want to dance all night" on the sleeve covers, because they were preprinted before the lyric change was made. Stanley Holloway's billing was also smaller than agreed, and Phil Lang's name was omitted.)[6] Also following tradition, the album was prepared based on providing the best aural experience for the listener, rather than simply recording what was heard in the theater. This had two main manifestations: changing details of the performance, and changing the text. In the former category, we can include modifications to the tempos—sometimes numbers would be done faster or slower in the theater according to the practical needs of the production, such as a scene change or accommodating a singer taking time to warm up at the start of the show—while the latter category includes increasing the number of players in the orchestra (for instance, to enhance the quality of the sound of the string section), re-arranging material, and omitting dialogue. Some of these considerations are especially interesting in relation to *My Fair Lady*. Although it was normal not to record an entire score,

Table 7.1. Examples of changes made to the text for the original cast album

Song title	Comments
Why Can't the English?	No introduction
Wouldn't It Be Loverly?	Spoken lines omitted; no introduction to the buskers' verse; dance break reduced
With a Little Bit of Luck	Introduction added; both instances of the song are combined into one number, with the dance music from the reprise
I'm an Ordinary Man	New introduction
The Servants' Chorus	Final verse only
The Rain in Spain	Dialogue reduced
I Could Have Danced All Night	Verse 3 uses Verse 1's orchestration
On the Street Where You Live	No verse; no dialogue in middle
You Did It	Introduction cut; no Mrs. Pearce
Show Me	Short introduction
Get Me to the Church	"For Gawd's sake" changed to "Be sure and get me"
A Hymn to Him	Only parts of Pickering's lines retained
Without You	New introduction and ending; Higgins's lines cut, including ending
I've Grown Accustomed to Her Face	Orchestration of strings in first chorus reduced to a solo violin, performed an octave lower; no dialogue at the end

it was curious that a musical highlight like "The Embassy Waltz" went unrecorded on the album. Some of the other changes are noted in table 7.1.

CHANGING CASTS

The three principal members of the original cast continued until November 28, 1957, when Rex Harrison left the show.[7] Stanley Holloway succeeded him on December 13, 1957, when he was granted permission to sever his contract early in order to be able to sail home on the Queen Mary before Christmas.[8]

Julie Andrews also asked to leave the show a little earlier than planned in order to have more of a break before starting rehearsals for the London production of the show. However, because Sally Ann Howes, who was to take over from Andrews,[9] was not available until February 3, 1958, Herman Levin refused Andrews's request, even though Lerner and Loewe were willing.[10] This meant that she departed on February 1 as originally planned, and started rehearsals for the London version on April 7.

Sally Ann Howes as the second Broadway Eliza Doolittle in
My Fair Lady *(Photofest)*

Filling the original cast's distinguished shoes was by no means an easy task. As early as 1956, Levin was already in discussion with agents about possible replacements. For instance, the British character actor Bill Owen auditioned for Doolittle's part, but after prolonged deliberation Levin balked at the idea of paying him $1,000 per week.[11] Lerner and Loewe also went to London to audition stage star Douglas Byng, but eventually Ronald Radd, best known for his television appearances, was hired to replace Holloway.[12] Levin also had ambitions to have major names succeeding Harrison in the role of Higgins: a letter dated March 20, 1956, indicates that the producer once more tried to interest Michael Redgrave in the show, even though it had only just opened on Broadway.[13] Since Harrison was committed to the production for only twelve months, Levin was concerned about sustaining its initial success: a telegram from Lerner to Levin on November 15, 1956, indicates that they had managed to get John Gielgud to agree to portray Higgins until March 1957 if Harrison refused to extend his contract. Lerner and Levin were intending to use Gielgud's commitment as a bargaining tool: "We can no[w] put pressure on Harrison to sign at least till June or lose London."[14] This reveals how important it was to Harrison to introduce the musical to British audiences.

A month later, Moss Hart took the role to Noël Coward, another star name who had been associated with the show at an early stage, but was again turned down.[15] In the end, Harrison's replacement was Edmund Mulhare, an Irish actor without Harrison's star name but who had filled in for his predecessor during vacations. Robert Coote (Pickering), Cathleen Nesbitt (Mrs. Higgins) and Christopher Hewitt (Karpathy) had long left the show, so with a fresh cast to review, Brooks Atkinson wrote an extensive article about the show on March 9, 1958.[16] He acknowledged that the new cast had "not been able to duplicate perfection," but still raved about the quality of the writing, design, and production. Nothing could stop *My Fair Lady* now. On July 12, 1961, it became the longest-running musical in Broadway history, and through several more cast changes, plus two changes of theater (to the Broadhurst and Broadway theaters) in the final year of the run (1962), it was clear that the public had taken the show to its hearts, regardless of who was in it.[17]

One curious aspect of its reception was the number of parodies that were written, especially during the original run. For example, in 1957 the composer Dean Fuller and the lyricist Marshall Barer wrote a sketch titled "My Late, Late Lady" for the *Ziegfeld Follies*, starring Beatrice Lillie; among the references to *My Fair Lady* was a pastiche of "The Rain in Spain" containing the lines "the sink doesn't stink any more" and "I had a bawth last night."[18] Another, more lasting project was a spoof recording put out on the Foremost record label in 1956, called *My Square Laddie*. This turned the *Fair Lady* story on its head and had Broadway veteran Nancy Walker (who had appeared in shows such as *On the Town*) teaching British actor Reginald Gardiner how to speak in an authentic Brooklyn dialect. Again, the references to Lerner's lyrics are numerous, with such song titles as "What Makes a Limey Talk so Square?" "It's De Oily Boid," and "I'm Kinda Partial to his Puss."[19] These and other such attempts to cash in on the success of *Fair Lady* invoked consternation in the Levin camp, yet in retrospect they are fascinating as items that show the extent to which the musical had been absorbed into American culture.

ORIGINAL LONDON PRODUCTION (1958)

My Fair Lady was always a natural choice for London's theater scene. As early as 1952, when Lerner and Loewe were still pursuing Mary Martin to play the role of Eliza, they even considered giving the piece its world premiere in the city of its original setting. The original London production was unusual in containing all four of the Broadway principals; notwithstanding isolated examples such as Mary Martin's appearance in the original London *South Pacific*, it was almost unheard of for a major Broadway show to be brought to England with production and cast practically in tact. Evidently, Harrison, Andrews, Holloway, and Coote wanted to return home victorious after conquering Broadway. Tickets for the London production went on sale on October 1, 1957, and Reuters reported that on the first day alone, more than $15,000 was taken by the box office (which was accepting sales up to October 1959).[20] Hugh Beaumont was finally able to benefit from the deal he had made with Levin in 1955 to release Harrison from *Bell, Book and Candle* so that rehearsals for *Fair Lady* could begin: the right to produce the show in London automatically gave him control over the hottest ticket in the West End. To complete the cast, he chose Betty Wolfe as Mrs. Pearce, Leonard Weir as Freddy, and Zena Dare as Mrs. Higgins. A veteran of the West End, Dare made her final stage appearance in this show. She stayed with the production for the entire five-and-a-half-year run, then going on tour with it until she decided to retire completely. Another important figure in the British production was Cyril Ornadel, a renowned West End musical director who also had considerable success as a composer of musicals.[21]

Loewe was unable to attend the London opening because he had suffered a heart attack on February 26 before he was due to leave New York. Hart, Levin, and Lerner had to go to London and open the show without him.[22] The premiere took place on April 30 at the Theatre Royal, Drury Lane, and the success of the Broadway run was repeated. In spite of such high expectations, arguably heightened because of the reverence for Shaw in England, the London critics were largely very positive: the *New York Times* described it as "triumphant," the *Evening News* said that it "came near perfection," and the *News Chronicle* even went so far as to note that "the critics themselves looked excited for once."[23] Kitty Carlisle Hart commented that "In London everyone was in a fever of excitement. The British felt that it was Shaw and Eliza Doolittle coming home." After a triumphant premiere on April 30, the Queen and Prince Philip attended a Royal Command Performance on May 5, coming backstage to meet the cast following the show.[24]

The production went on to run for 2,281 performances, again a huge achievement, especially given the much larger capacity of the Theatre Royal, Drury Lane (with more than 2,000 seats), compared to the Mark Hellinger on Broadway (approximately 1,500 seats). So successful was the London incarnation of the show that Columbia decided to record the British version, even though the four principals were the same. The introduction of two-track stereo recording equipment had taken off since the mono recording of the Broadway cast was made, so the opportunity to make a stereo version was irresistible. The recording took place on February 1, 1959, again under the direction of producer Goddard Lieberson. In general, the vitality and spontaneity of the original is not quite present on the London cast album, no doubt because the stars had performed it so many times, but Julie Andrews has recently declared her preference for the stereo version (which she describes as being "light years better than the original").[25]

RUSSIAN TOUR OF 1960

The international distribution of *My Fair Lady* was extraordinary for its time. Although it was by no means the first show to travel beyond the English-speaking peoples, it achieved an unprecedented success in important cities all over the globe, the only major exception being Paris. Australia was the first of many countries to follow the West End production in replicating the Broadway original in January 1959, and it was followed by locations as diverse as Germany (1961), Iceland (1962), Vienna (1963), Japan (1963), Italy (1963), and Israel (1964).[26] By far the most curious, though, was the ten-week tour of Russia undertaken in 1960. Never before had a musical been the subject of international diplomacy in the way that *My Fair Lady* became at this time. On May 6, 1959, the *New York Times* published an article indicating an interest in seeing the show travel to Moscow. Nikolai N. Danilov, Soviet Deputy Minister of Culture, had issued an invitation to bring the production to Russia as part of an ongoing series of Soviet-American cultural exchanges designed to foster better relations between the two nations during a difficult period of the Cold War. Levin had not been involved in the talks at this stage, but he was eager to be in charge of the tour, which he viewed as the beginning of a European tour that would then visit major cities all over the Continent.[27]

Initially, these plans were delayed as Lerner and Loewe objected publically to a separate Russian production of the show, to be given in translation, for which the authors would receive no royalties. The mastermind behind the production was a thirty-year-old Russian called Victor Louis, who thought nothing of requesting the orchestration from Lerner and Loewe while openly admitting that they would receive nothing in return.[28] This was front-page news in the *New York Times*, but instead of bringing the Russian *Fair Lady* to an end, it encouraged Danilov—only a few days later—to go ahead and invite the Broadway company to take their production to Russia. Taking a production of *Fair Lady*'s complexity (including the two turntables for Oliver Smith's set) to Moscow, Leningrad and Kiev, each with very different theaters, caused numerous logistical problems for Jerry Adler and Samuel Liff, the stage manager and production supervisor respectively. Ironically, Lerner and Loewe waived their royalties for the tour, in order to offset spiraling costs—a sign of how important the tour had become to them.[29]

But it became a triumphant success. The eighty-one-person company was greeted enthusiastically by the Russians, and all fifty-six performances were sold out. Franz Allers went with them to conduct the orchestra, which was drawn from the Bolshoi Theatre, and both the show itself and the cast (including Edward Mulhare as Higgins, Lola Fisher as Eliza, and Charles Victor as Doolittle) all received a rave review in the Soviet Culture newspaper from Grigory M. Yaron, a leading actor and director of the Moscow Operetta Theatre. The *New York Times* deemed it a landmark event in Russian-American relations, representing a new step in the development of *Fair Lady*'s growing international reputation.[30]

NEW YORK REVIVALS AT CITY CENTER IN THE 1960S

My Fair Lady had the longest consecutive road tour in musical theater history up to that time, crossing the continent five times since its launch in March 1957 and earning an estimated $21.5 million in its six years around the United States.[31] It finally ended its North American run on December 14, 1963, in Toronto. But the show had not been absent from Manhattan for eighteen months before plans were underway for its return. On January 30, 1964, the

New York Times announced plans for a revival at City Center in May of the same year.[32] The revival opened on May 20 for a six-week run. It starred Marni Nixon as Eliza, a role that she sang in place of Audrey Hepburn's vocals in the movie version of the show, due out in October of the same year. Ironically, given that he had appeared in the putative Henry Higgins role in the spoof *My Square Laddie*, Reginald Gardiner played Doolittle in the City Center revival, while the part of Higgins went to Myles Eason, an Australian-born actor of Shakespearean pedigree. John Canaday in the *New York Times* said the opening-night performance got off to a "hesitant start" but took fire during "The Rain in Spain," and went on to praise Gardiner in particular. Nixon and Eason got more mixed notices, but overall there was enthusiasm for the production, which used the original settings and costumes.[33]

Four years later, the production returned to City Center with an all-new cast. In the lead roles were Inga Swenson and Fritz Weaver, who had been seen playing opposite each other in the 1965 Sherlock Holmes–themed Broadway musical *Baker Street*; Doolittle was played by the British character actor George Rose, and it would later become his signature role. Richard F. Shepard in the *New York Times* raved about the entire experience, describing it as "delightful," referring to Swenson as "marvelous," Weaver as "splendidly vinegary," and Rose as "magnificently earthy." He concluded: "The style of the Broadway production has been kept, and who is to complain? . . . [W]e've grown accustomed to her face."[34] This statement is part of an emerging trend in the mid-1960s whereby the show was beginning to be discussed with an air of nostalgia. Six years after the end of the original Broadway run, the show had already become an important part of theater history—one which audiences had taken to their heart and turned into a classic.

THE 1964 MOVIE ADAPTATION

Even before it opened, Lerner and Loewe were hoping for a movie version of the show. In fact, before CBS came in and backed the whole production, the team had first approached Paramount Pictures in February 1955 with a view to their investing in the stage show in exchange for exclusive motion picture rights.[35] This fell through, but after the successful opening of the show the following year, many of the major studios and producers started approaching Levin, Lerner, and Loewe about a possible screen adaptation. These included Samuel Goldwyn, William Goetz, Columbia Pictures, and, most prominently, 20th Century-Fox, who wanted to cast Cary Grant as Henry Higgins.[36] Since the show was such a commercial success on the stage, though, the film version was postponed for the time being. Then in 1961, Jack Warner (of Warner Bros.) and Arthur Freed (of MGM) both became determined to produce the movie version. Lerner seems to have favored the MGM team who were behind his enormously successful movie *Gigi*, and lined up its director, Vincente Minnelli, to helm the project. Additionally, he wanted Julie Andrews and Richard Burton—stars of the most recent Lerner and Loewe stage show, *Camelot*—to play the lead roles.[37]

But although Warner's initial bid for the project was turned down, his determination to "outbid any offer by a million dollars" meant that in 1962, Warner Bros. won the rights to produce the movie for $5.5 million.[38] In June 1963, the *New York Times* announced that it was to be the most expensive film ever made, with a total cost of around $12 million. Contrary to Lerner's hopes of having the original Eliza (Julie Andrews) and a new Higgins (Richard Burton), Warner elected to retain Rex Harrison from the Broadway production and hire Audrey Hepburn—a bigger box office draw than Andrews—as Eliza. To Harrison's dismay, he earned only a fifth of Hepburn's deal—$200,000 to her $1 million—and neither of them was to participate in the movie's profits, although he went on to earn royalties from the soundtrack album.[39] Hepburn, however, received none, because her singing was dubbed by Marni Nixon. Hepburn had previously sung in a movie musical—*Funny Face* (1957)— as well as performing the Oscar-winning song "Moon River" in *Breakfast at Tiffany's* (1961), but her vocal ability was deemed inadequate for the lyric demands of *Fair Lady's* score, and Nixon was called in to replace her voice, just as she had done for Deborah Kerr in *The King and I* (1956) and Natalie Wood in *West Side Story* (1961). Stanley Holloway returned to play Doolittle, and Warner hired George Cukor to direct, best known for his work on classics such as *The Philadelphia Story* (1940) and *A Star Is Born* (1954). Cecil Beaton was brought in to reconceive his stage costumes for film, though the set designs were executed by Gene Allen, who is credited only for art direction; by all accounts (including their own), there was tension between Beaton and Cukor.[40] Rehearsals began on June 17, 1963, and the film was completed in about four months.[41]

Even though the movie is often cited for its fidelity, and (with some justification) even described as "stage-bound" or something similar, Lerner's screenplay is far from a literal transposition of the stage script. Indeed, Cukor himself later commented, "We used even more of Shaw's screenplay than the stage version did."[42] It is striking that when comparing the stage show's rehearsal script with the film, many of the lines that were cut before the Broadway opening were put back to their original version. Perhaps this is one reason why some portions of the film can seem overlong: the contraction and polishing done during rehearsals for the stage version was sometimes over-looked in the screen adaptation. On the other hand, bearing in mind that Lerner's stage script is based on Shaw's screenplay for *Pygmalion*, the movie of *My Fair Lady* returns the material to its source medium. Geoffrey Block has usefully summarized the changes to *Fair Lady* in its film adaption, which include everything from contracting Doolittle's first two appearances into one scene (so that the reprise of "Little Bit of Luck" is heard in the same scene as its first sounding) to showing Eliza's protestations in the bath while Higgins's servants try to clean her on the night of her arrival. The Ascot scene is expanded and elaborated so that we see the racecourse from more angles and also observe a brief conversation between Higgins and his mother after Eliza's gaffe. That said, the staging of this scene is the most stylized of the movie, and Block (among many others) considers it "a lost opportunity for cinematic extravagance."[43] Cukor said that "There was really no other way we could have done it. There's a big number sung during the sequence, so it couldn't be realistic. Nor could the picture as a whole. It had to take place in a kind of dream world." Perhaps for this reason, the movie was not filmed real-istically on location but in a stylized reinvention of Edwardian London.

There are, however, a few moments where Cukor uses cinematic tech-niques, such as the reprise of "Wouldn't It Be Loverly?" being heard as a voice-over to represent Eliza's emotional memory, and we see much more of the geography of Higgins's house, Wimpole Street, the Embassy, and the market locations than is possible on the stage. The movie also moves the in-termission to the end of the scene of Eliza and Higgins's departure for the ball (in which he shows her a newfound respect by extending his arm for hers), throwing further emphasis on their relationship by ending the first half of the film with a gesture about their ambiguous feelings toward one another. Another unusual feature of the movie was the decision to have Har-rison perform his numbers "live" on set rather than pre-record the vocals as was traditional with movie musicals. Cukor commented that this technique allowed "certain laughs in the lyrics that Rex said himself he could never get on the stage"; the director considered Harrison's performance "dazzling" and "even better on the screen than on the stage."[44]

The movie was first shown in New York on October 21, 1964, and garnered many fine reviews. The *New York Times* called it "superlative," the *New York Journal-American* said it was "enchanting," and the *New York World-Telegram* commented that Hepburn "must be the most delightful in the long proces-sion of Elizas."[45] It went on to win eight Oscars, including best picture, di-rector, actor, art direction, cinematography, sound, costume design, and original music score (for the musical director, André Previn). Additionally,

Lerner's screenplay, Holloway's Doolittle, Gladys Cooper's Mrs. Higgins, and William Ziegler's film editing were nominated, but Hepburn's performance was completely overlooked. In spite of having written the screenplay and been present for much of the filming, Lerner was unhappy with the results of the film, as he acknowledged numerous times in public. Privately, too, he quipped to Cecil Beaton: "I know how sad you will be to hear that George Cukor has not worked since *My Fair Lady*. As far as I'm concerned, since before *My Fair Lady*."[46]

1976 BROADWAY REVIVAL

It was inevitable that the show would return to Broadway for a full-fledged revival before long. In spite of the disparate directions the genre had taken during the first half of the 1970s—including such wide-ranging fare as *Company* (1970), *Grease* (1971), and *A Chorus Line* (1975)—*My Fair Lady* was a show for which there would always be a firm demand. So in 1976, Levin brought to bear a twentieth-anniversary revival at the St. James Theatre that would, in another sign of growing nostalgia about the show, aim to reinstate the original sets, costumes, and orchestrations. Jerry Adler, one of the stage managers of the 1956 production, was brought in to direct, while the original dance captain, Crandall Diehl, reproduced the choreography.[47] According to an article in the *New York Times*, Rex Harrison was approached to appear again as Higgins, but said he would do so only if Julie Andrews would return as Eliza; her availability at this point allowed for just "four to six weeks," so Levin turned, on Lerner's advice, to British actor Ian Richardson. Robert Coote returned to his original role of Pickering, while George Rose reprised his Doolittle from the 1968 revival. After many months of auditions, the role of Eliza was given to Christine Andreas, who had previously worked with Adler on the 1974 Sammy Cahn revue *Words and Music*. Hoping to follow their financial success with the original staging, CBS invested $500,000 in the production, which cost $750,000 overall.

Not everything was the same, though: Adler reported that Beaton's costumes had been reproduced with the exception of Eliza's ball gown, which had to be modified because Andreas was shorter than Andrews; the groupings in the choreography had to be changed because the St. James Theatre was shallower than the Mark Hellinger Theatre had been; and some of Oliver Smith's designs were reconceived. Adler also noted that Richardson's Higgins was "more mature" and "more intellectual," and was at great pains to emphasize the many different nuances being brought to their roles by the other leads in the new production.[48] Confirming the impetus for the revival, Levin commented in a separate article that "This is the classical musical show of the American theater. I think a classical musical has every right to be done over, just as a classical play is done."[49] A couple of weeks later, Richardson reported that the first-night audience agreed with Levin's view—"So electric was the audience, so desperately was it eager to have the show back," he said.[50] The revival opened on March 25 and ran until December 5, before transferring to the Lunt-Fontanne Theatre on December 9 for a brief run to February 20, 1977 (377 performances). In light of the success of the original production, this was a disappointment, but both Richardson and Rose were nominated for the Tony Award for best actor and Rose won.

1981 BROADWAY REVIVAL

The excitement was palpable when Rex Harrison announced that he would return to play Higgins on Broadway for a short run in 1981, following a U.S. tour. "There was a sense of expectation in the air" remarked Patrick Garland, the revival's director, who wrote a memoir about working with Harrison on the production.[51] The pre-Broadway tour was extensive and took in New Orleans, San Francisco, Detroit, Los Angeles, Chicago, and other major American cities. Garland recounts how, having given fine performances and inspired good reviews for much of the tour, Cheryl Kennedy, the British actress who played Eliza, developed vocal problems. Because of Harrison's extreme reluctance to play opposite her official understudy ("None of the others can play the comedy"), Kennedy was forced to perform through her illness until, after missing some of the latter part of the tour and performing only one of the New York previews, she was forced to withdraw due to laryngitis and nodes on her vocal cords. She was replaced by Nancy Ringham, a member of the company who had been the unofficial second understudy for the role of Eliza. The *New York Times* noted that Harrison had been adamant to have an English actress as Eliza, which explains his reticence about Ringham, who was American; the first cover for the role, Kitty Sullivan, was the wife of Milo O'Shea, who played Doolittle in the production, but Harrison refused to work with her, and she left the production the week before the Broadway opening.[52]

The revival opened on Broadway on August 18, 1981. It was reviewed at the final preview performance, much to Garland's alarm: he writes extensively about Harrison's antagonistic attitude toward Ringham during the performance, causing her to underperform, and comments that the reviews "were better than they deserved to be."[53] At the official opening night, however, Harrison "performed elegantly and beautifully" and Ringham "lifted her game, hit all the top notes with assurance, and performed with gusto and radiant charm." In the *New York Times*, Mel Gussow's review acknowledged that Ringham was clearly affected by the last-minute substitution, but absolutely raved about Harrison's performance, describing him as "triumphant" and "the quintessential Higgins." Gussow also had praise for the Mrs. Higgins of the ninety-three-year-old Cathleen Nesbitt, who returned to her original role and was "a graceful presence." There was praise for the choreography, which had once more been reproduced by Crandall Diehl, and for Garland's staging, though Oliver Smith's reconceived designs were perceived to be "short of the original elegance." The lighting and amplification also caused problems, yet overall Gussow's article stated that the piece "endures as a paragon of wit, romance and musicality."[54]

But the note of inhibition about Ringham's performance, which according to Garland resulted from Harrison's "ill-temper and unpleasantness," was to limit the New York engagement to three months, "because the aura of the Eliza Doolittle was never really there."[55] It closed on November 29 after 124 performances, including a four-week extension. The director and producers had all hoped for more, but in the end, the lack of "an inspirational Eliza" was to unhinge the balance in the Higgins-Eliza relationship, and the show could go no farther, even with its legendary male lead.[56]

1993 BROADWAY REVIVAL

In 1993 *Fair Lady* was booked to return to Broadway, and again it was to be the final destination in a U.S. tour. This time, though, the production was completely new. Attempts to cling to the original conception in all previous stagings were largely dismissed, with the only obvious connection found in the casting of Julian Holloway, Stanley's son, as Doolittle. The troubles experienced in the 1981 revival were nothing compared to the fate that befell the 1993 staging, which was reported to have cost somewhere in the region of $2.5 million. The pre-Broadway tour began in Fort Meyers, Florida, and already problems had started to emerge. A week before the opening, Melissa Errico, who was due to play Eliza, ruptured a capillary in her right vocal cord, and her understudy, Meg Tolin, had not sung the part in rehearsals; Errico's costumes did not fit Tolin, so replacements had to be hired locally. Ralph Koltai's sets did not fit the theater and had to be quickly changed; the first performance was then hijacked by a stagehands' strike, during which the actors managed to improvise their way through the performance. Two days later, the sets were being loaded into a truck to move to Orlando, when Fort Meyers was hit by a tornado; some of the sets and costumes were seriously damaged. The *New York Times* catalogued these and many other problems in an article on July 2, suggesting that the direction, choreography, sets, and cast (which included Richard Chamberlain as Higgins) each had major weaknesses.[57]

Howard Davies's production aimed for a radical interpretation of a well-loved show, which he implied had been treated with too much reverence in recent times. Fran Weissler, one of the producers, commented that "We asked for a new concept and supported one."[58] Davies's reading darkened the story, so that Higgins's library was now more reminiscent of a laboratory. A huge phrenological head and various pieces of apparatus dominated the set. Higgins's engagement with Eliza was more physical than before; at one point he sat astride her, and at another he prized open her mouth like a dentist. The Belgian painter Magritte's surrealistic work influenced certain aspects of the staging, especially the Ascot scene, in which some of the aristocrat spectators descended from the sky on swings and stood suspended in midair for the entire tableau. The "I Could Have Danced All Night" scene was set against a deep blue sky with only a window (hanging in midair) and a bed as scenery. On the other hand, Doolittle's scenes were staged fairly conventionally.

On the whole, the critics admired Davies's efforts to take a new look at the piece, but none of them found his view entirely successful. In the *New York Times*, for instance, David Richards said that the show wanted to be "a brave new *My Fair Lady*" but that it worked only "to a certain extent."[59] The production's drawn-out problems had been insurmountable, and it was ultimately neither revisionist nor traditional. After opening on December 9, 1993, at the Virginia Theatre, it closed on May 1, 1994, with only 165 performances under its belt. Subsequently, the show has not been seen on Broadway, though it was performed in concert by the New York Philharmonic four times between March 7 and March 10, 2007, at Avery Fisher Hall. The cast included the TV star Kelsey Grammer and Kelli O'Hara, a Broadway favorite who went on to star in the acclaimed 2008 revival of *South Pacific* at the Lincoln Center Theater. But *My Fair Lady* has yet to receive a full-blown Broadway revival for the new millennium.

BRITISH REVIVALS

During the 1960s, *My Fair Lady* went on a two-year tour around the UK, just as it had done for nearly seven years in America. Two separate companies toured England, and everywhere it went it caused a stir. When the production visited Birmingham in 1964, a flyer proclaimed: "Due to the tremendous reception given to this magnificent musical we are pleased to announce that its run must be EXTENDED INTO 1965! The best in entertainment at the finest theatre in the Midlands."[60] It was described as "A lavish new £60,000 production" but was clearly based in every way on the London staging. In 1977, however, all that was to change when Sir Cameron Mackintosh scored one of his earliest successes with a completely new staging, which would "recapture the spirit of the original but with new visual designs and modern stage technology."[61] The impetus for the staging was a grant from the British Arts Council that wanted to fund a big touring production, which would be a popular success in some UK regions, where many theaters were struggling to find material that would bring in audiences and keep the venues alive. Tim Goodchild created entirely new sets, and choreographer Gillian Lynne completely reinvented Hanya Holm's dances.

In the cast was the British actor Tony Britton as Higgins, a part he had played on tour and on record; Liz Robertson, a young actress who had previously made an impression in Mackintosh's *Side By Side By Sondheim*; and the veteran British actress Dame Anna Neagle as Mrs. Higgins. The production opened on November 9, 1978, in Leicester and visited key British cities (Leeds, Birmingham, Bristol, Liverpool, Nottingham, Newcastle, Oxford, and Cardiff) before coming to London the following year on October 25, 1979. By all accounts, Lerner himself had a significant impact on the production, in addition to the direction by Robin Midgley, and it was during this period that he met and fell in love with Liz Robertson, who became his wife and also went on to appear in his final completed musical, *Dance a Little Closer* (1983).[62]

The year 1992 saw a new touring *Fair Lady* in the UK that took a radically new look at the piece. Director Simon Callow enlisted the English fashion designer Jasper Conran to help him create a revisionist version, which placed the emphasis on the plight of the female protagonist. "*My Fair Lady* is about class, prejudice, feminism," commented Conran at the time. "Eliza is the most important person and the whole point of it is how she emerges as a strong woman."[63] Conran and Callow went back to Shaw's *Pygmalion* and explored Eliza's trajectory as the focal point of the show. Conran also took inspiration from the Greek myth, and even went so far as to dress Eliza in the style of a marble statue in the ball scene, including a laurel wreath for her head. David Fielding's set designs extended the idea of Eliza's struggle by covering the floor and many of the backdrops with Higgins's phonetic text, which in this version completely invaded her life. But although the performances by Edward Fox (Higgins) and Helen Hobson (Eliza) were praised in some quarters, neither their input nor the imagination of Callow's concept was deemed

Stanley Holloway (Doolittle) and Julie Andrews (Eliza) in the original Broadway production (Springer/Photofest)

to be enough by the critics to outweigh the production's problems, and it never transferred to London.[64]

The next major production of the show to be seen internationally once more stemmed from Cameron Mackintosh. In 2001 he supported a revival at London's National Theatre, directed by Trevor Nunn. Higgins was played by Jonathan Pryce, the esteemed British actor of stage and screen, while Eliza went to a genuine Cockney actress, Martine McCutcheon, who was prominent at the time for her appearance in the leading UK soap opera *EastEnders*. Although Nunn believed that Lerner had improved on Shaw, he added some lines from *Pygmalion* into the book of the *My Fair Lady* revival, making the already extensive text even longer.[65] This sort of thing typified Nunn's approach, which presented what seemed like a familiar version of the show but in truth changed it in various ways. William David Brohn's orchestrations and Chris Walker's dance arrangements revised certain aspects of the score, such as changing the thematic material in the overture (which was shortened) and adapting the "Little Bit of Luck" dance music to contain a percussive improvisatory section involving dustbin lids used for a tap dance in the manner of Gene Kelly in *It's Always Fair Weather*, "conducted" by Doolittle using a wooden spoon. Nunn moved the interval back, so that Higgins's and Eliza's departure for the ball was the end of the first act. Another striking aspect was the emphasis on historical context: the Ascot scene was costumed (by Anthony Ward) with the ensemble dressed in mourning for the late King Edward VII, and the staging of "Show Me" concluded with Eliza emerging from the London Underground and joining a line of Suffragettes demanding votes for women.

In general, the reviews were positive about Nunn's interpretation. Though Michael Billington in the *Guardian* complained that the piece itself "is a soft-centred betrayal of Shaw,"[66] Rhoda Koenig in the *Independent* wrote that, on the contrary, it is an improvement.[67] Having opened at the Lyttelton Theatre at the National Theatre on March 15, the production moved to the Theatre Royal, Drury Lane—home to the original London production—on July 21. Unfortunately, the initial cast was dogged by the frequent absence of Martine McCutcheon due to illness, mirroring the problems experienced during the 1981 Broadway revival. During one week, Pryce acted opposite three different Elizas, because McCutcheon's understudy also fell ill.[68] She was later replaced by the West End actress Joanna Riding, who continued in the role of Eliza with Pryce; he was then succeeded by Alex Jennings as Higgins in May 2002. In March 2003, a new cast took over, with Anthony Andrews (Higgins), Laura Michelle Kelly (Eliza), Russ Abbot (Doolittle), Hannah Gordon (Mrs. Higgins), and Stephen Moore (Pickering) providing such a fresh ensemble performance as to cause Edward Seckerson to declare in the *Independent* that "this is the cast that should have opened the show."[69] Charles Spencer in the *Daily Telegraph* went so far as to describe it as "musical theatre at the very summit of its achievement."[70]

The production then toured twelve cities in the UK from September 28, 2005, to August 12, 2006, again with a new cast, before launching a ten-month American tour in September 2007. The latter included two actresses as

Mrs. Higgins, both of whom had a strong connection to the show: first, Sally Ann Howes, who took over from Julie Andrews in the original Broadway production, and later Marni Nixon, who dubbed Audrey Hepburn's singing voice in the film version. Yet again, in spite of the idiosyncratic features of Nunn's production, nostalgia took over, and the staging took its place alongside all three Broadway revivals in retaining a connection to the original production in its casting.

8

THE LEGACY OF *MY FAIR LADY*

• • •

THE MUSICAL THEATER OF LERNER AND LOEWE

My Fair Lady was unquestionably the highpoint of the Lerner and Loewe relationship, both artistically and commercially. Yet even if they were not as popular, the experience of writing the earlier shows was crucial to the composer and lyricist's development. For one thing, the storylines of their four previous Broadway musicals—*What's Up?* (1943), *The Day Before Spring* (1945), *Brigadoon* (1947), and *Paint Your Wagon* (1951)—were broadly original, rather than adaptations of existing material. While the decision to set an established classic may partly explain the much greater success of *My Fair Lady* (which was their only show to date unhampered by a problematic book), writing their earlier musicals from scratch gave them the freedom to experiment with structure. For instance, they used extensive ballet sequences in both *What's Up?* (directed and choreographed by the ballet legend George Balanchine) and *The Day Before Spring* (choreographed by the British ballet dancer Antony Tudor) to manipulate the narrative through dance. So although the ballet was ultimately cut from *My Fair Lady*, its initial inclusion followed a pattern established in their early works.

The Day Before Spring was an important experience in other ways, too. The script, though flawed because of some peculiar moments of fantasy and perhaps a lack of action and excitement, was witty and mature in subject matter, just as *Fair Lady* was later to be. The story deals with the rekindling of an old romance during a college reunion, when a woman discovers that her former love has written a novel about her in the ten-year interim, and considers eloping with him and leaving her husband—comparatively risqué for a musical of this period. Musically, Loewe learned much from writing songs in contrasting styles. In particular, the Latin flair of "God's Green World" would later reap dividends in "The Rain in Spain" and "Show Me," while the title number and "You Haven't Changed at All" reveal Loewe's use of sophisticated chromatic movement to add interest and piquancy to romantic ballads.[1] Again, this is something that characterizes many of his later songs. The first-act finale has a different complexity, namely a fluid sequence of contrasting sections of music that reflects its intricate verse structure. The protagonist, Katherine, has to make up her mind—should she run off with her former love or stay with her husband?—so she asks statues of Plato, Voltaire, and Freud (who come to life) for their advice. They each answer differently, with individually-characterized music to match, and Loewe binds it all together in a large-scale structure based on tonal and thematic relationships. This model took on a more familiar form in *My Fair Lady* as "You Did It," the concerted number that opens the second act. The other important aspect of *The Day Before Spring* is that it contains music that was later reused—including sections of both the title song from *Gigi* and "On the Street Where You Live."[2]

A big step forward was taken with *Brigadoon*. There is a noticeable coherence about the piece, and the music hangs together more convincingly: Loewe learned how to create a kind of musical *tinta* (a unifying "color") so that the individual numbers had elements in common that gave them coherence. The use of dotted rhythms in many of the songs evokes Scotland, in an allusion to the folk music of the country, and thereby gives them stylistic unity. There are also several important dances and a strong role for the chorus, and in "The Chase" Lerner and Loewe evolved an extensive number that propels the action forward compellingly. It is an altogether more sophisticatedly conceived work, even if its atmosphere is far from sophisticated. Similar traits are found in *Paint Your Wagon* (1951), with gestures signifying the Wild West giving the score its unique character, and easily a third of the music consisted of dances. Both musicals are complex in construction, and show a composer and lyricist who knew what they were doing. These were the first two of their Broadway shows to be filmed, the first two to be revived, and the first containing a handful of songs that became standards.[3]

The problem was that neither show really gave Loewe the opportunity to compose the more lavish, glamorous music with which he was to excel in their next three musicals (*My Fair Lady*, *Gigi*, and *Camelot*). Similarly, Lerner's keenly romantic brand of poetry, coupled with a wordy sophistication, was not as much at home in the Scottish heather of *Brigadoon* or the plain desert of *Paint Your Wagon* as it would subsequently be when he turned to established sources of European literature for his three masterpieces with Loewe. He later commented that after *The Day Before Spring*, "I got off the track. Both *Brigadoon* and *Paint Your Wagon* were much more along the *Oklahoma[!]* road than the one I had set out on, and I was determined somehow to find my way back. So I, too, was as drawn to *Pygmalion* as Fritz was."[4] *Fair Lady* was a significant moment in the Lerner and Loewe collaboration, after years of never quite achieving the impact of certain of their rivals—notably Rodgers and Hammerstein.

SHADOWS OF THE PAST: RODGERS AND HAMMERSTEIN, SHAW, AND OPERETTA

Just as Lerner and Loewe's experiences with their early shows informed their composition of *My Fair Lady*, so too did the work of their contemporaries have an impact on the show. From 1943 on, the team of Richard Rodgers and Oscar Hammerstein II was the leading force on Broadway. The success of *Oklahoma!* (1943), *Carousel* (1945), *South Pacific* (1949), and *The King and I* (1951) was matched with an acute business sense on the part of both composer and lyricist that helped them to control every aspect of their productions, making them a legendary partnership, which had never before and, arguably, has never since been matched. It is in the context of these shows that *My Fair Lady* tends to have been read, and rightly so, up to a point.

But the comparisons between *My Fair Lady* and Rodgers and Hammerstein's musicals tend to rob Lerner and Loewe of some of their individuality. This was the case from the very beginning. In his review of the opening night of the show on Broadway, Robert Coleman of the *Daily Mirror* wrote that it was "a new landmark in the genre fathered by Rodgers and Hammerstein."[5] Immediately, this put the show under the shadow of the earlier team's output. Coleman went on to specify the elements of *Fair Lady* that particularly owed themselves to the supposed "Rodgers and Hammerstein model": "The Lerner-Loewe songs are not only delightful, they advance the action as well. They are ever so much more than interpolations or interruptions. They are a most important and integrated element in about as perfect an entertainment as the most fastidious playgoer could demand." This attitude has continued in the more recent secondary literature on Lerner and Loewe. For instance, Scott McMillin says that "the world of Rodgers and Hammerstein . . . is also the world of Lerner and Loewe."[6] Similarly, Thomas L. Riis and Ann Sears write that *My Fair Lady* has elements in common with "all the important Rodgers and Hammerstein shows" and uses "the Rodgers and Hammerstein formula."[7] The problem here is not that these and other writers are wrong, but that they capitulate to the canonic pull of Rodgers and Hammerstein rather than assessing the show on its own merit.

It is not just the shadow of Rodgers and Hammerstein that has been cast over the reception of *My Fair Lady*: that of George Bernard Shaw also continues to cloud the extent to which Lerner and Loewe are given credit for their work. The Shavian connection promotes an element of snobbery in the show's public profile, so that it has been seen as a cut above the average musical comedy simply because of its source material. In part, this has done *My Fair Lady* a service because it has given it the status of something almost approaching high culture, but it is also the reason why the perception that Shaw remains the brains behind the show first emerged. It is also perhaps the case that since productions of *Pygmalion* tend to resemble *My Fair Lady* in a broad sense—with period costumes and a study and library set, for instance—people might think that they have seen it all before, without initially realizing the rigorous job done by Lerner and Loewe in reworking the play on every level. This notion was cleverly anticipated by Al Hirschfeld in his now-iconic caricature of the show, which featured on the playbills and cast album. This image is associated more than any other with *My Fair Lady*. Not only is Higgins portrayed as the puppeteer, manipulating Eliza's every move, but Shaw himself is in charge of proceedings in the clouds, rising above as the master magician, as it were. Strikingly absent from the image are Lerner and Loewe, and the question Hirschfeld might be asking is, whose strings is Shaw really pulling—Higgins's and Eliza's or Lerner's and Loewe's?

Likewise, most of the reviews of the opening night on Broadway focused strongly on the way in which Lerner and Loewe had adapted *Pygmalion* for the musical stage (see chap. 7). Often, there is a tension between wanting to apologize for Lerner and Loewe's near-sacrilege in taking on the task in the first place and at the same time awarding *Fair Lady* extra kudos for its association with Shaw. Then again, perhaps the fact that the show strove to adapt Shaw's play as a piece of music theater rather than creating a brash piece of entertainment helped audiences to engage closely with the material. *My Fair Lady* is like other shows of its day in being a so-called book musical, with a strong storyline and script that give rise to plot-clinching songs and dances, but the way in which the book has achieved as legendary a status as the score has always made it stand out. Unusually for a musical, the script has never been out of print, and it has even been published in a volume side by side with *Pygmalion*—an especially singular move to bring a script of a musical and its source material together—as well as in an inexpensive paperback edition for popular use.[8]

The type of theater it constitutes has always struck critics and audiences as particularly absorbing. Brooks Atkinson's first-night review, for instance, mentions that "*My Fair Lady* is staged dramatically on a civilized plane.

*Julie Andrews (Eliza) and Rex Harrison (Higgins) in the final scene
from* My Fair Lady *(Photofest)*

Probably for the first time in history a typical musical comedy audience finds itself absorbed in the art of pronunciation and passionately involved in the proper speaking of 'pain', 'rain' and 'Spain.'"[9] The *Newark Evening News* reported that "The gaily perceptive Shavian fable of a Cockney flower vendor's transition into a lady of articulate charm by a bemused mentor of phonetics loses none of its classical zest in this retelling," a comment that promotes most avidly the idea that the articulate power of *Pygmalion* is maintained in *My Fair Lady*.[10] The reviewer in *Newsweek* claimed that "Shaw's pervasively witty malice guides their totality [i.e., the combined talent of Lerner, Loewe, Smith, and Beaton] toward something that is very close to great theater," while *Time* magazine said that the musical retains "all of Shaw's hardy perennial bloom."[11] More recently, Edward Jablonski, Stephen Citron, Geoffrey Block, and Scott McMillin have also focused strongly on the Shavian element of the show, demonstrating the irresistible pull of the very British *Pygmalion* on the reception of *My Fair Lady*.[12]

The third leading trend in the literature on the show concerns genre. In spite of opening on Broadway and being the product of a composer and lyricist whose careers centered around American musical theater, *My Fair Lady* has too often been interpreted as an operetta rather than a musical. Again, Lerner and Loewe are denied some credit for the originality of their work for this reason. It goes without saying that generic labels involve generalization and tend to homogenize works into groups rather than revealing their unique characteristics. But in the case of *My Fair Lady* the description "operetta" seems to have a pejorative connotation, loosely evoking the late-nineteenth-century Vienna of the Strauss family rather than 1950s Broadway. Perhaps the most notable writer to discuss *My Fair Lady* in this light is Richard Traubner, who devotes a chapter of his book *Operetta: A Theatrical History* to Broadway musicals. His attitude toward Broadway is that musicals "are very apparently and decisively operettas, though critics do not care to admit that they are. . . . [S]hows like *Oklahoma!*, *Brigadoon*, *The King and I*, *West Side Story*, *My Fair Lady* and *Camelot* are all to varying degrees romantic operettas."[13] More specifically on *My Fair Lady*, he writes: "The collaboration of Alan Jay Lerner . . . and Frederick Loewe . . . has provided the Broadway stage with three of the greatest operettas of the postwar era, though none of them was so termed."[14] Other writers to take this line include Thomas L. Riis and Ann Sears, who write that "Loewe's charming music . . . [is] redolent of the operetta of an earlier day";[15] Gervase Hughes, who includes Rodgers, Loesser, Bernstein, and Loewe in his book on operetta;[16] and William Zinsser, who says that Lerner and Loewe "won't be remembered for pushing the musical theater into new terrain . . . they were a throwback to the earlier generic team of Gilbert and Sullivan." Zinsser also goes on to say that "Loewe was . . . a residual product of the nineteenth century; he could have written melodies for Gilbert."[17]

Yet the fact that there is no census on the point makes this "operetta" label problematic. Genre is a two-way process: it exists so that audiences can access a set of identifiers to which they can relate and so that writers can function within some kind of framework. But it is not meant to be constrictive. Since each audience member brings a different set of experiences to his or her viewpoint, the generic markers have to be strong for a work's classification to be unambiguous. That might be the case with an action or horror movie, but much of *My Fair Lady* is so unlike anything else that it is easy to have sympathy with Ethan Mordden's view of the piece as *sui generis* ("without genre").[18] Mostly, generic readings do not tell us very much about *My Fair Lady*, yet it is interesting to ask why commentators might want to pursue them. The broadest reason is actually complimentary to the show: relating it to long-established pieces makes it part of a stronger historical lineage. And this is often related to the fact that Frederick Loewe was born and raised in Germany, and was therefore culturally allied to both Western art music and operetta. He also had a background in writing German cabaret songs, several of which were published.[19] Accounts of Loewe's life tend to emphasize the fact that his father sang in operettas in Berlin, and the composer himself propagated tales that he studied with Ferruccio Busoni while in Europe, supposedly alongside Kurt Weill, although this particular claim raises some doubt.[20] Loewe, a little like Weill, has always been regarded as slightly apart from his "American" colleagues. Lerner, too, has sometimes been connected with Europe more than America because of his British education, which is perhaps why Zinsser says that "Of all American lyricists, [he] was the nearest descendant of WS Gilbert; he could have written lyrics for Sir Arthur Sullivan."[21] But no specific example is given by Zinsser or any other writer making these assertions, and they ultimately tell us very little about the show or how it might be interpreted.

Nor does the claim that the score in some way evokes the nineteenth century or early twentieth century really ring true; Loewe is subtler than that. Even if one does not entirely accept the piece as being "beyond genre," there is surely too wide a range of generic markers to group the whole score under one umbrella. For instance, the dance-like elegance of "Why Can't the English?" may have an air of the archaic about it, but this is clearly intended to reflect Higgins's pomposity and arrogance: he is old-fashioned, and a stilted style is used to depict his arrogance. Likewise, Eliza's "Wouldn't It Be Loverly?" has moments of delicacy, but this is offset by the cockney roughness of the block chords that run through most of the number, not to mention the coarse all-male chorus. If anything, the "London musical" (for instance, Noel Gay's *Me and My Girl*) is the type being evoked here. Doolittle's "With a Little Bit of Luck" and "Get Me to the Church on Time" are a flagrant evocation of the music-hall background of Stanley Holloway, for whom the role was written.[22] Again, the gentlemanly elegance of the verses of "I'm an Ordinary Man" is a result of Loewe's gracefulness of line, and the loose, fluid structure of the song is sophisticated, but the dotted rhythms, thumb (tenor) line, and numerous chromatically modified chords are pure Broadway in their pedigree. Similar ingredients characterize "A Hymn to Him" and "I've Grown Accustomed to Her Face," and the short (twenty-bar) melody of the latter also signifies a freedom of form that put the composition firmly in the Broadway of the 1950s. The London-industrial East End brusqueness and characteristic Broadway tonic-dominant accompaniment of "Just You Wait" are also signs that the score is a long way from relying on the kind of musical language found in nineteenth-century operetta. "The Rain in Spain" and "Show Me" employ exotic, particularly Latin, styles of music that are very much in line with songs such as "Hernando's Hideaway" from *The Pajama Game* and "Whatever Lola Wants" from *Damn Yankees*, two musicals that opened in the years closely preceding *My Fair Lady* and which are quintessentially American in style and subject matter. Even "I Could Have Danced All Night," whose arpeggiated melody and relatively high tessitura require a performer of some vocal poise, has an unmistakable Broadway bounce and abandon.

Where the show does venture into artier waters, there is always a reason for it. Loewe deliberately makes "The Ascot Gavotte" sound archaic and affected, to reflect the artifice of the aristocracy at the races. Similarly, "The Servants' Chorus" is mannered and stiff in style to mirror the long, monotonous hours the servants have to endure as the clock ticks by during Eliza's lessons. "The Embassy Waltz" is a diegetic piece of music playing in the background at the ball, so its reliance on the Viennese waltz idiom is entirely appropriate, and the use of a concerted structure for "You Did It" is undoubtedly meant to be read in quotation marks, matching the satire of the lyrics; Lerner later referred to it, tongue-in-cheek, as "a sort of Hyde Park *Fledermaus*."[23] He also revealed that the most lyrical part of it, when Pickering originally had more lines, was cut specifically because he "was singing too long" and said that the number "is a sort of ruse to prevent the audience from realizing that a lot of bad singing is going on."[24] This is the opposite of the aim of the traditional operatic *largo concertante*, in which all the characters are united precisely to show off the quality and power of the cast's singing.

In fact, the only song in the score that should be read through the lens of an operetta aria is "On the Street Where You Live." Here, Freddy Eynsford-Hill sings of his love for Eliza in both musical and lyrical cliché, with several melodramatic vocal peaks in the melody and numerous romantic flights of fancy in the lyric, such as "All at once am I several stories high" and "Does enchantment pour out of every door?" The ways in which the number was heavily revised during the out-of-town tryouts show that Lerner and Loewe were striving for an amusing effect. We are meant to laugh at Freddy, and thereby realize why he is an impossible match for Eliza: his song is superficially pretty but a little dull and insipid, rather like himself. Therefore, the employment of an operetta style in this number is deliberate and fulfills its intended effect of making the singing Freddy an outsider, while the dismissal of the rest of the score as being stylistically anachronistic is too much of a generalization to be convincing.

The three aspects of the show's reception discussed earlier are interwoven: *My Fair Lady* has often been presented as beholden, whether to Rodgers and Hammerstein, to Shaw, or to the operetta genre, the implication being that it is not completely "original" and that the adaptation is passive. Yet there were several hundred changes to Shaw's text, along with the addition of completely new episodes. More than this, the realignment of the Eliza-Higgins relationship allowed Lerner and Loewe to create a much more tantalizingly ambiguous situation than in *Pygmalion*. By using all the elements of musical theater to the full, they created something that is obviously quite separate and unique from the play.

AN ACTIVE ADAPTATION

As much as anything, the problem with writers' inclination to read *Fair Lady* as subservient to various precedents has been one of formulation. It is still important to understand that Shaw and Rodgers and Hammerstein belong in the reception of *My Fair Lady*, but not in a way that denies Lerner and Loewe the full extent of their contribution. For instance, it is undeniable that Rodgers and Hammerstein brought in a more substantial type of musical theater with their collaboration, as Lerner himself was always ready to acknowledge.[25] This particularly applies to the books (librettos), which are so much more than soufflés or mere star vehicles. *The King and I* is an especially important precursor. Like *Fair Lady*, it is based on a substantial literary source and takes several ideas from the screen adaptation of that book.[26] More significantly, Rodgers and Hammerstein deal not only with a serious subject involving racial tensions and the death of the male protagonist but also with a central relationship that is not unlike that of Higgins and Eliza, both socially and emotionally. Anna Leonowens comes from England to become tutor to the offspring of the King of Siam, and the show charts a clash of cultures as Anna attempts to bring Western, democratic values to the pantheistic, feudal culture she finds in the East. This theme is propelled by a series of tautly woven interactions between the principal characters. What emerges is the attraction between the polygamous king and the prudish, Christian teacher. Consummation of this attraction is rendered impossible by their situation—she does not approve of his moral code and seems to have embraced widowhood as a permanent way of life, while he would probably not accept a Western wife and would certainly not treat her as an equal, as Anna would demand—yet Rodgers and Hammerstein tantalize us with the possibility quite brilliantly. He is clearly attracted when she stands up to him, and the climax of the show is their second-act duet, "Shall We Dance?," in which they unite in a grand polka. This drives the relationship to its most intimate, yet the number is interrupted and the next time they meet, the king is on his deathbed.

Obviously, the tragic ending of *The King and I* is quite different to the final scene of *My Fair Lady*, but there is no doubt that this kind of musical helped pave the way for Lerner and Loewe. In both shows, the musical numbers and spoken dialogue have equal weight, rather than the dialogue merely filling in the spaces between the lyric moments; they both explore wider social issues as well as painting psychologically complex relationships in the foreground; and neither of them capitulates to the cliché of the romantic ending, albeit in different ways. We can also see the reinvention of Rodgers and Hammerstein's work in "I've Grown Accustomed to Her Face," which is a complex monologue related to the models of the king's "It's a Puzzlement" in *The King and I* and, before that, Billy Bigelow's iconic "Soliloquy" from *Carousel* (even if, in a broader sense, the idea is just as obviously borrowed from the big *scena* form of Italian opera). Still, it is the magnetic and complex relationship between Anna and the king which is the most important precedent for the portrayal of the connection between Higgins and Eliza.

The work of composers other than Rodgers also helped. Cole Porter's *Kiss Me, Kate* (1948), for instance, is a loose musical adaptation of Shakespeare's *The Taming of the Shrew*. Although the play is liberally interpreted through the lens of a backstage musical, substantial portions of Shakespeare's verse remain intact thanks to the show's meta-theatrical format. While *Kiss Me, Kate* was far from being the first Broadway musical based on a Shakespeare play, Porter and his collaborators' fearlessness in using large sections of a classic piece of English literature is an obvious precedent for the retention of big portions of Shaw's period dialogue in *Fair Lady*. This meant that Lerner and Loewe could confidently write a dialogue-heavy show, and thereby create characters who were psychologically complex and could engage in a complicated relationship.

The flip side is that it is less obvious to read *My Fair Lady* in the context of American society because of its English setting, and in this respect it is completely unlike many of the other shows of the period. Contrasts between the pastoral and the urban in *Oklahoma!* (1943), the representation of the Wild West in *Annie Get Your Gun* (1946), the depiction of trade unions in *The Pajama Game* (1954), baseball in *Damn Yankees* (1955), McCarthyism in *Candide* (1956), ethnic clashes in *West Side Story* (1957), small-town America in *The Music Man* (1957), the assimilation of Asian-Americans in *Flower Drum Song* (1958), and the dilution of Jewish religious traditions in *Fiddler on the Roof* (1964) are all examples of how the Broadway musical engaged directly with American society. Several of Lerner and Loewe's other shows can be read in similar ways, too, be it the idolizing of an untouched historico-pastoral idyll by urban Americans in *Brigadoon*, the gold rush in *Paint Your Wagon,* or the posthumous association of the story of *Camelot* with the rise and fall of the John F. Kennedy administration.

However, *My Fair Lady* pursues a more latent "American" agenda in the form of the character of Eliza Doolittle. Like other Broadway classics, it has optimism at its centre. Whether during the boom of the 1920s (Gershwin's *Girl Crazy*), the Depression of the 1930s (Porter's *Anything Goes*), the Second World War (Berlin's *This is the Army*), or the Cold War (Porter's *Silk Stockings*), Broadway musicals had often provided either a reflection of the good times they were written in or a flicker of hope to overcome the bad times; in a broad sense, songs such as "You'll Never Walk Alone" from Rodgers and Hammerstein's *Carousel* or "Somewhere" from Bernstein and Sondheim's *West Side Story* seem to epitomize much of what musicals are about. Eliza Doolittle is the ultimate Broadway musical heroine, therefore, because from start to finish she embodies the triumph of aspiration as well as being a representative of feminism, women's suffrage, and social mobility—themes which chime with aspects of the American Dream such as getting rich, getting on in the world, and the equality of the sexes. Eliza's first song, "Wouldn't It Be Loverly?," makes this connection clear at once, showing us that she wants to be warm and comfortable. Her line "I want to be a lady in a flower shop, 'stead of selling at the corner of Tottenham Court Road" (24), initially representing her goal in life, functions as a prominent leitmotif in the show because it is repeated on the gramophone record of Eliza's voice that Higgins plays in the final scene (155). Higgins also refers to this ambition in act 2 during the great clash between the characters, when he says, "What about that old idea of a florist's shop?" (111).[27] She also remains a strong character in act 2, singing of her independence in "Without You" and demanding something more concrete than empty promises in "Show Me." Thus the broader atmosphere is very much in keeping with other Broadway musicals of the period.

Still, the main reason why the show is so compelling is the brilliant depiction of the relationship between Higgins and Eliza. The tension between them is palpable from start to finish, yet at no point is it explicitly referred to as a signifier of love. This aspect of the piece is by far the one most often remarked upon by critics, and has been from its premiere; the disagreements as to whether the final scene represents romantic union between the two characters or mere reconciliation after a disagreement are constant. In contrast to some of the reviews such as Brooks Atkinson's in the *New York Times* (see chap. 7), which perceived the show to depict a love story, the review in *Variety* by Hobe Morrison more cautiously referred to "the development of the romantic angle that Shaw scorned" without making it clear whether this "development" meant consummation.[28] John Beaufort in the *Christian Science Monitor* gave a thorough account of how the musical's book was adapted from the 1938 film of *Pygmalion*, complete with its "liberating revisions": "Lerner winds up the story with a wry reunion between Eliza and Henry Higgins."[29] The resolution of the relationship can therefore be viewed in three different ways: overt romance (Atkinson), developed romance (Morrison), and "wry reunion" (Beaufort), the latter in particular the antithesis to Atkinson's use of the word "love."

Are Higgins and Eliza really in love, then? The fact is that Lerner and Loewe were careful to avoid discussion of the subject in the show. When *My Fair Lady* was nearing its third birthday on Broadway, Herman Levin approached various journalists with a standard letter, suggesting that they should write an editorial about the anniversary. The second paragraph of Levin's letter in every case reads:

> Though it is without kiss, embrace or tap dance, many authorities, exclusive of this partisan, think it is the best musical comedy ever produced in this country. Critics on both sides of the Atlantic have commended it for its taste, its freedom from vulgarity, and the fidelity with which is clings to the plot and dialogue of Shaw's *Pygmalion*.[30]

Of course, these letters were not written for public consumption and were created for a commercial function, but Levin underlined an undeniable truth when he said that the show is without "kiss or embrace." Their relationship is without physical or verbal confirmation of their love, surely a stumbling block for anyone who wants to read the final reunion of Eliza and Higgins as a capitulation to conventional romantic "happy endings"—whether in musical comedy, the *lieto fine* of eighteenth-century *opera buffa*, or the traditional conclusion to Shakespearean comedy, featuring the marriage of one or more couples. Ultimately, these precedents are probably what make people want to believe the show *must* end with the main characters in love.

The theme has been taken up in all the secondary literature on the musical. Joseph Swain, for instance, writes of "the transformation of Higgins, from a self-imagined misogynist to someone who has become accustomed to love a woman."[31] He then embarks on a detailed analysis of "I've Grown Accustomed to Her Face," at one point highlighting broad similarities between the melodies of part of this song and Eliza's "Just You Wait," and goes on to ask: "Does this turnabout on the revenge motive imply a mutual affinity between the two protagonists, who have been portrayed so differently throughout?"[32] He then has to admit, however, that the "relationship between Higgins and Eliza is developed with consistent subtlety—the word 'love' never comes between them—through the music of the play, which is, of course, the principal addition to *Pygmalion*. The tone of even their music is so understated that it demands a compromise of style: Lerner and Loewe forswear all serious devices of romantic expression that the Broadway tradition makes available to them, so that even 'I've Grown Accustomed to Her Face', the weightiest number of the play, is restrained in overt expression."[33] With good reason, Swain reads the show as subverting convention in terms of negating the need for a central romance—the word "love" never comes between them, he admits—so it is perhaps surprising that he should pursue the idea that Higgins is unambiguously in love with Eliza.

Swain is not alone in pursuing a romantic reading of the show. Geoffrey Block also assumes that the final scene represents "a romantic resolution between Higgins and Eliza" and asserts that "Despite Shaw's desire to grasp at this perceived ambiguity and despite the fact that audiences of both film and musical do not actually see Eliza fetch Higgins's slippers, most members of these audiences will probably conclude that Freddy is not a romantic alternative."[34] With good reason, Block describes how Higgins is softened as a character in the musical, perceiving this to be a way of grooming him as a more conventional "leading man" type and paving the way through "The Rain in Spain" to romance in the final scene. Certainly, this is a valid way of reading Lerner's epigram to the published stage script, in which he explains that he omitted Shaw's epilogue to *Pygmalion* "because in it Shaw explains how Eliza ends not with Higgins but with Freddy and—Shaw and Heaven forgive me!—I am not certain he is right." Yet even Block admits that "Readers of Shaw's play know, as Shaw knew, that Higgins would "never fall in love with anyone under forty-five" [a line of Mrs. Higgins's from *Pygmalion*]. Indeed, marrying Freddy might have its drawbacks, but marrying Higgins would be unthinkable."[35] Block concludes by saying that the greatest achievement of *My Fair Lady* is that in it, "the unthinkable has become the probable."

But is this happy ending really implied? What seems to confuse many writers is the odd progression of events leading to the finale. First, Eliza and Higgins meet and are poles apart in social rank and education. They unite as pupil and teacher, and the fact that Eliza takes up residence in Higgins's house increases their level of intimacy above the norm. When she finally masters the language in the "Rain in Spain" scene, they sing and dance together, and in a song of triumph Eliza sings the lines, "I only know when he / Began to dance with me / I could have danced all night" (68). Other than this, Eliza never sings or speaks with joy about Higgins. Following the Ascot scene, the next step in their relationship is more tactile, when they are about to depart for the ball in act 1, scene 9. Eliza appears on the stairs in her evening gown, Pickering tells her she looks beautiful, and Higgins says that she is "Not bad. Not bad at all" (91). The stage directions tell us that as Higgins is at the threshold of the house, "he pauses, turns and gazes at Eliza. He returns to her and offers his arm. She takes it and they go out of the door, Pickering following after." This represents an unprecedented gesture of respect from Higgins. He then dances with her at the ball in scene 11 (98), again taking their relationship to a new level with the act of touching.

But his self-congratulatory behavior in "You Did It" indicates that things have not significantly changed, and there is no suggestion here that Higgins might be in love with Eliza. He thanks God that the experiment is over (106); he says, "What does it matter what becomes of you?" (107); and he suggests that Eliza might get married, specifically to someone else ("I daresay my mother could find some chap or other who would do very well," 111). On the flip side, he admits to Eliza at the height of the scene that "You have wounded me to the heart" (113) and refers to his folly in having lavished "the treasure of my regard and intimacy on a heartless guttersnipe!" (114), emotive language that shows an attachment but still does not necessarily imply romantic love.

For her part, Eliza is deeply upset by Higgins's behavior, since he does not care what is to become of her and she does not know what to do. She feels lost and abandoned, but if her resentment is derived from unrequited love, she does not really show it. The only gesture of possible significance here is Eliza's returning of the ring Higgins gave to her during an unseen visit to Brighton, a symbol of the dissolution of a romantic relationship. But even this is outwardly just the return of a gift given out of friendship. Both the dancing in act 1 and the ring in act 2 are examples of how Higgins and Eliza are associated with tantalizing conventional symbols of love whose meaning is subverted:

Pickering is part of their "Rain in Spain" dance, whose context is far from romantic; their Embassy Ball dance is part of their experiment; and the ring is rejected, having never been exchanged as part of the story in the first place. In each case, attraction glimmers between them but soon subsides.

After her tearful reprise of "Just You Wait," Eliza departs the house and sings "Show Me." Had this song been delivered to Higgins it would undeniably function as a demand for a tangible expression of love, but as Eliza sings it to Freddy it functions more generally as an articulation of her frustration with men. The exchange that really reveals the most about the Higgins-Eliza relationship takes place in act 2, scene 5, at Mrs. Higgins's house. Here they discuss their unusual association for the first time. Higgins softens briefly and asks, "You never wondered, I suppose, whether I could get along without you" (143), later admitting "I shall miss you, Eliza. I've learned something from your idiotic notions. I confess that humbly and gratefully" (145). When Higgins proposes that she return to live with him, he adds that she can walk out at any point and go back to selling flowers, or perhaps marry Pickering. She responds directly: "I wouldn't marry you if you asked me" (145). If this were not clear enough, she goes on to say that she does not want Higgins to be infatuated with her; she just wants "a little kindness. I know I'm a common ignorant girl, and you a book-learned gentleman; but I'm not dirt under your feet. . . . What I did was not for the dresses and the taxis: I did it because we were pleasant together and I come—came to care for you; not to want you to make love to me, and not forgetting the difference between us, but more friendly like" (146). The argument continues, and Eliza sings that she can live "Without You," to which Higgins reacts alone with "I've Grown Accustomed to Her Face." But even though Eliza then returns to the house at the end of the song, it is difficult in light of the dialogue about friendship to see how this could be construed as a sign that they will marry. Indeed, the characters lay out quite explicitly the kind of terms in which they could live under the same roof together again. That is not to say, however, as Raymond Knapp has done, that Higgins must be homosexual, or that he is engaged in a sexual relationship with Pickering just because they both choose to live in a largely homosocial environment.[36] As Shaw indicated in his epilogue, there must be a certain attraction between Eliza and Higgins in order for the tension to exist between them. What we don't know is the degree to which they feel it, and *this* is at the heart of the show's success. Nor is the fact that Higgins is a non-lyric role particularly significant in the interpretation of his sexuality: all along, Lerner and Loewe were looking for a male classical actor to carry Higgins's huge, complex speeches, and it was to be expected that such an actor would not be a strong singer.

It is not just on the basis of the published text that the status of the Eliza-Higgins relationship can be understood as ambiguous rather than romantic. In this book chapters 1–6 show numerous examples of the writers initially going down more conventional routes with the lyrics, dialogue, music, and even the casting, and then retracing their steps. For instance, we saw in chapter 1 that their initial idea for the show was to pursue Mary Martin to play the lead role. Lerner's letter to Gabriel Pascal, in which he says "I'm ready to do anything short of homicide to see Mary as Liza," suggests that the show was to be written around her talents. This in itself would have had huge implications, since Martin was the hugely popular star of quintessential Broadway shows such as *South Pacific*, *Annie Get Your Gun* (on tour), and *One Touch of Venus*. Furthermore, not only was she American but she was also approaching her thirty-ninth birthday when the idea was first proposed and would probably have been over forty by the time the show went into production. In both these respects she was the complete antithesis of the English, twenty-year-old Julie Andrews, who eventually got the part. The two singers' vocal ranges and timbres were also completely different, with Andrews at the lighter soprano end and Martin at the warmer, lower end, which would obviously have had an effect on the style and range of the music. Though we do not know exactly what would have happened if the show had been built around Martin, it seems almost sure that it would have had much more of an extrovert "Broadway" feel to it, and with this would probably have come a more conventionally romantic relationship between the two main protagonists.

Certainly, many of the initial attempts at writing songs for the show were in line with this. Sketches for numbers such as "What is a Woman?" and "The Undeserving Poor" suggest generic Broadway numbers, while the complete lead sheet for "Please Don't Marry Me" shows that both the lyric and the music for this song deals with the subject of love in a more head-on way than is the case in "I'm an Ordinary Man." Eliza's "There's a Thing Called Love" is similar in this respect, and the fact that the music for the number was recycled in the stage version of *Gigi* as a full-blown love song indicates that Lerner and Loewe did not want Eliza to have quite the same kind of romantic number that someone like Gigi sings; the avoidance of such a number is also shown in the removal of the sentimental "Shy" from the score late in the compositional process. Even more strikingly, Higgins refers to Eliza as becoming "my lady" in the unused song "Lady Liza," a direct nomination of her as his consort. The removal of the long sequence in act 1 ("Come to the Ball," the ballet, and "Say a Prayer") was largely due to the running time of the previews in New Haven, but it also served an interpretative purpose. "Come to the Ball" was intensely seductive and featured Higgins persuading Eliza to do his will, again in waltz-time, again with reference to himself as consort ("Come to the ball with me"), while the original lyric for "Say a Prayer" had Eliza singing such sentiments as "If I were a work of art / Would I wake his sleeping heart?" and "Say a prayer that he'll discover / I'm his lover." That this material did not make it into the show is no accident.

Lerner and Loewe undertook this sort of anti-romantic modification even in the songs that remained in the score at the musical's Broadway opening. For instance, changes to "On the Street Where You Live" helped soften the impact of Freddy as a feasible suitor to Eliza, whereas the original had more actively posited him as a rival to Higgins for her affections. The removal of some of the more sadistic lines in "You Did It" helped prevent demonizing Higgins to too much of an extent, so that we understand his attitude in the number as simply not noticing Eliza, rather than being actively nasty, while Eliza's "Without You" was similarly toned down from its original extended version. It was important not to make either character seem too actively furious at the other, since this is traditionally a signifier of people who exaggerate their hatred of each other to mask the fact that they are in love (classic Shakespearean examples being Katherine and Petruchio in *The Taming of the Shrew*, and Benedict and Beatrice in *Much Ado About Nothing*).

Additionally, it is notable that the songs that stayed in the show tend to avoid being too specific where they could have been overt expressions of love. For instance, "Why Can't the English?" contains some initial addresses to Eliza but broadens out to include the crowd (and indeed people from all over the world). Eliza's equivalent opening statement, "Wouldn't It Be Loverly?" talks about "Someone's head resting on my knee" but does not refer to anyone specific, and it would certainly be difficult to register this as an allusion to Higgins. "I'm an Ordinary Man" expresses a negative attitude toward women but does not involve Eliza directly (nor does it discuss romance or matrimony, for that matter), while the more direct "Just You Wait" comes so obviously in the aftermath of Higgins's strict treatment of her as his pupil that it would take a stretch of the imagination to receive it as an "anti-love" love song. As noted above, "Show Me" is sung not to Higgins but to Freddy, so that the brief mention of the Professor in Eliza's opening verse ("I get words all day through / First from him, now from you") goes by relatively unnoticed. She has sickened of the behavior of men in general, and there is little sense of Freddy acting as an object against whom Eliza can vent her anger toward Higgins in the physical absence of the latter. Similarly subtle is the brief reference to him in the line "I only know when he / Began to dance with me" from "I Could Have Danced All Night": certainly it strikes us that

Julie Andrews in the final scene of My Fair Lady *(Photofest)*

some kind of feeling has been aroused inside Eliza, but the thought is so fleeting that we cannot conclude too much from it.

Lerner and Loewe delay confrontation of the issue until the pair's last two songs, when Eliza sings that she can live "Without You," and Higgins admits that "I've Grown Accustomed to Her Face." Along with "I Could Have Danced All Night," the latter is surely the only strong reason to infer a romantic connection between the two: lines such as "She almost makes the day begin" and "I've grown accustomed to the trace of something in the air" undoubtedly represent a very personal expression of feeling for Eliza on Higgins's part. Yet

Lerner never takes either of them any farther than this. Whereas song is traditionally a conduit through which a character's heightened emotions can flow, in *My Fair Lady* the musical numbers contribute to the grander scheme of creating a central relationship whose full implications we can never fully understand.

In other words, the triumph of *My Fair Lady* is not its resolution of the romance between Higgins and Eliza but that Lerner and Loewe resolve the characters' ongoing battle without defining their relationship any more explicitly than it has been earlier in the show. It is a stroke of genius: because the argument is over, the audience can enjoy the conventional satisfaction of a happy ending, but because there is no duet, no physical connection, and no verbal expression of love, the ambiguity that has been achieved during the previous three hours is maintained even at the final curtain. In that respect, and in spite of Lerner's epigram to the script, they avoid negating Shaw's beliefs about what the relationship means, and yet send a Broadway audience home entirely satisfied in the knowledge that the characters they care about are friends once more. Now that Eliza has gained her independence from Higgins, she can return to his company as her own woman: both her breaking away and her decision to come back are signs of Lerner's retention of the latent feminism in Shaw's play. Their reconciliation is clear-cut, but an uncertain note remains. When Higgins utters his final line, "Where the devil are my slippers?" Lerner tells us in the stage directions that Eliza "understands." Exactly *what* she understands is perhaps up to the individual, and can also vary according to the director and performer. Trevor Nunn's 2001 production, for instance, had the two characters standing up, folding their arms, and laughing, during the final bars of the show, implying that the whole thing had been a joke; the staging of the 1964 film is more poignant but still does not depict a romantic union. Since Higgins is too independent and emotionally immature to let a woman in his life, and Eliza is too strong to allow herself to become beholden to him, there can never be love between them. In an article written a few years after the show's opening, Lerner indicated his agreement on the matter: "It was impossible for Higgins to love Eliza; for them to admit to themselves that they felt anything emotional about each other."[37] What Higgins really wanted, he said, "was a friend. He wanted Eliza, but he wanted her to behave as a friend because he didn't understand the emotional pressure of an intimate relationship."[38] For that reason, Lerner wrote the perfect ambiguous conclusion: the "serenely independent" Higgins cannot love Eliza but is happy to admit that he has grown accustomed to her face.

APPENDICES

APPENDIX 1 "WITHOUT YOU" (EARLY VERSIONS)

Copyist

There'll be spring every year without you.
England still will be here without you.
There'll be fruit on the tree and a shore
by the sea;
There'll be crumpets and tea without you!
I can thrill to a play without you;
Take a bath ev'ry day without you.
I can still have a dream and it's liable to
seem
Even more like a dream without you.
I can do without you!
The world without your smiling face,
Still will be a highly agreeable place!
They can still rule the land without you;
Windsor Castle will stand without you.
And without much ado
We can all muddle through without you!
Without your pulling it, the tide comes in.
Without your twirling it, the earth can spin.
Without your pushing them, the clouds
roll by.
If they can do without you, ducky, so can I!
There'll be fog ev'ry year without you;
When it clears, it'll clear without you.
And there still will be rain on the plain
down in Spain;
Even that will remain without you!
I can laugh till it hurts without you;
Order fat'ning desserts without you!
I can prosper and thrive, and be glad I'm
alive;
Be the mother of five without you.

Bennett

There'll be spring every year without you.
England still will be here without you.
There'll be fruit on the tree and a shore by
the sea;
There'll be crumpets and tea without you!
I can thrill to a play without you;
Take a bath ev'ry day without you.
I can still have a dream and it's liable to
seem
Even more like a dream without you.
I can do without you!
The world without your smiling face,
Still will be a highly agreeable place!
They can still rule the land without you;
Windsor Castle will stand without you.
And without much ado
We can all muddle through without you!
Without your pulling it, the tide comes in.
Without your twirling it, the earth can spin.
Without your pushing them, the clouds
roll by.
If they can do without you, ducky, so can I!
There'll be fog ev'ry year without you;
When it clears, it'll clear without you.
And there still will be rain on the plain
down in Spain;
Even that will remain without you!

I can do without you!
You, dear friend, can jolly well
Plumb go straight to Hartford, Hereford
   and Hampshire!
I can carve out a niche without you!
Even scratch where I itch without you.
So go back in your shell, I can do bloody
   well without you!
(Higgins interrupts with "By George, I
   really did it!")

I can do without you!
You, dear friend, can jolly well
Plumb go straight to Hartford, Hereford
   and Hampshire!
I can carve out a niche without you!
Even scratch where I itch without you.
So go back in your shell, I can do bloody
   well without . . .
(Higgins interrupts with "By George, I
   really did it!")

APPENDIX 2 "WHY CAN'T THE ENGLISH?" (ORIGINAL VERSION)

Higgins
Look at her, a prisoner of the gutters;
Condemned by ev'ry syllable she utters.
By right she should be taken out and hung
For the cold-blooded murder of the English tongue!
Daily her barbaric tribe increases,
Grinding our language into pieces.

Hear them down in Soho Square,
Dropping aitches everywhere,
Speaking English any way they like.
"You, sir, did you go to school?"

Cockney
"What d'you take me fer, a fool?"

Higgins
No-one taught him "take" instead of "tike."
Hear a Yorkshireman converse,
Cornishmen are even worse,
A national ensemble singing flat.
Chickens cackling in a barn,
Just like this one.

Eliza
Garn!

Higgins
I can see the writing on the wall.
Soon we'll have no language left at all!

Why can't the English teach their children how to speak?
In every other nation
They stress pronunciation.

In France, mispronounce a word
And the French are fit to kill,
And frequently add it to your bill.

Rumanians learn Rumanian although why remains a riddle;
Hungarians learn Hungarian once they've learned to play the fiddle.
But well-spoken English you will hardly ever get!
Oh why can't the English learn to
Set a good example to people whose English is painful to your ears?
Canadians pulverise it
In Ireland they despise it.
There even are places where English completely disappears.
Americans haven't used it for years.

Why can't the English teach their children how to speak?
In Norway there are legions of literate Norwegians.
In German a wee mistake and the Germans rant and roar;
And promptly prepare to go to war.

In Italy ev'ry tenor learns his language like the gospel.
The Hebrews learn it backwards which would seem to be imposs-bel.
But use proper English, you're regarded as a freak.
Oh why can't the English
Use standard English?
Why can't the English learn to speak?

APPENDIX 3 "ON THE STREET WHERE YOU LIVE" (ORIGINAL VERSION)

The original lyric was as follows (with the cut passages in bold text):

Love appears at the most peculiar places.
You can never foresee when it will start.
Love attacked me while I was at the races;
And I lost my money and my heart.

(dialogue with Mrs. Pearce)

There's the tree she rushes under when it starts to rain.
See the way it's filled with bloom.
And isn't there a garland all around that window-pane?
That could only be her room!

This street is like a garden
And her door a garden gate.
What a lovely place to wait.

I have often walked down this street before;
(as published, up to:)
No, it's just on the street where she lives"

Some men hate to wait and wait
If by chance the girl is late.
I don't mind the waiting part at all.
Some get bored and wander on;
Curse their fate and soon are gone.
I would wait through winter spring and fall.

For oh! the towering feeling
(etc.)

Verse 2
Now they're at the gate
For the second run.
Now the cue is sounding;
They are bounding
Forward—
Look! It has begun!

What a burst of pandemonium!
Never heard the like of it any place.
'Twas a thrilling, absolutely chilling
Running of the Ascot Second Race!

End of Scene
There they are again
For another run.
Now they're holding steady,
Each equestrian is ready
For it—
Look! It has begun!

APPENDIX 5 "YOU DID IT": CUT PASSAGE

Pickering
Tonight, old man, you did it!
You did it! You did it!
You said that you would do it
And indeed you did.
I thought that you would rue it;
I doubted you'd do it.
But now I must admit it
That succeed you did.

Servants
Congratulations,
Professor Higgins!
For your glorious
Victory!
Congratulations,
Professor Higgins!
You'll be mentioned
In history!

Pickering
You should get a medal
Or be even made a knight.

Servants
They should honour you
By making you a knight.

Pickering
All alone you hurdled
Ev'ry obstacle in sight.

Higgins
I must confess
Without undue conceit,
It was an electrifying feat!

Pickering
And you're the one who did it!
Who did it . . . who did it!
I said you couldn't do it
But you pulled her through.
Tonight, old man, you did it!
You did it! You did it!
I know that I have said it
But you did it and the credit
For it all belongs to you!

Servants
Congratulations,
Professor Higgins!
Who would dream you
Could pull her through?
Congratulations,
Professor Higgins!
Sing a hail and halleluiah!
Ev'ry bit of credit
For it all belongs to you!

NOTES

ABBREVIATIONS

FLC   Frederick Loewe Collection, Library of Congress

HLP   Herman Levin Papers, Wisconsin Center for Film and Television Research, Madison, Wisconsin

HRP   Harold Rome Papers, Yale University

TGC   Theatre Guild Collection, Yale University

WCC   Warner-Chappell Collection, Library of Congress

CHAPTER 1

1. Ovid (trans. John Dryden), *Metamorphoses*, Wordsworth Classics Edition (London: Wordsworth, 1998), 325.

2. Alan Jay Lerner, *The Street Where I Live* (London: Hodder and Staughton, 1978), 29–119. Page numbers refer to the 1989 English paperback edition with a foreword by Benny Green (New York: Da Capo Press, 1989).

3. Steven Bach, *Dazzler: The Life and Times of Moss Hart* (New York: Knopf, 2001). David Mark D'Andre, "The Theatre Guild, Carousel, and the Cultural Field of American Musical Theatre" (PhD diss., Yale University, May 2000).

4. Dan Laurence, ed., *Bernard Shaw: Collected Letters 1926–50* (New York: Viking, 1988), 528. In an earlier letter to novelist and playwright Siegfried Trebitsch, Shaw revealed that he had suggested that Straus's score for *The Chocolate Soldier* be provided with "a new libretto bearing a new name" and referred to the operetta as "the abominable C.S." Letter of April 28, 1931, Shaw to Trebitsch in ibid, 236–37.

5. Letter of August 28, 1921, Shaw to Trebitsch, in Dan Laurence, ed., *Bernard Shaw: Collected Letters 1911–25* (New York: Viking, 1985), 730–31.

6. In a letter of December 18, 1907, to Trebitsch on hearing that Straus intended to set his play to music rather than merely use an idea from act 1, Shaw wrote: "Such a musical version would simply drive the play off the boards," in Dan Laurence, ed., *Bernard Shaw: Collected Letters 1898–1910* (New York: Dodd, Mead, 1972), 742.

7. Letter of February 3, 1948, Shaw to E. A. Prentice in ibid., 813.

8. Letter of April 5, 1948, Shaw to Fanny Holtzmann in ibid., 817.

9. Lewis Funke, "The Long View of Mary Martin's Plans after *South Pacific*," *New York Times*, May 20, 1951, 11.

10. Sam Zolotow, "Goldsmith Writes Play for Mitchell," *New York Times*, October 5, 1951, 38.

11. Memorandum of October 24, 1951, Marshall to Langner, *TGC*, 137.

12. Interoffice memorandum of January 4, 1952, by Langner, *TGC*, 137.

13. Letter of February 15, 1952, Langner to Pascal, *TGC*, 137.

14. Lewis Funke, "Theatre Guild Mentioned as Producer of *Pygmalion* Musical," *New York Times*, January 27, 1952, X1.

15. A complete score for *Spring* was rediscovered by the author during the course of the research for this book and received its first complete performance since the original 1945 Broadway run by the London-based Lost Musicals organization in June 2010.

16. "On the 21st he dangled in front of Anderson a play that was certainly among those he was to discuss with Alan Jay Lerner a year or two later—*Pygmalion*." David Drew, *Kurt Weill: A Handbook* (London: Faber, 1987), 419–20. Lerner and Weill eventually collaborated on *Love Life* (1948).

17. See Valerie Pascal, *The Disciple and his Devil* (New York: McGraw-Hill, 1970), 239.

18. Telegram of March 22, 1952, Langner to Pascal, *TGC*, 137.

19. Lerner, *Street*, 49–51.

20. Letter of May 10, 1952. Lerner to Pascal, *TGC*, 137.

21. Letter of May 22, 1952, Langner to Fitelson. *TGC*, 137.

22. Sam Zolotow, "Michael Todd Eyes *Ninotchka* Script," *New York Times*, May 30, 1952, 12.

23. Lewis Funke, "Plans for Musicalizing *Pygmalion* Are Making Progress," *New York Times*, June 1, 1952, X1.

24. Letter of June 17, 1952, Langner to Helburn; letter of June 19, 1952, Marshall to Helburn, *TGC*, Box 62.

25. Letter of June 20, 1952, Helburn to Langner. *TGC*, Box 62. Less than three months later, Lawrence died of cancer, which was undoubtedly the cause of her problems in performance. Sheridan Morley, *Gertrude Lawrence* (New York: McGraw-Hill, 1981), 197–98.

26. Telegram of June 25, 1952 (10:15 a.m.), Langner to Helburn, *TGC*, 137.

27. Telegram of June 25, 1952 (11 a.m.), Langner to Helburn, ibid.

28. Letter of June 27, 1952, Langner to Helburn. *TGC*, 62. Quoted in D'Andre, "Theatre Guild," 248; Valerie Pascal, *Disciple*, 220.

29. Crawford describes her difficulties in her autobiography, *One Naked Individual: My Fifty Years in the Theatre* (New York: Bobbs-Merrill, 1977). Letter of July 1, Helburn to Langner, *TGC*, 62.

30. D'Andre, "Theatre Guild," 248. D'Andre does not cite a source for this piece of information.

31. Letter of July 18, Langner to Helburn. *TGC*, 137.

32. Telegram of August 7, 1952, Harrison to Langner. *TGC*, 59.

33. Interestingly, Noël Coward's published diary for July 28, 1952, indicates that he had been approached by the Theatre Guild to write a *Pygmalion* musical for Mary Martin at this time. Graham Payn and Sheridan Morley, eds., *The Noel Coward Diaries* (London: Macmillan, 1983), 196.

34. Both D'Andre and Valerie Pascal agree on this date, though neither cites a source. D'Andre, "Theatre Guild," 249; Pascal, *Disciple,* 221. Pascal's copy of the contract is held in the Pascal Collection, Howard Gottlieb Archival Research Center, Boston University.

35. Lerner, *Street*, 38.

36. Letter of October 20, 1954, Helburn and Langner to Lerner, *TGC*, Box 137.

37. Bach says, "There were rumors that the collaborators had quarreled, for neither the first nor the last time." Bach, *Dazzler*, 338.

38. Interoffice memorandum of February 17, 1953, Jo Mielziner to Marshall, *TGC*, 137.

39. D'Andre, "Theatre Guild," 250. D'Andre does not state the sources for this information.

40. Lewis Funke, "News and Gossip Gathered on the Rialto," *New York Times*, February 8, 1953, X1.

41. Brooks Atkinson, review of *Maggie*, *New York Times*, February 19, 1953.

42. Letter of February 20, 1953, Helburn to Langner. *TGC*, 137.

43. Although D'Andre states this date with certainty, he does not cite a source for the information.

44. Sam Zolotow, "*Saints and Sinners* Stage News Again," *New York Times*, May 27, 1953, 28.

45. Letter of July 8, 1953, Benjamin Aslan to Charles Abramson of the Famous Artists Corp., *HRP*, folder 79/57.

46. Sam Zolotow, "Decision Awaited on Hit's Transfer," *New York Times*, August 28, 1953, 13.

47. Sam Zolotow, "*Saints and Sinners* Is Postponed," *New York Times*, September 18, 1953, 16. *The Girl with Pink Tights* had a score by Sigmund Romberg; it opened on March 5, 1954, at the Mark Hellinger Theatre, which would eventually be the home of *My Fair Lady*.

48. Letter of October 27, 1953, Benjamin Aslan to Jane Rubin of the Richard J Madden Play Company, Inc., *HRP*, 79/57.

49. Sam Zolotow, "*Richard III* Back on Stage Tonight," *New York Times*, December 9, 1953, 9.

50. Letter of January 26, 1954, Benjamin Aslan to Michael Halperin of Wilzin and Halperin, *HRP*, 79/57. A copy of the contract also lies in the same box of *HRP* at Yale.

51. Sam Zolotow, "Guinness Stymied in Bid to Act Here," *New York Times*, June 11, 1954, 20; Zolotow, "Katzka Discusses Spewack Musical," *New York Times*, July 21, 1954, 19. Hal Prince went on to become one of Broadway's leading producers and directors, with shows such as *West Side Story* and *The Phantom of the Opera* to his credit.

52. Letter of September 8, 1954, Aslan to Herbert P. Jacoby of Schwartz and Frohlich, *HRP*, 79/57.

53. Letter of September 10 from Aslan to Rome, Fields, Loewe, and Chodorov; letter of September 12, 1956, Rome to Aslan; letter of October 31, Aslan to Herbert Jacoby; letter of March 14, 1957, Aslan to Loewe, Rome and Fields, *HRP*, 79/57.

54. Typescript for *Saints and Sinners*, *HRP*, folder 65/85. Sale of Frederick Loewe's manuscripts at Christie's, Los Angeles, November 18, 1999, Lot 99, Sale 9292. Demo recording of *Saints and Sinners*, Library of Congress, call number RGB 0465.

55. Louis Calta, "*Li'l Abner* Bagged by Two Showmen," *New York Times*, March 17, 1953, 26. Lewis Funke's column briefly mentions the same project in his column five days later. Funke, "News and Gossip of the Rialto," *New York Times*, March 22, 1953, X1.

56. Arthur Schwartz's successes include *The Band Wagon*, written for Fred Astaire on Broadway in 1931 and later fitted out with a new book and additional songs as an MGM film, again with Astaire (1953), and *A Tree Grows in Brooklyn* (1951).

57. Thomas M Pryor, "Cinerama Slates Full-Length Film: *Paint Your Wagon*, with New Music and Lyrics, on Tap as First Feature in Process," *New York Times*, February 11, 1953, 35.

58. Edwin Schallert, "Cinerama Start Looms," *Los Angeles Times*, February 11, 1953, B9.

59. A song with the title "There's Always One You Can't Forget" was written for Lerner and Charles Strouse's *Dance a Little Closer* in 1983 but with an otherwise completely new lyric.

60. My thanks to Mr. Schwartz and Erik Haagensen for bringing this script to my attention and for generously providing me with a copy.

61. Louis Calta, "News of the Stage," *New York Times*, November 12, 1953, 37.

62. Stephen Holden, "A Composer's Son Remembers Life with Father, Through Music," *New York Times*, October 4, 1988, 17.

63. Sam Zolotow, "Lewis Wondering about Three Musicals," *New York Times*, June 21, 1954, 20.

64. Howard Thompson, "The Local Screen Scene," *New York Times*, August 15, 1954, X5.

65. I thank Richard C. Norton for this piece of information about Olsen, which comes from his forthcoming biography of Loewe. Olsen also mentions her part in this reunion in the Camera Three Productions documentary *Lerner and Loewe: Broadway's Last Romantics* (1988).

66. Lerner, *Street*, 45.

CHAPTER 2

1. Sam Zolotow, "Bow Set Tonight for *On Your Toes*," *New York Times*, October 11, 1954, 31.

2. Letter of October 19, 1954, Lerner to Helburn and Langner, *TGC*, 137.

3. Letter of October 20, 1954, Helburn and Langner to Lerner, ibid.

4. *HLP*, 25/7. On December 4, 1956, Moss Hart would approach Coward with a view to him appearing in the London production of the show (*HLP*, 23/5). Nothing came of this offer, but Coward later wrote a musical for production by Levin, *The Girl Who Came to Supper* (1963).

5. *HLP*, 26/6.

6. Ibid.

7. Lerner, *Street*, 60. Certainly Lerner, Loewe, and Levin met with Beaton in London, but Lerner leaves the reader with the impression that all discussions about the show took place there rather than having started in New York with Levin.

8. *HLP*, 23/5.

9. Ibid.

10. Diary, 1955. Michael Redgrave Papers, Theatre Museum Archive, Victoria and Albert Museum, TH 17/31/41/12. The "Clurman-Giraudoux" project was a play about the Trojan wars called *Tiger at the Gates*, in which Redgrave would play Hector.

11. Memo of telephone conversation with Richard Halliday, December 14, 1954, *TGC*, Box 137.

12. D'Andre, "Theatre Guild," 253. I was not able to access the interoffice memos D'Andre cites for this information.

13. Letter of December 27, 1954, Langner to Paul Ramsay, *TGC*, 137.

14. Theatre Guild Memo of January 18, 1955, *TGC*, 137.

15. Summary of conversations with Rodgers and Hammerstein, February 9, 1955, *TGC*, 137.

16. *HLP*, 25/8.

17. Lerner, *Street*, 81. In the end, Hanya Holm's choreography received unanimous praise, but the cutting of the ballet—which would have been her great moment—meant that the amount of choreography was reduced even further.

18. Ibid. Lerner finished the story: "Moss had nothing to say and obviously could not wait for the meeting to end. After Mike left, Moss looked at Fritz and me and from his lips came an over-articulated, 'No.'"

19. In a letter of June 13, 1955, Levin wrote to Laurence Evans: "We have made a deal with Moss Hart to direct the show," *HLP*, 25/7. Hart's contract, dated June 18, 1955, is also in *HLP*, 25/8.

20. Telegram of January 25, 1955, Lerner to Levin, *HLP*, 25/7. Letter of April 1, 1955, Levin to Laurence Evans, *HLP*, 25/7. Letter of April 1, 1955, Levin to Beaton, *HLP*, 24/7.

21. *HLP*, 26/6. One assumes that the reference to *Show Boat* is sarcastic rather than the person referred to in the phrase "I'm meeting him today . . . ," if nothing else because Sammy Lee, the choreographer of the original *Show Boat*, did no further work on Broadway after 1932.

22. Lerner, *Street*, 81.

23. *HLP*, 25/7. In his book on Moss Hart, Steven Bach cites an interview he carried out with production assistant Bud Widney by way of explaining Holliday's brief connection with the show, Bach, 343–44.

24. *HLP*, 26/6.

25. Agreement between Levin and Andrews of March 31, 1955, to which are attached various riders of May-June 1955, *HLP*, 25/5.

26. Julie Andrews, *Home* (New York: Hyperion, 2008), 180–81.

27. Lerner, *Street*, 52.

28. Andrews, *Home*, 182.

29. *HLP*, 23/5.

30. Letters of February 7, 1955, Levin to Martin Jurow and David Hocker, *HLP*, 23/5.

31. Letter of April 11, 1956, Basil Geoffrey of Renée Stepham Ltd. to Levin, *HLP*, 23/5. Geoffrey had read about *My Fair Lady* in the *Daily Express* and wrote to Levin to suggest three of his artists: Barry Sinclair for Higgins, Stanley Beard for Doolittle, and Petula Clark for Eliza.

32. Lerner, *Street*, 54.

33. Ibid.

34. Ibid., 49.

35. Ibid., 60.

36. Ibid., 62–63.

37. *HLP*, 23/5.

38. Lerner, *Street*, 53.

39. Letter of April 1, 1955, Levin to Beaton, *HLP*, 24/7. Beaton was designing both costumes and sets for Selznick's production of Enid Bagnold's play *The Chalk Garden*, which was to open on Broadway in October 1955 and star Gladys Cooper (who later played Mrs. Higgins in the 1964 movie version of *My Fair Lady*)

40. Letter/agreement of March 18, 1955, Levin to Harrison and countersigned by the latter, *HLP*, 25/7.

41. See, for instance: Jared Brown, *Moss Hart: A Prince of the Theatre* (New York: Crown, 2006), 338.

42. Letter of February 24, 1955, Lillian Aza to Herman Levin, *HLP*, 25/9.

43. Lerner, *Street*, 60.

44. Letter of March 14, 1955, Aza to Levin, *HLP*, 25/9.

45. Letter of March 25, 1955, Levin to Aza, *HLP*, 25/9.

46. Letter of March 31, 1955, Aza to Levin, *HLP*, 25/9.

47. Letter of April 6, 1955, Levin to Aza, *HLP*, 25/9.

48. Lerner writes: "We . . . promised him that we would fly over to see him to show him his songs as we wrote them, to make certain he felt comfortable with them," Lerner, *Street*, 62–63.

49. Letter of April 1, 1955, Levin to Laurence Evans, *HLP*, 25/7.

50. Letter of April 1, 1955, Levin to Smith, *HLP*, 26/6.

51. Four telegrams between Levin and Van Druten. Only Van Druten's first telegram is dated (April 6), so the dates of the others remain conjectural.

52. Memorandum of Telephone Message, Monica McCall to Herman Levin of May 9, 1955, *HLP*, 25/7.

53. Letter of April 14, 1955, Aza to Levin, *HLP*, 25/9.

54. Letter of April 29, 1955, Aza to Levin, *HLP*, 25/9.

55. Letter of May 6, 1955, Levin to Aza, *HLP*, 25/9.

56. Letter of May 12, 1955, Aza to Levin, *HLP*, 25/9.

57. Letter of May 17, 1955, Levin to Aza, *HLP*, 25/9.

58. Letter of May 31, 1955, Aza to Levin, *HLP*, 25/9.

59. Telegram of June 13, Levin to Aza, *HLP*, 25/9.

60. Letter of June 27, Aza to Levin, *HLP*, 25/9.

61. Telegrams of July 13, 1955 between Levin and Aza, *HLP*, 25/9.

62. Letter of April 4, 1955, Evans to Levin, *HLP*, 25/7.

63. Letter of April 20, 1955, Levin to Evans, *HLP*, 25/7.

64. Letter of April 25, 1955, Evans to Levin, *HLP*, 25/7.

65. Letter of May 2, 1955, Evans to Levin; letter of May 6, 1955, Levin to Evans, *HLP* 25/7.

66. Letter of May 9, 1955, Evans to Levin, *HLP*, 25/7.

67. Letter of May 17, 1955, Levin to Evans, *HLP*, 25/7.

68. Letter of May 18, 1955, Evans to Levin, *HLP*, 25/7. Lerner describes how Harrison was having an affair with Kay Kendall at the time Harrison was appearing onstage with Lilli Palmer. Lerner, *Street*, 55.

69. Letter of May 23, 1955, Evans to Levin, *HLP*, 25/9.

70. Letter of May 27, 1955, Levin to Evans, *HLP*, 25/9.

71. Letter of April 6, 1955, Beaton to Levin, *HLP*, 25/9.

72. Letter of May 13, 1955, Arnold Weissberger to Levin, *HLP*, 24/7.

73. Letter of May 24, 1955, Weissberger to Levin, *HLP*, 24.7.

74. Letter of June 13, 1955, Weissberger to Levin, *HLP*, 24/7. On June 17, Levin wrote to Beaton to inform him that he had received the contracts the previous day. Letter of June 17, 1955, Levin to Beaton, *HLP*, 24/7.

75. Letter of April 20, 1955, Levin to Actors' Equity Association, *HLP*, 25/5.

76. Letter of April 27, 1955, Actors' Equity Association to Levin, *HLP*, 25/5.

77. Letter of May 14, 1955, Smith to Levin, *HLP*, 26/6.

78. Letter of May 17, 1955, Levin to Smith, *HLP*, 26/6.

79. Letters of May 20 and June 2, 1955, between Smith and Levin, *HLP*, 26/6.

80. Lerner, *Street*, 61–62.

81. "Suggested Deal—CBS" of May 23, 1955, *HLP*, 27/10. The fruits of the advertising aspect of the deal came to bear in February 1956. A letter from CBS to Levin lists fourteen television spots in the following week in which the opening of *My Fair Lady* would be announced. Letter of February 10, 1956, Sam Cook Digges of CBS to Levin, and attached list, *HLP*, 33/5.

82. Letter of June 15, 1955, Irving Cohen to Levin, *HLP*, 27/10.

83. Agreement of July 18, 1955, between Levin and CBS, *HLP*, 28/5.

84. Letter of June 13, 1955, Levin to Evans, *HLP*, 25/7.

85. Letter of June 24, Beaton to Levin, *HLP*, 24/7.

86. Letters of March 16 and May 19, 1955, Geoffrey to Levin; letters of June 12 and July 27, Levin to Geoffrey, *HLP*, 23/5. Michael King would go on to earn $200 a week in this role.

87. Letter of June 29, 1955, Lou Wilson to Levin, *HLP*, 25/5.

88. Letter of June 28, 1955, Levin's amanuensis—presumably his secretary—to W. H. Worrall (Levin's London broker for this negotiation), *HLP*, 25/7.

89. Letter of July 6, 1955, Levin to Evans, *HLP*, 25/7.

90. Letter of July 6, 1955, Levin to Beaton, *HLP*, 24/7.

91. Telegrams of July 12 and 13, 1955, between Levin and Evans, and letter of July 15, Levin to Evans, *HLP*, 25/7.

92. Letter of July 15, Levin to Beaumont, *HLP*, 25/7. Evans's secretary wrote a further letter to Levin that day to inform him of an error in the letter regarding the date of *Nina*'s opening: she had written August 27 instead of August 7, but it had now been changed to July 27. Letters of July 15, 1955, Evans and Eileen Rutherford to Levin, *HLP* 27/5.

93. Letter of July 15, Levin to Evans, *HLP*, 25/7.

94. Letter of July 18, Levin to Evans, *HLP*, 25/7.

95. Letter of July 18, 1955, Levin to Aza, *HLP*, 25/9.

96. Letter of July 29, 1955, Levin to Evans; telegram, Levin to Evans of July 28, *HLP*, 25/7.

97. Letter of July 19, 1955, Beaumont to Levin. In another letter, of July 26, he restated the complexity of his position, *HLP*, 25/7.

98. Telegram of July 20, 1955, Evans to Levin, and telegram of July 20, Levin to Evans, *HLP*, 25/7. Levin wrote snappily to Evans: "IMPOSSIBLE WAIT AUGUST 21 SITUATION HERE INTOLERABLE. LERNER AND LOEWE ARRIVE LONDON JULY 31. I ARRIVE AUGUST 3. PLEASE ARRANGE HOTEL."

99. Telegram of July 28, 1955, Levin to Evans, *HLP*, 25/7.

100. Letter of July 28, 1955, Gielgud to Hugh Wheeler. Richard Mangan, ed., *Gielgud's Letters* (London: Weidenfeld and Nicolson, 2004), 183.

101. Telegram of August 1, 1955, Levin to Evans, *HLP*,, 25/7.

102. Telegram of August 12, 1955, Evans to Levin, *HLP*, 25/7.

103. Memorandum of telephone conversation 5:15 p.m., August 17, 1955, between Levin and Moskowitz, *HLP*, 25/7.

104. Memorandum of telephone conversation between Levin and Evans at 3:10 p.m. on August 18, 1955, *HLP*, 25/7.

105. Telegram of August 26, 1955, Evans to Levin, *HLP*, 25/7.

106. Untitled memorandum of August 30, 1955, *HLP*, 25/7. A couple of annotations in Levin's handwriting indicate the memo is probably his.

107. Letter of September 1, 1955, Beaumont to Levin (with a draft version attached), *HLP*, 25/7.

108. Contract between Levin and Harrison, September 2, 1955, *HLP*, 23/10.

109. Contract between Levin and Andrews, September 8, 1955, *HLP*, 23/10

110. Contract between Levin and Holloway, September 13, 1955, *HLP*, 23/10

111. Contract between Levin and Michael King, September 23, 1955, *HLP*, 26/8.

112. Memorandum Re: Robert Coote, September 27, 1955, *HLP*, 23/9. On March 26, 1956, Tom Helmore was hired as Rex Harrison's understudy.

113. Rider dated June 15, 1955, between Levin and the Trebuhs Realty Company, *HLP*, 24/3. Telegram of September 2, Levin in London to Lerner in New York, *HLP*, 25/7. Contract between Levin and Farrell of 9 September, *HLP*, 25/7. The choice of the Mark Hellinger was considered a bad omen, since that venue had not enjoyed success before, but after the triumph of *My Fair Lady* Lerner went on to use it for *On a Clear Day You Can See Forever* and *Coco*.

114. Contract of September 15, 1955, between Levin and the Shuberthaven Operating Company, *HLP*, 24/3.

115. Contract of October 3, 1955, between Levin and 265 Tremont Street Inc. for the Shubert Theatre, Boston. Contract of November 2, 1955, between Levin and Goldlawr, Inc, for the Erlanger Theatre, *HLP*, 24/3.

116. Elliott Norton, "Fair Lady Twice Passes Up Hub, Waits 'til 59," *Boston Daily Record*, November 11, 1957. Accessed from a photocopy in *HLP*, 33/5.

117. Agreements of June 27 and September 12, 1955, between Levin and Allers, c/o Meyer Davis Music, *HLP*, 26/3.

118. Letter of September 20, 1955, Albert Sirmay to Levin; contract of August 31, 1955, between Levin and Chappell's, *HLP*, 26/3.

119. Letter of September 12, 1955, in which Levin asks Irving Cohen to draw up new contracts with Beaton and Smith to provide for the possible television transmission that may take place under the agreement with CBS, *HLP*, 24/7. On September 19, David Grossberg of Reinheimer and Co. sent Smith's contract to

Levin, who then passed it on to Rudy Karnolt of United Scenic Artists the next day. At the same time, the producer submitted Abe Feder's contract to do the lighting for the show. Letter of September 19, 1955, David Grossberg to Herman Levin, and letter of September 20, Levin to Rudy Karnolt. Smith's contract is dated September 20, 1955, *HLP*, 26/6. Beaton's contract is dated September 22, 1955, and was submitted to Arnold Weissberger that day by Levin. Weissberger returned them, signed, on September 28. Contract and letter from Levin to Weissberger, *HLP*, 24/7. Of the circumstances of Hanya Holm's joining the show, very little documentary evidence exists. The Hanya Holm Collection in the New York Public Library contains no correspondence related to this period of the show's genesis, and the Levin Papers contain only the contract of September 25, 1955, *HLP*, 25/10.

120. Contract of September 7, 1955, between W. Spencer Harrison of CBS and Lerner, Loewe, and Levin. The television company's investment was recouped by November 16, 1956, whereupon Levin wrote to Spencer Harrison in great satisfaction: "From now on, it's all gravy," Letter of November 16, 1956, Levin to W Spencer Harrison, *HLP*, 27/10.

121. Letters of September 13 and 19, 1955, Levin to Evans; letter of September 15, Evans to Levin, *HLP*, 25/7.

122. Letter of September 19, 1955, Levin to Evans, and letter of September 29, Evans to Levin, *HLP*, 25/7. Roy Lowe was Harrison's vocal coach.

123. Letters of September 27 and October 4, 1955, Levin to Evans, *HLP*, 25/7.

124. Letter of October 12, 1955, Levin to Evans, *HLP*, 25/7. In his diary for November 1955, Beaton mentions completing the *Pygmalion* designs during the final days of his three-month visit. Diary 1954–5, vol. 98, Papers of Sir Cecil Beaton, St. John's College Library, Cambridge.

125. Contract of October 4, 1955, between Levin and Nesbitt; contract of October 10, 1955, between Levin and Hewett, specifying at that stage that he could be called upon to understudy Higgins, Pickering, or Doolittle, and resignation letter of mid-March 1956 (following a conversation with Lerner, Loewe, and Levin on March 13), attached, *HLP*, 23/9.

126. On October 21, Levin wrote to the U. S. Passport Department to support Holm's application for passport renewal. "The purpose of Miss Holm's trip, so far as it concerns this organization, is to collect material and study various types of Cockney life and dancing in connection with *My Lady Liza*." Letter of October 21 from Levin to U.S. Passport Dept. A list from the Helene Pons costume studio of New York, addressed to Beaton on October 31 indicates the costumes to be made in London for Harrison. In addition, wigs for Eliza, costumes and wigs for the footmen, costumes for the policemen, a hat for Doolittle, and an outfit for a Street Cleaner were to be bought in London. Letter of October 31, 1955, Helene Pons Studio to Beaton, *HLP*, 35/4.

127. Memo to Oliver Smith from Levin, October 27, 1955, *HLP*, 26/6.

128. Letter of November 1, 1955, Levin to Evans, *HLP*, 25/7.

129. Letter of November 7, 1955, Evans to Levin. On November 17, Evans requested that Alan Jay Lerner pay Roy Lowe's account for Harrison's "tuition and coaching" between October 27 and November 10; Levin sent him a check for $77.30 six days later.

Then on December 29, Evans requested an additional payment for Lowe's account from November 12 to December 2, giving a clear indication of when Harrison's vocal lessons took place. Letter of November 17, Evans to Alan Jay Lerner, and Levin's reply of November 23; letter of December 29, Evans to Levin, *HLP*, 25/7.

130. Letter of November 1, 1955, Aza to Levin; letters of October 26 and November 4, Levin to Aza. Prior to this, Aza had informed Levin that "Julie Andrews had excellent publicity when she arrived in this country [i.e., returned to England after finishing *The Boy Friend* on Broadway]. Strangely enough her birthday is on the same day as Stanley, so they should get on well together," letter of October 5, Aza to Levin, *HLP*, 25/9.

131. Letters of November 9 and December 13, Aza to Levin, *HLP*, 25/9.

132. Andrews, *Home*, 184–87.

133. Letter of November 18, 1955, , Levin to Charles Tucker, *HLP*, 25/5.

134. Letter of November 23, 1955, , Tucker to Levin, *HLP*, 22/5.

135. Letter of December 5, 1955, Lerner to Julie Andrews, *HLP*, 25/5.

136. Contracts of November 15 between Levin and Bevans, December 12, between Levin and Coote and December 12 between Roache and Levin, *HLP*, 23/9; contracts between Rod McLennan and Levin of December 5 and Olive Reeves-Smith of December 9, *HLP*, 23/10.

137. Press releases and clippings, *HLP*, 23/6.

138. Contract of November 26, 1955, between Levin and Maney; agreements of November 30, 1955, between Levin and Rittman; agreement of December 2, 1955, between Levin and Ernest Adler, *HLP*, 24/2.

139. For an introduction to Rittman and her work, see Steven Suskin, *The Sound of Broadway Music: A Book of Orchestrators and Orchestrations* (Oxford: Oxford University Press, 2009), 155 and 196.

140. Letter of November 26, 1955, Eileen J Hose on behalf of Cecil Beaton to Levin, *HLP*, 24/7.

141. Letter of November 28, 1955, Levin to Hose, *HLP*, 24/7.

142. Letter of December 6, 1955, Levin to Harrison. The reference to $450 is made in a letter of January 4, 1956, Jerry Leider of MCA Artists to Philip Adler, c/o Levin, *HLP*, 25/7.

143. Letter of December 6, 1955, Levin to Beaton, *HLP*, 24/7.

144. Estimates from Imperial Scenic Studios of December 13, 1955; TB McDonald Construction Co, Inc, of December 19; and the Nolan Brothers of December 14. On December 16, the Nolan Brothers submitted a new estimate, and on the same day Levin drew up a contract to hire them to make the sets, *HLP*, 35/8.

145. Letter of December 28, 1955, Levin to Coote, *HLP*, 26/8.

146. Lerner, *Street*, 75–76.

147. Ibid, 91.

148. Letter of November 29, 1955, Lerner to Harrison, *HLP*, 25/7.

149. December 16 is the latest date on which Levin refers to *My Lady Liza* (in the contract with the Nolan Brothers); the letter to Coote of December 28 is the earliest mention of *My Fair Lady*.

150. Letter of December 30, 1955, Levin to Lieberson, and attached billing sheet, *HLP*, 24/11.

151. Letter of January 4, 1955, Levin to Evans, *HLP*, 25/7.

152. Letter of December 29, 1955, Levin to Julie Andrews, *HLP*, 25/5.

153. Lerner, *Street*, 87.

154. Ibid.

155. Andrews, *Home*, 193.

156. Lerner, *Street*, 88.

157. Ibid., 89.

158. Ibid., 90.

159. Andrews, *Home*, 194–95.

160. Lerner, *Street*, 90.

161. Ibid.

162. Contract of January 5, 1955, between Levin and Tutrinoli; contract of January 8, between Levin and Russell Bennett, *HLP*, 23/6.

163. Letter of February 11, 1956, Robert Russell Bennett to Levin, *HLP*, 24/2.

164. Letter of January 9, 1956, Doris Prober of Decorative Plant Corp to Levin, *HLP*, 25/1. Letter of January 10, 1956, Philip Alder to Miss Brown of Coro Jewelry, *HLP*, 24/13. Letter of January 10, 1956, Beaton to Levin and Sales Contract between Levin and the Helene Pons Studio, January 18, 1956, *HLP*, 35/4.

165. Contract of December 30, 1955, between The Liza Company and the New Haven Jewish Community Center, *HLP*, 24/3.

166. Lerner, *Street*, 94.

167. Ibid., 96.

168. Ibid., 97.

169. Ibid, 98.

170. Bone, "Shows Out of Town: *My Fair Lady*," *Variety*, February 8, 1956, 56.

171. Letter of February 15, 1956, Hyman to Adler, *HLP*, 25/8.

172. Letter of February 23, Weissberger to Levin, *HLP*, 24/7.

173. Letter of June 8, 1956, Langner to Lerner, *TGC*, 83.

CHAPTER 3

1. Basic factual details about Shaw's biography and the history of *Pygmalion* come from L. W. Conolly's magnificent introduction to his scholarly edition of the play published in the New Mermaids series (London: Methuen, 2008) and Michael Holroyd's seminal *Bernard Shaw* (one-volume ed., London: Chatto and Windus, 1997), unless otherwise stated.

2. Conolly, "Introduction: The Author," in *Pygmalion*, xiv–xv.

3. Michael Holroyd reports on Shaw's activities: "As early as September 1897 everything 'has been driven clean out of my head by a play I want to write . . . in which [Sir Johnston Forbes-Robertson] shall be a west end gentleman and she an east end dona in an apron and three orange and red ostrich feathers.'" Holroyd, *Bernard Shaw*, 415–16.

4. Conolly, *Pygmalion*, xvii.

5. Tree "loved to disguise himself with beards, uniforms, vine leaves, ear-trumpets. In this respect, Professor Higgins was a disappointment." Holroyd, *Bernard Shaw*, 441.

6. Conolly, *Pygmalion*, 74. Eliza's line comes in response to Freddy's question, "Are you walking across the park, Miss Doolittle?"

7. Conolly, *Pygmalion*, xxiv.

8. Ibid. 146.

9. Shaw, *Complete Letters*, vol. 3, 227–28.

10. Conolly, *Pygmalion*, xxvi.

11. "Sequel," ibid., 129.

12. *Pygmalion*, 139–40.

13. Ibid., 132.

14. Ibid.,129–30.

15. Ibid., xxvii.

16. Ibid., 149.

17. Ibid., 150–51.

18. Ibid., 147.

19. Ibid., 154.

20. Ibid., 20.

21. The correspondence of Shaw and Pascal has been collected into a convenient volume edited by Bernard F. Dukore, with extensive reference to *Pygmalion*. Bernard F. Dukore, ed., *Bernard Shaw and Gabriel Pascal: Selected Correspondence* (Toronto: University of Toronto Press, 1996). Dukore is also the editor of a beautiful volume of Shaw's screenplays that discusses various versions of *Pygmalion*, including the foreign-language films. Bernard F. Dukore, ed., *The Collected Screenplays of Bernard Shaw* (London: George Prior Publishers, 1980).

22. *Pygmalion*, xxviii.

23. Paul Bauschatz, "The Uneasy Evolution of *My Fair Lady* from *Pygmalion*" in Fred D. Crawford, ed., *The Annual of Bernard Shaw Studies*, xviii (University Park, PA: Penn State University Press, 1998), 192 and 195. Curiously, Bauschatz also claims early on that "virtually all of *My Fair Lady*'s dialogue can be found in *Pygmalion*," but then goes on to relate various departures from Shaw's text. Bauschatz, "Uneasy Evolution," 181.

24. Joseph P. Swain, *The Broadway Musical: A Critical and Musical Survey* (New York: Oxford University Press, 1990), 185.

25. Lerner, *Street*, 36.

26. "After a private showing of *Pygmalion*, [Lerner and Loewe] became enthusiastic." V. Pascal, *Disciple*, 219.

27. Telegram of March 22, 1952, Langner to Pascal, *TGC*, box 137.

28. Letter of May 10, 1952, Lerner to Pascal, *TGC*, box 137.

29. Holroyd, 436. Holroyd also describes Doolittle as being "of Dickensian vitality."

30. Richard Traubner, *Operetta: A Theatrical History* (New York: Doubleday, 1983), 409.

31. Dukore, *Complete Screenplays of Bernard Shaw*, 46.

32. "Lady Liza—Brief Outline," *HLP*, 34/2.

33. One possibility is that Higgins was there doing "research," and that Pickering simply arrived from India there, but if this was Lerner's thinking, he does not say so here.

34. *Pygmalion*, 69.

35. *My Fair Lady* script, 91.

36. Lerner, *Street*, 99.

37. Outline 2 survives because it was included in an appendix to an early dissertation on the musical by Gerald Harold Weissman, who seems to have been given access to it by Lerner during the musical's original Broadway run. Gerald Harold Weissman, "The musicalization of *Pygmalion* into *My Fair Lady*" (master's thesis, Stanford University, 1957).

38. Lerner, *Street*, 44.

39. *My Fair Lady*, "Mimeographed Rehearsal Script," *HLP*, 34/7.

40. Kitty Carlisle Hart, *Kitty: An Autobiography* (New York: Doubleday, 1988), 177; Bach, *Dazzler*, 341.

41. Page numbers in brackets in this chapter refer to the first British edition of the script of *My Fair Lady* (London, 1958). I use this edition because it contains a few corrections of typographical errors in the American first edition. References to "the published script" are to this British text.

42. *Pygmalion*, 11.

43. Ibid., 36.

44. Ibid., 73.

45. Though even after reinstating these lines, Lerner still did not merely lift the *Pygmalion* text. For instance, Shaw's Higgins tells Mrs. Pearce to pay Eliza out of the housekeeping money, as well as reflecting tangentially about the difficulty of getting Eliza "to talk grammar." *Pygmalion*, 37.

46. Ibid., 45.

47. Ibid., 78.

48. *Pace* Swain, who opines that "the lyrics no longer convey fantasy: Eliza now has the power to do what she says." In fact, the opposite is the case, since Eliza has to run away in order to elude Higgins's power, rather than enacting the violence described in the song. Swain, *Broadway Musical*, 190.

49. Ethan Mordden has noticed this aspect of the show, too: "[M]idway through Act One, there's a sequence made of alternating song and dialogue that is generally conceded to be the point at which critics and public realized that *My Fair Lady* was not just very enjoyable but very special." Ethan Mordden, *Coming Up Roses: The Broadway Musical in the 1950s* (New York: Oxford University Press, 1998), 155.

50. *Pygmalion*, 7.

CHAPTER 4

1. See the outlines in chap. 3 for corroboration the position of these two songs. Location of the manuscripts in *FLC*: "What Is a Woman," 5/25; "Who Is the Lady?," 8/45; "Dear Little Fool," 5/4; "Over Your Head," 8/27, "Limehouse," 8/20; and "The Undeserving Poor," 8/40.

2. "What's to Become of Me?," *FLC*, 8/44. Eliza's speech quoted from *My Fair Lady* script, 110.

3. *FLC*, 8/37.

4. "Who Is the Lady?" is not substantially different from this extract. In bars 3, 7, 35, and 39, D and E are written instead of E and F-sharp, and the melody ends with bar 46.

5. Lerner, *Street*, 57.

6. *FLC*, 5/18.

7. *My Fair Lady* script, 55–56.

8. "Please Don't Marry Me" in folder marked "Lyrics and Songs Not Used," *HLP*, 34/8.

9. *FLC*, 5/24.

10. The lyric is also similar in mood to that of "Shy," which is known to have been the precursor to "I Could Have Danced."

11. Rex Harrison, *Rex* (London: Macmillan, 1974), 161.

12. Rex Harrison, *A Damned Serious Business* (London: Bantam, 1990), 140.

13. *Lady Liza*: Brief Outline, 4. *HLP*, 34/2.

14. Ibid.

15. Lerner, *Street*, 65–66 and 91–92.

16. Julie Andrews, *Home*, 201.

17. *My Lady Liza*: outline of scenes and musical numbers, 2. *HHP*, Series 4, 21/518.

18. Both versions are in *FLC*, 5/23.

19. My thanks to Elliot J. Cohen for sharing the transcript of his interview with Trude Rittmann (dated October 3, 1995) with me.

20. "I finished the lyric in twenty-four hours, but not to my satisfaction . . . I thought my lyric was earth-bound. There was one line in particular that made me blush when I sang it to Fritz. The line was: "And [*sic*] all at once my heart took flight." I promised Fritz I would change it as soon as I could. As it turned out, I was never able to . . . [T]o this day the lyric gives me cardiac arrest." Lerner, *Street*, 86.

21. A document titled "*My Fair Lady*: timing sheet" in the Levin Papers shows that the final version of act 1, scene 9 took 3′15″ to run. By contrast, the duration of "Come to the Ball" in the appendix of the Jay recording of *My Fair Lady* runs 3′24″, which does not include the repeated choruses for the dancing; and "Say a Prayer for Me Tonight" on the original soundtrack recording of *Gigi* runs 1′13″.

22. Lerner, *Street*, 76–77 and 98.

23. Loewe's autograph and his annotated copy of a copyist's score are in *FLC*, 5/2 and 5/3; the full score is in *WCC*, 142/1; the remaining manuscripts are in *WCC*, 142/3.

24. *My Fair Lady* script, 121–22.

25. Ibid, 123.

26. Rittmann diverges from Bennett's orchestrated version only from bar 212 on, where her version is a minor third higher than his.

27. The location of the scores in *WCC* is as follows: Freda Miller's score, 142/7; conductor's score for "Intro to Dress Ballet" plus a copy of Rittmann's piano score, 142/6; the copy of the piano score with the modified ending in Rittmann's hand, 142/7; Rittmann's autograph for the new "Intro to Dress Ballet," 142/7; Lang's autograph full score for the "Intro" is at the back of the autograph full score for "Come to the Ball," 142/1; Bennett's autograph full score, 142/5.

28. Lerner to Pascal, May 10, 1952, *TGC*, box 137.

29. *Lady Liza*—Brief Outline, 4. *HLP*, 34/2.

30. Untitled scenic outline, 2, *HLP*, 34/2.

31. *My Lady Liza* outline, 2. Hanya Holm Papers, New York Public Library. Series 4, 21/518. All of Hanya Holm's notes referenced in the rest of this chapter are from this same folder, unless otherwise noted.

32. Clearly by "vanishes" Holm means "removes" with added connotations of speed and of the dancers' disappearance.

33. "Intro to Dress Ballet," *WCC*, 142/7.

34. Full score to "Intro to Dress Ballet," *WCC*, 142/1.

35. Lerner, *Street*, 152.

36. "Say a Prayer for Me Tonight" in folder marked "Lyrics and Songs Not Used," *HLP*, 34/8. The line "Gracious, proud and refine" was probably intended to read "refined."

37. "Say a Prayer for Me Tonight" piano-vocal score, marked "FA," *WCC*, 147/2. "Say a Prayer for Me Tonight" from *Gigi* Song Album (London, 1958), 11–13.

38. "Say a Prayer for Me Tonight" and "Bridge after Prayer" orchestrations, *WCC*, 151/5.

39. Jeremy Gerard, "Stars Perform in Memorial Tribute to Composer Frederick Loewe," *New York Times*, March 29, 1988.

CHAPTER 5

1. The main difference is in the line "With one enormous chair," which originally read "With one gigantic chair"; the copyist's lyrics read "gigantic," but the word has been struck through in pencil and replaced with "enormous." "Wouldn't It Be Loverly?," copyist's piano-vocal score, marked "Russell" in Trude Rittmann's handwriting on the front cover, *WCC*, 154/5.

2. Loewe, "Overture" autograph, *FLC*, 5/17.

3. 'Lang takes credit for *My Fair Lady*'s "With a Little Bit of Luck," "The Ascot Gavotte," "On the Street Where You Live," "The Embassy Waltz," "Get Me to the Church on Time," and "Without You," the remainder (including the Overture) being Bennett's contributions. Robert Russell Bennett with George J Ferencz, ed., *The Broadway Sound: The Autobiography and Selected Essays of Robert Russell Bennett*, Eastman Studies in Music, (Rochester, NY: University of Rochester Press, 1999), 228.

4. See Lerner, *Street*, 59–60. Lerner also says that the lyric for this song initially caused him agony, as a result of the lack of confidence he derived from Mary Martin's negative reaction to the songs. After receiving psychiatric help, however, Lerner says that the words took him only two days to write. *Street*, 66–67.

5. "Wouldn't It Be Loverly" lyric sheet, *HLP*, 34/8.

6. "Wouldn't It Be Loverly" lyric sheet, *WCC*, 151/6.

7. There is one notational discrepancy: Loewe has a D sharp in the second beat of the two-bar introduction to the refrain, which is adhered to in Bennett's orchestration but is left as a natural in the copyist's vocal score and both of the published vocal scores.

8. See chap. 5. For Rodgers's approach to song writing, see Tim Carter, *Oklahoma! The Making of an American Musical* (New Haven, CT: Yale University Press, 2007), 118–20. "As is typical of Rodgers's sketches, the *Oklahoma!* ones are presented on a single stave, with the melody, some indications of one or more inner parts, and, very

occasionally, roman numerals to indicate the harmony." This is almost the same as Loewe's apparent evolution of "Say a Prayer for Me Tonight" (and a large number of non-*My Fair Lady* songs), though the roman numerals are less of a feature of his method than they are of Rodgers's.

9. Lerner, *Street*, 49–50.

10. "Just You Wait": lyric sheet, *HLP*, 34/8; copyist's score, *WCC*, 148/3.

11. The score is initialed "R.B." in the top righthand corner.

12. "Musical Synopsis (2)," envelope titled "Franz Allers Lyrics," *WCC*, 151/6.

13. Lerner, *Street*, 84.

14. Julie Andrews confirms this chronology. Andrews, *Home*, 201.

15. Lerner, *Street*, 86.

16. Marni Nixon is well known as the singing voice for Audrey Hepburn in the film version of *My Fair Lady* and also sang for Deborah Kerr in *The King and I* and Natalie Wood in *West Side Story*. Her story does not fit in with the facts at all: we know that Lerner and Loewe were not writing *My Fair Lady* in the first half of 1954 and that the song was one of the last to be composed. Marni Nixon, *I Could Have Sung All Night* (New York: Billboard Books, 2006), 139.

17. "I Could Have Danced All Night" from folder marked "Vocal Score" in *HLP*, 30/1.

18. "I Want to Dance All Night," copyist's score with title in Loewe's hand, *WCC*, 146/8. That the score has also been marked "Peter"—indicating Peter Howard, the conductor's assistant—also suggest that this title was used during rehearsals rather than as the original title of the song.

19. Script, *HLP*, 34/4.

20. Script, *HLP*, 34/3.

21. Copies of the playbills and the early pressing of the album are in the author's collection.

22. *My Fair Lady* script, *HLP*, 34/5.

23. Her lines are: "I understand, dear. / It's all been grand, dear. / But now it's time to sleep."

24. There is also an amusing copying error in the second refrain: instead of writing "[Why all at once] my heart took flight," Bennett has put "my heart stood still," probably an unconscious reference to the Rodgers and Hart song "My Heart Stood Still."

25. We saw in chap. 5 that in the New Haven version of the show, Eliza had an additional solo, "Say a Prayer for Me Tonight," before setting off to the ball, but it was cut during the first week of tryouts. The return of "Just You Wait," therefore, has all the more impact.

26. The same can probably be said of "The Rain in Spain," whose use of habanera rhythms is connected simply to the reference to Spain in the song's title.

27. "Just You Wait," Rittmann's autograph, *WCC*, 148/3.

28. "On the Street Where You Live" reprise, original orchestration, *WCC*, 148/1.

29. "Street Reprise," Rittmann's autograph, *WCC*, 148/3.

30. "Show Me," Loewe's autograph, *FLC*, 5/22.

31. Lerner, *Street*, 92–94.

32. "Without You," various scores, *WCC*, 153/7. The autograph in *FLC*, like so many of the others, presents only the final version of the text. *FLC*, 5/29.

33. It is partly a performance issue, too: Rex Harrison brings appeal to the part in the film, which other actors might not do on the stage.

34. Lerner, *Street*, 77. Lerner specifies "In Norway there are legions / Of literate Norwegians" as an example of a short, Cowardesque lyric.

35. Harrison, *Rex*, 164.

36. Letter of November 29, 1955, Lerner to Harrison, *HLP*, 25/7.

37. The pages from this manuscript are divided between four other songs in the Loewe Collection and used as covers to bind them: "Show Me," "I Could Have Danced All Night," "The Street Where She Lives," and the final version of "Why Can't the English?"

38. However, it is clear that while Rittmann wrote the eighth notes in the melody line in bars 2, 3, 5, 9, 10, and 11, Loewe contributed those in bars 6, 7, and 8; Rittmann's eighth notes are smoothly rounded while Loewe's tend to have a distinctive groove in the tail.

39. Lerner, *Street*, 92–94.

40. Curiously, a copy of this score was registered with the Library of Congress for copyright on April 3, 1956, (three weeks after the show opened), rather than the final version. "Why Can't the English?," *WCC*, 152/8; Library of Congress copyright deposit, Eu 432970.

41. The new couplet reads: "Make one slip in German and, Good Lord, how the Germans roar! / In fact, you'll be lucky if they all don't go to war." The words "you'll be lucky if they" are set to a new descending F-major scale of sixteenth notes to fit in the extra words.

42. The three differences are: the use of the past tense in relation to the Hebrews (who "learnt" it backwards in this lyric but "learn" it backwards in its published form); a witty mention of ancient Greek ("But soon proper English will be dead as ancient Greek!"); and a line asking why the English can't use "decent English."

43. "The English," *WCC*, 152/8.

44. The only difference is that "The Scotch and Irish" later became "The Scotch and the Irish" in the final song, necessitating the modification of an eighth note into two sixteenths. Both the early autograph and the copyist's score for the initial version of the song feature a clumsier melody and harmonic rhythm at this point.

45. The front indicates that the copy belonged to Franz Allers, the conductor, though it is difficult to determine whether he was responsible for the modifications. Loewe's autograph score for "Why Can't the English?" is located in *FLC*, 5/26.

46. The lyric sheet is with the other "Why Can't the English?" documents in *WCC*, 152/8.

47. Lerner, *Street*, 68.

48. Ibid., 68–69 and 77.

49. It reads "With no eccentric whim" instead of "Of no eccentric whim," "Who wants to live his life" instead of "Who likes to live his life," "For let a woman in your life" instead of "Oh, let a woman in your life" (in two places), and instead of ending "Oh, let a woman in your life . . . / Let a woman in your life. . . . / Let a woman in your life," the original lyric read "For let a woman in your life . . . / But let a woman in your life. . . . / Just let a woman in your life . . ."

50. As an aside, the original American edition of the script omitted the line "Just a very gentle man" at the end of the relevant verse—apparently an oversight, because the English edition reinstates the line, as do the published scores.

51. This is based on the lyric from the rehearsal script, not the published lyric.

52. The autograph full score for the scene change music is also in Bennett's hand, but it is titled "New No. 5a (Ordinary Man)," suggesting that something different might originally have been planned.

53. Lerner, *Street*, 87.

54. Harrison, *Rex*, 166.

55. "A Hymn to Him," *WCC*, 146/4.

56. Loewe wrote "They're nothing but exasperating, irritating, agitating, calculating, aggravating, maddening and infuriating hags," but the published version modifies "agitating" to "vacillating" and "aggravating" becomes "agitating" instead.

57. Further discussion of Lang's orchestration is not made here because it contains no changes or additions other than during the final four bars, which have evidently been rewritten. Since they are firmly taped down, it is not possible to see what was originally written.

58. Letter of November 29, 1955, Lerner to Harrison, *HLP*, 25/7.

59. Lerner, *Street*, 85–86.

60. "I've Grown Accustomed to Her Face," copyist's vocal score and choral score, *WCC*, 147/5.

61. In another difference, the original has "She rather makes the day begin" instead of the published version's "She almost makes the day begin."

62. "New Intro to I've Grown Accustomed," *WCC*, 147/3.

63. There were a couple of other small differences. Later, when Higgins sings "Poor Eliza! How simply frightful! How humiliating! How delightful!" the original version had an extra exclamation, "How ghastly!" after "Poor Eliza!" The spoken section that follows was also slightly different—"How shall I react on that inevitable night . . ." rather than "How poignant it will be . . ."—and the underscoring was more extensive.

64. Originally it read "I will slam the door and let the villain freeze" rather than "let the hellcat freeze."

65. The manuscript has "Finale Ultimo" on the front and "Incidental Insert Into: Accustomed to her Face" as the title inside.

66. "Tempo di Rodgers—ma molto espressivo!!" is evidently a joke (about Richard Rodgers's preference for slightly slow tempi) between Rittmann and Bennett, both of whom worked on the musicals of Rodgers and Hammerstein.

67. Bennett's score says "rather makes the day begin" instead of "almost," and "villain" instead of "hellcat"; the former case has then been corrected in pencil but the latter still says "villain."

CHAPTER 6

1. For the reprise in act 1, scene 4, the autograph full score is the only existing primary source.

2. This lyric is common to both the Warner-Chappell Collection and the rehearsal script.

3. Another example is "To tend his needs and see his food is cooked," which becomes "To share his nest and see his food is cooked."

4. The reprise of the song in act 1, scene 4, also contains a small deviation from the published lyric: Lerner writes "[A man was made to help support his children; /] Which is the proper thing for him to do" rather than "Which is the right and proper thing to do" (Jack Mason's full score also uses this "original" lyric). Again, the change is small but the addition of the word "right" helps to assert the image of the "correctness" of taking fatherhood seriously in contrast to the end of the verse when Doolittle sings of his hope that "They'll go out and start supporting you."

5. "With a Little Bit of Luck," *FLC*, 5/27.

6. It is possible that Loewe was reusing an old piece of manuscript paper, which had contained a completely different piece of music. Based on a survey of all the manuscripts in the Loewe Collection, many of which contain fragments from more than one song (sometimes from more than one show), this seems to have been standard procedure for him, either in other to save paper or because he had to use whatever paper was available.

7. This is corroborated by the copyist's fair copy of the orchestration, which starts simply with the first fully accompanied bar and misses out "The Lord a-." "With a Little Bit of Luck," copyist's full score, *WCC*, 153/1.

8. Also included in the folder with the song is Lang's full score for the scene change music (No. 4a).

9. Lerner, *Street*, 85.

10. "Get Me to the Church on Time," lyric sheet, *WCC*, 151/6.

11. "Get Me to the Church on Time," Rittmann's piano score and Miller's photocopy, *WCC*, 145/4.

12. "Get Me to the Church II," choral arrangement, *WCC*, 145/3.

13. Lerner, *Street*, 76.

14. *Lady Liza*, Brief Outline, *HLP*, 34/2.

15. The New Haven playbills give the song its final title, but the copyists scores in the Warner-Chappell Collection all direct the lyric to the third person.

16. Lerner, *Street*, 98.

17. The presentation was given on December 12, 1971, as part of the *Lyrics and Lyricists* series at the Kaufmann Concert Hall of the 92nd Street Y in New York. It is now available on CD as *An Evening with Alan Jay Lerner*, DRG Records 5175 (1977).

18. This backs up the idea of a link with "Please Don't Marry Me," which had been cut long before the orchestration was made.

19. Unusually for Bennett, it is written in pencil rather than in pen.

20. The other key players are, clearly, Eliza, Higgins, and Doolittle. I discount Pickering, Mrs. Pearce, and Mrs. Higgins here because they do not have a significant solo numbers and are mostly on the periphery of the drama.

21. Geoffrey Block, *Enchanted Evenings* (New York: Oxford University Press, 1997), 379. n.28.

22. They are written in Roman numerals, starting with "I—Gm."

23. Keith Garebian, *The Making of My Fair Lady* (Toronto: ECW Press, 1993), 108. Bennett's full score is relatively free of corrections, although the cut verse is crossed out.

24. Lerner, *Street*, 83–84. Harrison, *Rex*, 161. Block compares the accounts in *Enchanted Evenings*, 379, n.26.

25. "Dance—Rain in Spain," *WCC*, 151/3.

26. A copy of the published sheet music (New York: Belwin, Inc.) for this song is found in *FLC*, 8/36.

27. "Ascot Gavotte," *FLC*, 5/1.

28. "Gavotte Repr.," Untitled manuscript starting "Presto furioso" with a message from Rittmann to Bennett, *WCC*, 141/3. "Intro to Gavotte" and "Gavotte Dance," *WCC*, 144/1.

29. "Ascot Gavotte," annotated "Freda" on front, with associated loose photocopies of "Intro to Gavotte" and "Gavotte Dance," *WCC*, 141/1.

30. This version also appears in two separate lyric sheets in the Warner-Chappell Collection, a lyric sheet in Levin's papers, and the rehearsal script.

31. Lyric sheet in envelope titled "Franz Allers Lyrics," *WCC*, 151/6.

32. "Ascot Gavotte," choral score, 141/6; "Gavotte," conductor's score, *WCC*, 141/3.

33. Untitled original "End of Ascot" music and "Gavotte Repr.," *WCC*, 141/3.

34. This is demonstrated by the orchestration of this original ending to the Ascot Scene, housed in the Warner-Chappell Collection. "Fainting Music" and "End of Ascot (out)," *WCC*, 144/3 and 141/1.

35. "Ballroom Intro," *WCC*, 141/7.

36. Block, *Enchanted Evenings*, 231.

37. Unnumbered folder titled "The Embassy Waltz: parts," *WCC*, box 143.

38. Bennett's orchestration, titled "The Embassy Waltz," is in the *WCC*, 143/2.

39. "Promenade," orchestration, *WCC*, 150/1.

40. "Entr'acte," Rittmann piano score, *WCC*, 143/8.

41. Clearly, the "glorious Russell Bennett finish" was in fact to be a "glorious Phil Lang" one.

42. "Finish of Entr'acte," Lang's full score, *WCC*, 143/6.

43. Lerner, *Street*, 77 and 81.

44. Ibid., 100.

45. As was the case with several earlier numbers, the version of the song in *FLC* contains Loewe's handwriting only in the music of the first three systems of the first page and all the lyrics; Rittmann is responsible for all the remainder of the music. *FLC*, 5/31.

46. Although the published vocal scores contain this section and indicate that it was not performed on Broadway, the British first edition of the published libretto does not include it nor do the original cast albums (Broadway and London).

47. One of the copyist's scores has the word "Silly" crossed out and replaced by "Utter" at this point, perhaps to avoid the alliteration with so many "s" sounds in the line. *WCC*, 155/3.

48. Geoffrey Block correctly refers to "the uncharacteristically inconsiderate Pickering" in his analysis of the number, but the Colonel was in fact even more inconsiderate in the original version of the number. Block, *Enchanted Evenings*, 236.

49. William Zinsser, *Easy to Remember: The Great American Songwriters and Their Songs* (Jaffrey, NH: David R. Godine Publisher, 2000), 229.

CHAPTER 7

1. "Shows Out of Town: *My Fair Lady*," *Variety* (February 8, 1956), 56. My thanks to Richard C. Norton for providing me with a copy of this and various other reviews.

2. "*Lady Fair* Cut 15 Mins. During New Haven Bow," *Variety*, February 15, 1956, 67.

3. Unless otherwise stated, the reviews from this section are quoted from Rachel W. Coffin, ed., *New York Theatre Critics' Reviews* 17, no.7: 345–48.

4. Brooks Atkinson, "*My Fair Lady*: Shaw's *Pygmalion* Turns into One of the Best Musicals of the Century," *New York Times*, March 25, 1956, Arts and Leisure supplement, X1.

5. Bob Rolontz, "Exit a Winner: *My Fair Lady* Leaves Mark on Disk Mkt. as well as the Theater," *Billboard Music Week*, March 3, 1962, 5.

6. Copy in the author's collection.

7. Sam Zolotow, "Huxley Disowns Staging of Novel," *New York Times*, November 29, 1957, 33. My thanks to Richard C. Norton for pointing out this article.

8. Letter, Herman Levin to Lillian Aza (November 4, 1957); agreement between Herman Levin and Stanley Holloway (November 4, 1957). *HLP*, 25/9.

9. Letter, Levin to Howes (January 31, 1959), 25/11. Howes played the role on Broadway for twelve months, leaving on January 31, 1959.

10. Letter, Charles Tucker to Herman Levin (August 27, 1957); reply, Levin to Tucker (August 30) *HLP*, 25/5.

11. Letter, Levin to Felix de Wolfe (August 21, 1957), 23/5.

12. Letter, Levin to Lerner and Loewe in Paris (July 19, 1957), *HLP*, 23/5.

13. Letter, Michael Redgrave to Levin (March 20, 1956), *HLP*, 26/1.

14. Telegram, Lerner to Levin (November 15, 1956), *HLP*, 23/5.

15. Telegram, Moss Hart to Coward (December 4, 1956), *HLP*, 23/5. In a letter to Laurence Olivier on January 12, 1957, Coward confirmed that he had "refused haughtily but graciously to play *My Fair Lady* for three months." Quoted in Barry Day, ed., *The Letters of Noël Coward* (London: Methuen, 2007), 618.

16. Brooks Atkinson, "Two Fair Years: Shavian Musical Is Still a Delightful Show," *New York Times*, March 9, 1958, X1.

17. After Julie Andrews and Sally Ann Howes, Eliza was played by Pamela Charles, and in January 1961 Margot Moser became the first American girl to play the role. Higgins was played by Edward Mulhare, Michael Evans, and Michael Allison.

18. Quoted in Robert Baral, *Revue: A Nostalgic Reprise of the Great Broadway Period* (New York: Fleet Publications, 1962), 98.

19. The recording is now available on CD via Sepia Records (SEPIA 1090).

20. Reuters, *New York Times*, October 2, 1958, 28.

21. His scores for the West End include *Pickwick* (his greatest success), 1963; *Treasure Island*, 1973; and *Great Expectations*, 1975. London productions for which he had served as musical director include *Wonderful Town*, *Pal Joey*, *Kismet*, *Call Me Madam*, and Lerner and Loewe's own *Paint Your Wagon*.

22. Loewe's illness is related in Andrews, *Home*, 237–38 and Lerner, *Street*, 112–13.

23. Drew Middleton, "Londoners Greet Their *Fair Lady*; Spiritual Home of Musical Discovers It Is as Good as the Yanks Said It Was," *New York Times*, May 1, 1958, 34.

24. K. Hart, *Kitty*, 191. Hart was present at the Royal Gala and accompanied her husband, Moss, to the Royal Box during the intermission, making for an amusing anecdote in her book.

25. Andrews, *Home*, 255.

26. For a list of the countries in the years immediately following the premiere, see Sam Zolotow, "Israeli Players to do *Fair Lady*," *New York Times*, December 18, 1963, 46. For this section of the chapter, I am particularly indebted to Richard C. Norton for allowing me to read the unpublished manuscript of his forthcoming book on Loewe.

27. Howard Traub, "Soviet Union Asks for a Troupe to Sing *Fair Lady*," *New York Times*, May 6, 1959, 1.

28. Philip Benjamin, "*Fair Lady* Faces Russian Pirating," *New York Times*, May 1, 1959, 1.

29. Max Frankel, "Moscow Sizes Up a Grand *Lady*," *New York Times*, April 3, 1960, X1.

30. Osgood Carruthers, "*Fair Lady* Hailed by Moscow Critic," *New York Times*, April 24, 1960, 85.

31. Anonymous, "*My Fair Lady* Ending Its North American Run," *New York Times*, December 13, 1963, 39.

32. Sam Zolotow, "Eliza Doolittle to Dance Again," *New York Times*, January 30, 1964, 25.

33. John Canaday, "Audience as well as Cast Has Grand Time at *My Fair Lady*," *New York Times*, May 21, 1964, 43.

34. Richard F. Shepard, "*My Fair Lady* Wins Again," *New York Times*, June 14, 1968, 42.

35. Memorandum by Levin, February 10, 1955. *HLP*, 24/8.

36. Testimony of Herman Levin, May 15, 1960, *HLP*, 27/14.

37. Handwritten notes, *HLP*, 25/12.

38. See Hugh Fordin, *MGM's Greatest Musicals* (New York: Da Capo Press, 1996), 517, for more information on Warner's position. The refusal of the first bid in September 1961 is discussed in a telegram from Levin to the studio's negotiator, *HLP*, 23/8.

39. Details of Harrison's deal are described in Alexander Walker's excellent biography of the actor, *Fatal Charm: The Life of Rex Harrison* (London: Orion, 2002), 307.

40. In his diary, Beaton wrote that after one clash, "it took George Cukor two hours to recover from his displeasure with me enough to continue." Richard Buckle, ed., *Self-Portrait with Friends: The Selected Diaries of Cecil Beaton* (London: Pimlico, 1981)367. In turn, Cukor acknowledged in an interview that "As everyone knows, we didn't get on very well."

41. Murray Schumach, "*Fair Lady* to Set a Film-cost Mark," *New York Times*, June 5, 1963. Gavin Lambert, *On Cukor* (New York: G. P. Putnam, 1972; rev. ed. New York: Rizzoli, 2000), 186.

42. Lambert, *On Cukor*, 192.

43. Block, *Enchanted Evenings*, 323–27.

44. Lambert, *On Cukor,* 192.

45. Reviews quoted in Jerry Vermilye, *The Complete Films of Audrey Hepburn* (New York: Citadel, 1995), 178–80.

46. Letter, Lerner to Cecil Beaton, April 21, 1967, Cecil Beaton Papers, St. John's College, Cambridge.

47. Much later, Diehl wrote a detailed reminiscence of working with Holm for a specific dance publication. Crandall Diehl, "*My Fair Lady* and other Broadway Memories," *Choreography and Dance* 2, pt. 2, 73–87.

48. Robert Berkvist, "Will this *Fair Lady* be as Loverly?," *New York Times,* March 21, 1976, 57.

49. Richard Eder, "Levin Back on Street Where She Lived," *New York Times,* March 22, 1976, 21.

50. Mel Gussow, "Richardson Finds 'Iggins a Lovely Change of Pace," *New York Times,* March 31, 1976, 29.

51. Patrick Garland, *The Incomparable Rex* (London: Macmillan, 1998).

52. Anonymous, "*Fair Lady* Understudy Is Going On," *New York Times,* August 18, 1981, C8.

53. Garland, *Incomparable Rex,* 205.

54. Mel Gussow, "*My Fair Lady* Returns," *New York Times,* August 19, 1981, C17.

55. Garland, *Incomparable Rex,* 206.

56. Ibid., 205.

57. Glenn Collins, "On Stage and Off," *New York Times,* July 2, 1993, C2.

58. Bruce Weber, "Fighting for the Soul of Eliza Doolittle," *New York Times,* December 15, 1993.

59. David Richards, "*My Fair Lady*: A Darker Side to the Fable of a Flower Girl," *New York Times,* December 10, 1993.

60. Copy in the author's collection.

61. Sheridan Morley and Ruth Leon, *Hey, Mr Producer! The Musical World of Cameron Mackintosh* (London: Weidenfeld and Nicholson, 1998), 52–53.

62. See Gene Lees's *Inventing Champagne: The Musical Worlds of Lerner and Loewe.* (New York: St. Martin's Press, 1990), 288–89.

63. Quotation from an article on Conran's website, http://www.jasperconran. com/performing-arts/my-fair-lady/#nav=path_%252Fperforming-arts%252Fmy-fair-lady%252Fmy-fair-lady-press%252C7%252CSLS.html%253Fid%253D953%2526m odule%253Dgallery (accessed November 19, 2010).

64. See, for instance, Charles Spencer's review of the production in the *Daily Telegraph,* February 19, 1992.

65. The day before the revival opened, Nunn published an article in the *Guardian,* containing the headline "In George Bernard Shaw's original play, Eliza and Henry don't even get it together. No wonder My Fair Lady is miles better than Pygmalion." *Guardian,* March 14, 2001, accessed online at http://www.guardian.co.uk/culture/2001/mar/14/ artsfeatures.georgebernardshaw on November 19, 2010. In an article in the program booklet for the production (copy in the author's collection), the choreographer Matthew Bourne referred to Nunn's addition of lines from *Pygmalion.*

66. Michael Billington, review of *My Fair Lady*, *Guardian*, March 17, 2001. Accessed online at http://www.guardian.co.uk/stage/2001/mar/17/theatre.artsfeatures1, November 23, 2010.

67. Rhoda Koenig, review of *My Fair Lady*: "Cockney Charmer is Set Fair for Success," *Independent*, March 2011. Accessed online at http://www.independent. co.uk/arts-entertainment/theatre-dance/reviews/cockney-charmer-is-set-fair-for-success-687653.html, November 23, 2010.

68. See Hugh Davies, "Martine Will Soon Be Back on Song," *Daily Telegraph*, April 13, 2001. Accessed at http://www.telegraph.co.uk/news/uknews/1316079/Martine-will-soon-be-back-on-song.html, November 23, 2010. Jonathan Pryce commented on the situation in an interview connected with the Drury Lane transfer: Dominic Cavendish, "Life With Lots of Doolittles," *Daily Telegraph*, July 24, 2001. http://www.telegraph. co.uk/culture/4724679/Life-with-lots-of-Doolittles.html, November 23, 2010.

69. Edward Seckerson, review of *Our House* and *My Fair Lady*, *Independent*, May 19, 2003. Accessed at http://www.independent.co.uk/arts-entertainment/theatre-dance/reviews/our-house-cambridge-theatre-london-brmy-fair-lady-theatre-royal-druary-lane-london-590799.html, November 24, 2010.

70. Charles Spencer, "New Eliza is just loverly," *Daily Telegraph*, March 26, 2003. Accessed at http://www.telegraph.co.uk/culture/theatre/3591872/New-Eliza-is-just-loverly.html, November 24, 2010.

CHAPTER 8

1. These characteristics can also be found in "You Wash and I'll Dry" and "You've Got a Hold on Me" from *What's Up?*, most of whose score is currently lost.

2. Sections of "Katherine receives advice" were later reworked for "The Contract," one of Lerner and Loewe's new additions to the score of *Gigi* when it was adapted for the stage in 1973.

3. MGM bought the rights to *The Day Before Spring*, but in spite of several attempts it never reached the screen.

4. Lerner, *Street*, 35.

5. Quoted in Steven Suskin, *Opening Night on Broadway: A Critical Quotebook of the Golden Era of the Musical Theatre* (New York: Schirmer, 1990), 470.

6. Scott McMillin, *The Musical as Drama* (Princeton, NJ: Princeton University Press, 2006), 91.

7. Thomas L. Riis and Ann Sears, "The Successors of Rodgers and Hammerstein from the 1940s to the 1960s," in William A Everett and Paul R Laird, eds., *The Cambridge Companion to the Musical* (Cambridge: Cambridge University Press, 2002), 149.

8. *Pygmalion* and *My Fair Lady* (New York: Signet Classics, 1969). *My Fair Lady* (London: Penguin Readers, 1999, repr. 2008).

9. Quoted in Suskin, *Opening Nights*, 470.

10. Rowland Field, "Musical Shaw: *Fair Lady* Is a Rare Inspiration," *Newark Evening News*, March 16, 1956.

11. Anonymous, "A Memorable Musical," *Newsweek*, March 26, 1956; anonymous, "New Musical in Manhattan," *Time*, March 26, 1956.

12. Edward Jablonski, *Alan Jay Lerner: A Biography* (New York: H. Holt and Co., 1996), 106–45; Stephen Citron, *The Wordsmiths: Oscar Hammerstein 2nd and Alan Jay Lerner* (New York: Oxford University Press, 1996), 240–80; Geoffrey Block, *Enchanted Evenings*, 231–34; McMillin, *Musical as Drama*.

13. Richard Traubner, *Operetta*, 378.

14. Ibid., 407.

15. Riis and Sears, "The Successors of Rodgers and Hammerstein from the 1940s to the 1960s," in Everett and Laird, *Cambridge Companion to the Musical*, 149.

16. Gervase Hughes, *Composers of Operetta* (London: Macmillan, 1962), 249.

17. Zinsser, *Easy to Remember*, 229.

18. Mordden, *Coming Up Roses*, 155.

19. These are all in *FLC* and include "Cath'rine" (1925) (*FLC*, 8/6); "Love is Blind" (1924) (8/23); and "Sag' ja" (1923) (8/33).

20. See Lees, Zinsser, and Block's accounts of Loewe's life as typical examples of the emphasis placed on Loewe's early life in Europe.

21. Zinsser, *Easy to Remember*, 229.

22. Lerner himself said that "Luck" was intended to be "an English music hall song." Alan Jay Lerner, "Creation of a Lady," *Alpha RHO Journal* 1, no. 2 (Fall, 1960): 7.

23. Ibid., 10.

24. Ibid., 11.

25. Lerner once wrote an article mentioning "the deep and true influence of *Oklahoma!* . . . [S]ince that spring of 1943, no musical could ever again aspire to success with a sketchbook foundation, and no amount of unrelated choreographic virtuosity could rescue a raggedy second act." Alan Jay Lerner, "Oh What a Beautiful Musical," *New York Times Magazine*, May 12, 1963, 29–33. When he later wrote a book on the history of the genre, Lerner devoted an entire chapter to the importance of *Oklahoma!* Alan Jay Lerner, *The Musical Theatre: A Celebration* (London: Collins, 1986), 150–53.

26. Margaret Landon's part-novel, part-biography *Anna and the King of Siam* was published in 1944 and filmed in 1946. The novel was based on Anna Leonowens's two memoirs, *The English Governess at the Siamese Court* (1870) and *Romance of the Harem* (1872).

27. Page numbers in parentheses refer to the published script. Ultimately, of course, the fact that Eliza's desire to better herself has been over-satisfied—because she is fit to be "a consort to a king" (again Higgins's words, 147)—means that this ambition is now too modest, and perhaps impossible now that she has entered high society. One of the tensions of the story, indeed, is that Eliza's ambition to become a lady is realized by the end of act 1. The remainder of the story concerns the resolution of the Eliza-Higgins relationship, but in truth Eliza's question to Higgins—"What's to become of me?" (110)—is never really answered.

28. Hobe Morrison, review of "My Fair Lady," *Variety*, March 21, 1956.

29. John Beaufort, "My Fair Lady from Pygmalion," *Christian Science Monitor*, March 24, 1956.

30. Letter of March 2, 1959, Levin to Kenneth Allen, ed., *Tribune*, HLP, 33/6. The exact same wording is used in numerous letters to similar journalists and editors contained in this folder, which is marked "Editorial Campaign."

31. Swain, *Broadway Musical*, 199.

32. Ibid., 197.

33. Ibid., 200.

34. Block, *Enchanted Evenings*, 231 and 234.

35. Ibid., 242.

36. Raymond Knapp, *The American Musical and the Performance of Personal Identity* (Princeton, NJ: Princeton University Press, 2006), 284–93.

37. Lerner, "Creation of a Lady," 9.

38. Ibid., 12.

BIBLIOGRAPHY

PUBLISHED SCRIPTS

Lerner, Alan Jay. *My Fair Lady*. New York: Coward-McCann, 1956.

Lerner, Alan Jay. *My Fair Lady*. London: Signet, 1958.

Lerner, Alan Jay. *My Fair Lady*. London: Penguin 1999, repr. 2008.

Shaw, George Bernard, and Alan Jay Lerner. *Pygmalion and My Fair Lady*. New York: Signet Classics, 1969.

PUBLISHED SCORES

Loewe, Frederick. *My Fair Lady*. London: Warner-Chappell, 1956.

Loewe, Frederick. *My Fair Lady*. New York: Chappell/Intersong, 1969.

SECONDARY LITERATURE

Altman, Rick, ed. *Genre: The Musical*. London: Routledge and Kegan Paul, 1981.

Andrews, Julie. *Home*. New York: Hyperion, 2008.

Atkinson, Brooks. *Broadway*. New York: Macmillan, 1970.

Bach, Steven. *Dazzler: The Life and Times of Moss Hart*. New York: Knopf, 2001.

Barrios, Richard. *A Song in the Dark: The Birth of the Musical Film*. New York: Oxford University Press, 1995.

Beaton, Cecil. *Cecil Beaton's Fair Lady*. London: Weidenfeld and Nicolson, 1964.

Beaton, Cecil. *The Restless Years: Diaries 1955–63*. London: Weidenfeld and Nicolson, 1976.

Bennett, Robert Russell. *The Broadway Sound: The Autobiography and Selected Essays of Robert Russell Bennett*. Edited by George J Ferencz. Eastman Studies in Music. Rochester, NY: University of Rochester Press, 1999.

Block, Geoffrey. *Enchanted Evenings: The Broadway Musical from "Show Boat" to Sondheim and Lloyd Webber*. New York: Oxford University Press, 1997; rev. ed., 2008.

Block, Geoffrey. *Richard Rodgers*. New Haven, CT: Yale University Press, 2003.

Brahms, Caryl, and Ned Sherrin. *Song by Song: 14 Great Lyric Writers*. London: R. Anderson Publishers, 1984.

Buckle, Richard, ed. *Self-Portrait with Friends: The Selected Diaries of Cecil Beaton*. London: Pimlico, 1981.

Bush Jones, John. *Our Musicals, Ourselves: A Social History of the American Musical Theatre*. London: Praeger, 2003.

Carter, Tim. "In the Workshop of Rodgers and Hammerstein." In Colleen Reardon and Susan Parisi, eds., *Music Observed: Studies in Memory of William C Holmes*. Warren, MI: Harmonie Park Press, 2004.

Carter, Tim. *Oklahoma! The Making of an American Musical*. New Haven, CT: Yale University Press, 2006.

Castle, Charles. *Noël*. London: W. H. Allen, 1972.

Citron, Stephen. *The Wordsmiths: Oscar Hammerstein 2nd and Alan Jay Lerner*. New York: Oxford University Press, 1996.

Crawford, Cheryl. *One Naked Individual*. New York: Bobbs-Merrill, 1977.

D'Andre, David Mark. "The Theatre Guild, Carousel, and the Cultural Field of American Musical Theatre." PhD diss., Yale University, May 2000.

Day, Barry, ed. *The Letters of Noël Coward*. London: Methuen, 2007.

Drew, David. *Kurt Weill: A Handbook*. London: Faber, 1987.

Dukore, Bernard F., ed. *Bernard Shaw and Gabriel Pascal: Selected Correspondence*. Toronto: University of Toronto Press, 1996.

Dukore, Bernard F., ed. *The Collected Screenplays of Bernard Shaw*. London: Prior, 1980.

Dunne, Michael. *American Film Musical Themes and Forms*. Jefferson, NC: McFarland and Co., 2004.

Emmet Long, Robert. *Broadway: The Golden Years*. New York: Continuum, 2001.

Engel, Lehman. *The American Musical Theater*. New York: Macmillan, 1967.

Engel, Lehman. *Words with Music*. New York: Macmillan, 1972.

Everett, William A., and Paul R Laird, eds. *The Cambridge Companion to the Musical*. Cambridge: Cambridge University Press, 2002.

Feuer, Jane. *The Hollywood Musical*. Bloomington: Indiana University Press, 1982.

Fordin, Hugh. *MGM's Greatest Musicals*. New York: Da Capo Press, 1996.

Gänzl, Kurt, and Andrew Lamb. *Gänzl's Book of the Musical Theatre*. London: Bodley Head, 1988.

Garebian, Keith. *The Making of My Fair Lady*. Toronto: ECW Press, 1993.

Garland, Patrick. *The Incomparable Rex*. London: Macmillan, 1998.

Gottfried, Martin. *Broadway Musicals*. New York: Abrams, 1979.

Green, Benny, ed. *A Hymn to Him: The Lyrics of Alan Jay Lerner*. London: Pavilion Books, 1987.

Green, Benny. *Let's Face the Music: The Golden Age of Popular Song*. London: Pavilion Books, 1989.

Green, Stanley. *Encyclopaedia of the Musical Film*. New York: Oxford University Press, 1981.

Green, Stanley. *Encyclopaedia of the Musical Theatre*. New York: Dodd Mead 1976.

Green, Stanley. *The World of Musical Comedy*. 3rd ed. New York: Da Capo, 1974.

Guernsey, Otis L. Jr., ed. *Playwrights, Lyricists, Composers on Theater*. New York: Dodd, Mead, 1974.

Harrison, Rex. *A Damned Serious Business: My Life in Comedy*. London: Bantam Press, 1990.

Harrison, Rex. *Rex: An Autobiography by Rex Harrison*. London: Macmillan, 1974.

Hart, Kitty Carlisle., *Kitty: An Autobiography*. New York: Doubleday, 1988.

Hart, Moss. *Act One: An Autobiography*. New York: Random House, 1959.

Holloway, Stanley with Dick Richards. *Wiv a Little Bit O' Luck: The Life Story of Stanley Holloway*. London: Frewin, 1967.

Hughes, Gervase. *Composers of Operetta*. London: Macmillan, 1962.

Inglis, Ian, ed. *Popular Music and Film*. London: Wallflower Press, 2003.

Jablonski, Edward. *Alan Jay Lerner: A Biography*. New York: Henry Holt and Co., 1996.

Kirle, Bruce. *Unfinished Business: Broadway Musicals as Works-in-Progress.* Carbondale: Southern Illinois University Press, 2005.

Knapp, Raymond. *The American Musical and the Formation of National Identity.* Princeton, NJ: Princeton University Press, 2005.

Knapp, Raymond. *The American Musical and the Performance of Personal Identity.* Princeton, NJ: Princeton University Press, 2006.

Kortus, Günter. *My Fair Lady: Musical von Friedrich Loewe.* Die Oper: Schriftenreihe über Musikalische Bühmnenwerke. Berlin: Robert Lienau Verlag, 1977.

Lambert, Gavin. *On Cukor.* New York: G. P. Putnam, 1972; rev. ed. New York: Rizzoli, 2000.

Laufe, Abe. *Broadway's Greatest Musicals.* New York: Funk and Wagnalls, 1970.

Laurence, Dan, ed. *Bernard Shaw: Collected Letters 1898–1910.* New York: Dodd, Mead, 1972.

Laurence, Dan, ed. *Bernard Shaw: Collected Letters 1911–25.* New York, Viking, 1985.

Laurence, Dan, ed. *Bernard Shaw: Collected Letters 1926–50.* New York: Viking, 1988.

Lawson-Peebles, Robert, ed. *Approaches to the American Musical.* Exeter: University of Exeter Press, 1996.

Lees, Gene. *Inventing Champagne: The Worlds of Lerner and Loewe.* New York: St. Martin's Press, 1990.

Lerner, Alan Jay. *The Musical Theatre: A Celebration.* London: Collins, 1986.

Lerner, Alan Jay. *The Street Where I Live.* London: Hodder and Staughton, 1978.

Loney, Glenn, ed. *Musical Theatre in America.* Westport, CT: Greenwood Press, 1984.

Mangan, Richard, ed. *Gielgud's Letters.* London: Weidenfeld and Nicolson, 2004.

Matthew-Walker, Robert. *Broadway to Hollywood.* London: Sanctuary Press, 1996.

McMillin, Scott. *The Musical as Drama.* Princeton, NJ: Princeton University Press, 2006.

Miletich, Leo N. *Broadway's Prize-Winning Musicals: An Annotated Guide for Libraries and Audio Collectors.* New York: Haworth Press, 1993.

Mordden, Ethan. *Beautiful Mornin': The Broadway Musical in the 1940s.* New York: Oxford University Press, 1999.

Mordden, Ethan. *Broadway Babies: The People Who Made the American Musical.* New York: Oxford University Press, 1983.

Mordden, Ethan. *Coming Up Roses: The Broadway Musical in the 1950s.* New York: Oxford University Press, 1998.

Morley, Sheridan. *A Talent to Amuse: A Biography of Noël Coward.* London: Weidenfeld and Nicolson, 1975.

Nixon, Marni. *I Could Have Sung All Night.* New York: Billboard Books, 2006.

Pascal, Valerie. *The Disciple and his Devil.* New York: McGraw-Hill, 1970.

Payn, Graham, and Sheridan Morley, eds. *The Noël Coward Diaries.* London: Macmillan, 1982.

Rodgers, Richard. *Musical Stages: An Autobiography.* New York: Random House, 1975.

Rosen, Jody. *White Christmas: The Story of an American Song.* London: Fourth Estate, 2002.

Shapiro, Doris. *We Danced All Night: My Life Behind the Scenes with Alan Jay Lerner.* New York: Wm. Morrow, 1990.

Sorrell, Walter. *Hanya Holm: The Biography of an Artist.* Middletown, CT: Wesleyan University Press, 1969.

Stirling, Richard. *Julie Andrews: An Intimate Biography.* London: Portrait Books, 2007.

Strachan, Alan. *Secret Dreams: A Biography of Michael Redgrave.* London: Orion, 2004.

Steyn, Mark. *Broadway Babies Say Goodnight: Musicals Then and Now.* London: Faber, 1997.

Suskin, Steven. *Opening Night on Broadway: A Critical Quotebook of the Golden Era of the Musical Theatre.* New York: Schirmer, 1990.

Suskin, Steven. *The Sound of Broadway Music: A Book of Orchestrators and Orchestrations.* Oxford: Oxford University Press, 2009.

Swain, Joseph P. *The Broadway Musical: A Critical and Musical Survey.* New York: Oxford University Press, 1990.

Traubner, Richard. *Operetta: A Theatrical History.* New York: Doubleday, 1983.

Vickers, Hugo. *Cecil Beaton: The Authorised Biography.* London: Weidenfeld and Nicolson, 1985.

Walker, Alexander. *Fatal Charm: The Life of Rex Harrison.* London: Orion, 2002.

White, Mark. *You Must Remember This: Popular Songwriters 1900–80.* London: Frederick Warne Publishers, 1983.

Wilk, Max. *They're Playing Our Song.* New York: Viking, 1973.

Windeler, Robert. *Julie Andrews: A Biography.* New York: St. Martin's Press, 1983.

Zinsser, William. *Easy to Remember: The Great American Songwriters and their Songs.* Jaffrey, NH: David R. Godine Publisher, 2000.

ARCHIVAL MATERIAL CONSULTED
Library of Congress, Washington DC:
Frederick Loewe Collection (by box/folder number):
5/1: Ascot Gavotte (3pp, Loewe autograph)
5/2: Come to the Ball (4pp, Loewe autograph)
5/3: Come to the Ball (11pp, Ozalid of copyist's piano-vocal score, ann. in pencil)
5/4: Dear Little Fool (1p, Loewe autograph; lead sheet, no lyric)
5/5: Finale Act 1/(Procession—Embassy Waltz) (8pp, Loewe autograph)
5/6: Entr'acte (8pp, Loewe autograph)
5/7: Flower Market (5pp, Loewe autograph)
5/8: Get Me to the Church on Time (4pp, Loewe autograph)
5/9: A Hymn to Him (13pp, Loewe autograph)
5/10: I Could Have Danced All Night (inside cover: crossed out pp. 3–4 of early version of "Why Can't the English?") (7pp, Loewe autograph)
5/11: I'm an Ordinary Man (13pp, Loewe autograph)
5/12: I've Grown Accustomed to Her Face (13pp, Loewe autograph)
5/14: Just You Wait (8pp, Loewe autograph)

5/15: Lady Liza (1p, lead sheet); Liza—counterpoint (2pp, lead sheet) (Loewe autographs)

5/16: On the Street Where She Lives (inside cover: crossed out pp. 7–8 of early version of "Why Can't the English") (7pp, Loewe autograph)

5/17: Overture (2pp, Loewe autograph)

5/18: Please Don't Marry Me (lead sheet) (3pp, Loewe autograph)

5/19: The Pygmalion Waltzes (Embassy Waltz) (7pp, Loewe autograph)

5/20: The Pygmalion Waltzes (4pp, Photocopy of copyist's autograph piano score with ann. in pencil)

5/21: The Rain in Spain (5pp); The Servants' Chorus (2pp) (Loewe autographs)

5/22: Show Me (inside cover: crossed out pp. 5–6 of early version "Why Can't the English?") (7pp, Loewe autograph)

5/23: Shy (3pp, Loewe autograph); Shy (4pp, Rittmann arrangement, Latin version)

5/24: There's a Thing Called Love (lead sheet; typed lyric sheet laid in) (2pp, Loewe autograph)

5/25: What Is a Woman? (lead sheet) (1p, Loewe autograph)

5/26: Why Can't the English? (inside cover: crossed out pp. 1–2 of early version of the same song, Rittmann arrangement) (10pp, Loewe autograph)

5/27: With a Little Bit of Luck (6pp, Loewe autograph)

5/29: Without You (7pp, Loewe autograph)

5/30: Wouldn't It be Loverly? (5pp, Loewe autograph)

5/31: You Did It (23pp, Loewe autograph)

8/20: Limehouse (melody without lyric) (1p, Loewe autograph)

8/27: Over Your Head (melody without lyric) (1p, Loewe autograph)

8/36: The Son of the Wooden Soldier (1941); lyrics by John W. Bratton (5pp, published piano-vocal score)

8/37: There's Always One You Can't Forget (melody without lyric) (1p, Loewe autograph)

8/40: The Undeserving Poor (sketch) (1p, Loewe autograph)

8/44: What's to Become of Me? (lead sheet; "There's Always One" written below) (1p); Say Hello For Me (lead sheet without lyric) (1p); "What's To Become of Me?" (sketches) (1p) (Loewe autographs)

8/45: Who Is the Lady? (lead sheet without lyric) (1p, Loewe autograph)

9/2: Say a Prayer for Me Tonight (sketch) (1p, Loewe autograph)

9/9: Who Is the Lady? (lead sheet) (1p, Loewe autograph)

9/10: Say a Prayer for Me Tonight (sketches)

Warner-Chappell Collection (By Box/Folder Number):

141/1: End of Ascot (1p, Bennett's full score for original end of scene)

141/1: New 24 (2pp, Lang's score for change of scene)

141/1: Ascot Gavotte (16pp, Copyist's full score)

141/1: Ascot Gavotte (9pp, Freda Miller's dance pianist's piano score: mixture of copyist's score and Rittmann's score for the dance; intermediate stage of number)

141/1: Ascot Gavotte (3pp, photocopy of Rittmann's piano score for 'Intro to Gavotte' with pencil annotations)

141/3: Intro to Gavotte (2pp, photocopy of Rittmann's piano score (ann.))

141/3: Ascot Gavotte (7pp, copyist's score plus Rittmann's score (ann.); final version)

141/3: Middle of Ascot (untitled) (1p, piano score with instructions; possible Loewe score; music depicts the entrance of Higgins)

141/3: Ascot Gavotte Reprise (1p, photocopy of Rittmann's score with pencil annotations)

141/3: Gavotte (9pp, copyist's piano-conductor score, original version of ending/ second verse)

141/3: Ascot Gavotte Reprise (1p, photocopy of Rittmann's score with pencil annotations; at bottom is the original end of scene)

141/3: End of Ascot (untitled) (1p, Rittmann's piano score; cut)

141/5: Ascot Gavotte (7pp, choral score; includes extra verse which was later cut)

141/6: I've Grown Accustomed to Her Face (33pp, copyist's full score)

141/7: Ballroom Intro + Continuation (5pp, Lang full score; original version)

141/7: Ballroom Intro (4pp, conductor's short score; First page in Bennett's hand, other three in unknown hand)

141/8: Changes of scene: 4a, 5a, 6a, 10a and 23 (copyist's full scores)

142/1: Come to the Ball (27pp, Bennett's full score)

142/1: Intro to Dress Ballet (2pp, Lang's full score)

142/3: Come to the Ball (16pp, copyist's conductor's score; includes dance section)

142/3: Come to the Ball (12pp, copyist's piano score; includes early version of transitional section)

142/5: Dress Ballet (34pp, Bennett's full score)

142/6: Intro to Dress Ballet (1p, copyist's version of conductor's v score)

142/6: Dress Ballet (14pp, photocopy of Rittmann piano score)

142/7: Intro to Dress Ballet (1p, Rittmann's piano score)

142/7: Dress Ballet (14pp, Freda Miller's photocopy of Rittmann piano score (ann.))

142/7: Dress Ballet (16pp, annotated photocopy of Rittmann piano score; contains final pages at end which represent a revision)

143/2: The Embassy Waltz (24pp, Bennett's full score, crossed out; early version)

143/4: Embassy Waltz (7pp, copyist's piano score)

143/4: Embassy Waltz (10pp, photocopy of Loewe/Rittmann piano score with completely new Rittmann ending)

143/5: End of Gavotte and Blackout (6pp, copyist's full score)

143/6: Finish of Entr'acte (5pp, Lang's full score)

143/6: Entr'acte (28pp, copyist's full score)

143/8: Entr'acte (3pp, Rittmann's piano score (ann.))

143: The Embassy Waltz (13pp, copyist's conductor's short score)

144/1: Exit Music (29pp, copyist's full score)

144/3: Fainting Music (Instrumental parts for early version of the end of the Ascot scene)

144/5: End of Finale (Recording only) "Fair Lady" (6pp, Bennett's full score, as used on the Original Broadway Cast album)

144/6: Intro to Finale One/Finale One (1p + 11pp, copyist's version of conductor's short score)

144/7: Finale Ultimo (5pp, Rittmann's piano score for the end of the show [ann.])

145/1: Get Me to the Church On Time (47pp, Copyist's full score)

145/1: Church (old) version (29pp, Lang's full score of original version of "Get Me to the Church on Time")

145/3: Get Me to the Church II (2pp, choral arranger's score)

145/4: Church On Time Dance (11pp, Rittmann's piano score)

145/4: Church on Time Dance (8pp, photocopy of Rittmann's piano score [ann.])

145/5: Get Me to the Church on Time (6pp, copyist's piano-vocal score; annotations by Rittmann indicating how the dance music is to be created)

145/Unnumbered folder: Get Me to the Church on Time (Utility) (9pp, Lang's full score)

146/1: A Hymn to Him Utility (10pp, Lang's full score for utility)

146/1: A Hymn to Him (30pp, copyist's full score)

146/4: Hymn Continued and Scene Change (4pp, copyist's conductor's short score of final verse of "A Hymn to Him" and the scene change)

146/4: A Hymn to Him (10pp, Loewe/Rittmann piano score, with some annotations. Loewe's handwriting on the lyric, but Rittmann's on the music.)

146/4: A Hymn to Him (10pp, photocopy of Loewe/Rittmann piano with annotations)

146/4: A Hymn to Him (18pp, copyist's score in two parts, with pp. 13–18 stuck on end; contains earlier version of lyric)

146/5: I Could Have Danced All Night (utility) (10pp, Lang full score for utility)

146/5: I Could Have Danced All Night (21pp, copyist's full score)

146/6: I Should Have Danced All Night (copies of the Reed parts for "I Could Have Danced All Night"—Reeds 1 and 2 use "Should" in the title, but Reed 3 has "Could")

146/7: Bridge after Prayer (1p, viola part; stuck on back of viola part for different number

146/8: I Want to Dance All Night (14pp, copyist's score; Loewe has written the title on in pencil)

146/8: I Could Have Danced All Night (12pp, Copyist's Score)

147/2: Say a Prayer for Me Tonight (3pp, copyist's score)

147/5: I've Grown Accustomed to Her Face (16pp, copyist's piano-vocal score; original version, includes "Gay Females" singing "Without You," comments by Rittmann, and small note on final page "Danced All Night in B Flat, low and pretty, by FL")

147/3: Intro to Accustomed (3pp, Rittmann's piano score for final version of start of song, but title page in Loewe's hand)

147/5: I've Grown Accustomed to Her Face (16pp, copyist's piano-vocal score)

147/6: I've Grown Accustomed to Her Face (2pp, copyist's choral score)

148/1: Reprises (7pp, original orchestration for the double reprise and Freddy's verse of Show Me; all Bennett)

148/1: Just You Wait (17pp, copyist's full score)

148/2: Yost Jew Wait (1p, percussion score)

148/3: Just You Wait (7pp, copyist's piano score of original version)

148/3: Intro to Reprise of Just You Wait (2pp, Rittmann's piano-vocal score [ann.])

148/3: Street Reprise (2pp, Rittmann score on p.1; second page includes Loewe manuscript)

148/3: Just You Wait (8pp, copyist's score [ann.])

148/4: Just You Wait (Reprise) (3pp, copyist's full score)

148/6: On the Street Where She Lives (41pp, Lang's full score; complete original version of song, including different verse)

148/8: On the Street Where She Lives (7pp, copyist's piano-vocal score)

149/1: Ordinary Man (36pp, copyist's full score)

149/2: Street Where You Live (Reprise) (8pp, copyist's full score)

149/3: Opening Act 1 (6pp, Rittmann's autograph piano score, early version)

149/5: Overture (6pp, Rittmann's score, early version)

149/6: Overture and Opening (35pp, copyist's full score)

150/1: Promenade (11pp, Bennett/Lang full score with notes and missing pages)

150/1: Promenade (10pp, Lang's full score of original music)

150/3: The Pygmalion Waltzes (9pp, photocopy of Loewe/Rittmann's piano score with annotations)

151/1: The Rain in Spain (14pp, copyist's full score)

151/3: Dance: Rain in Spain (2pp, photocopy of Rittmann's piano score)

151/5: Say a Prayer for Me Tonight (10pp, Jack Mason's full score)

151/5: Bridge after Prayer (2pp, Bennett's full score)

151/10: Servants (4pp, Loewe and Rittmann score; contains a lyric sheet titled "Servants")

151/10: Servants (8pp, copyist's choral score; contains an extra verse)

152/1: Show Me (12pp, copyist's full score)

152/3: Show Me (front cover) (1p, Bennett's piano score cover; contains notes indicating how the double reprise into "Show Me" is to be created)

152/5: (New) Waltz (11pp, Rittmann's piano score [ann.])

152/6: English (Utility) (5pp, Lang's full score)

152/8: The English (10pp, Intermediate version of "Why Can't The English"; mixture of Loewe, Rittmann, and copyist's score)

152/8: Why Can't the English (10pp, old version of the song with some additions/appendages)

152/8: Why Can't the English (10pp, copyist's score)

153/6: End of Without You (1p, Rittmann's piano score for the end of the number)

153/1: With a Little Bit of Luck (18pp, copyist's full score)

153/4: With a Little Bit of Luck Reprise (10pp, copyist's full score)

153/5: Without You (13pp, copyist's full score)

153/7: Without You (11 p + loose insert, copyist's vocal score + one page of Rittmann/unknown hand)

153/7: Without You (RRB) (7pp, copyist's conductor's short score [ann.])

153/7: Without You (11pp, copyist's piano score)

154/1: Without You—You Did It (23pp, Lang's full score, original version)

154/3: Wouldn't It be Loverly Utility (10pp, full score in unknown hand)

154/3: Wouldn't It Be Loverly (22pp, copyist's full score)

154/4: Flower Market (7pp); Rittmann piano score of "Flower Market" (3pp); Rittmann piano score of pre-Processional Music to Embassy Waltz (2pp); sketches in unknown hand (2pp)

154/5: Loverly (11pp, choral score)

154/5: Wouldn't It be Loverly (6pp, copyist's piano score)

154/5: Wouldn't It Be Loverly (1p, choral score)

154/5: Wouldn't It Be Loverly (1p, choral arranger's draft choral score)

155/1: You Did It (44pp, copyist's full score)

155/3: You Did It (23pp, copyist's piano-vocal score, original version of number)

155/4: You Did It (Choral Score) (8pp, copyist's chorus score, original version)

Wisconsin Historical Society
Herman Levin Collection (By Box/Folder Numbers):

19/10–12: Advertising Reports

20/1–4: Advertising Reports

20/5—23/1–4: Box Office Statements

23/5: Casting miscellany

23/6: Clippings 1956–65

23/7: Crew

23/8: Dancers

23/9: Principals

24/1: Singers

24/2: Staff

24/3: Theatres

24/4: Actors Equity correspondence

24/5: Julie Andrews correspondence

24/6: Bankers Trust Co. correspondence

24/7: Cecil Beaton correspondence

24/8: CBS correspondence

24/9: Pamela Charles correspondence

24/10: Chorus and crew correspondence

24/11: Columbia Records correspondence

24/12: Commercial rights correspondence

24/13: Costumes correspondence

24/14: Dramatists' Guild correspondence

25/1: Equipment correspondence

25/2: Abe Feder and Joe Davis correspondence

25/3: Foreign correspondence

25/4: Form letters and memoranda

25/5–6: General correspondence

25/7: Rex Harrison correspondence

25/8: Moss Hart correspondence

25/9: Stanley Holloway correspondence
25/10: Hanya Holm correspondence
25/11: Sally Ann Howes correspondence
25/12: Richard Lamarr correspondence
25/13: Legal correspondence
25/14: License Renewal correspondence
26/1: Miscellaneous correspondence
26/2: Edward Mulhare correspondence
26/3: Musicians and conductor correspondence
26/4: Pascal arbitration correspondence
26/5: Protection of Rights correspondence
26/6: Oliver Smith correspondence
26/7: Summer tent theaters correspondence
26/8: Supporting actors correspondence
26/8–27/11: Financial Statements
26/9, 27/12–29/11: Legal records
30/1: Vocal score (ann.)
30/2: Voice parts, printed score
30/3–32/3: Payroll
32/5: Publicity correspondence
32/6: Editorial campaign
33/1: Letters from the public
33/2: Richard Maney correspondence
33/3: Thank You letters
33/4: Publicity miscellany
33/5–33/11: Royalties
34/2: Early script outlines
34/3: Mimeographed script by Lerner
34/4–6: Mimeographed scripts (ann.)
34/7: Rehearsal script
34/8: Unused/cut lyric sheets
34/9: Stage manager's script
35/1: Technical script
35/2: Bus and truck script
35/3: Taxes
35/4–9: Technical production
60/1: Piano-conductor score
60/2–5: Act I instrumental parts
61: Act 2 instrumental parts
62/2: Light plots and hanging plots by Abe Feder

Moss Hart Collection:
12/5: *My Fair Lady* typescript, personal copy

Beinecke Rare Book and Manuscript Library, Yale University
Theatre Guild Collection:
Box 83: Correspondence (Alan Jay Lerner)
Box 59: Correspondence (Rex Harrison)
Box 62: Correspondence (Theresa Helburn)
Box 137: Correspondence (George Bernard Shaw)

Harold Rome Papers:
MSS 49: 65/85 and 79/57: Script and correspondence for *Saints and Sinners*

New York Public Library
Hanya Holm Papers:
Series 4, 21/518: Choreographic notation and correspondence on *My Fair Lady*

Library of St John's College, Cambridge
Cecil Beaton Papers:
Vol. 98: Diary, 1954–45.

Harvard University Library
Harvard Theatre Collection, Houghton Library:
MS Thr 225: *My Fair Lady* "script prepared for publication"

Theatre Museum Collections, Victoria and Albert Museum
Michael Redgrave Papers:
TH 17/31/41/12: Redgrave's Diary for 1955

CREDITS

INDEX